Burning to Read

BURNING TO READ

English Fundamentalism and
Its Reformation Opponents

JAMES SIMPSON

THE BELKNAP PRESS OF
HARVARD UNIVERSITY PRESS
Cambridge, Massachusetts
London, England
2007

Library of Congress Cataloging-in-Publication Data

Simpson, James, 1954–
Burning to read : English fundamentalism and its
Reformation opponents / James Simpson.
p. cm.
Includes bibliographical references and index.
ISBN-13: 978-0-674-02671-1 (alk.paper)
ISBN-10: 0-674-02671-3 (alk. paper)
1. Great Britain—Church history—16th century.
2. Reading. I. Title.
BR375.S54 2007

274.2'06—dc22   2007011203

I dedicate this book to my friends Christopher Clark and Amitav Ghosh,
whose "gentle conference" over many years contributed to it
(and very much more) in such rewarding
and pleasurable ways.

Acknowledgments

I LOVE writing books. Whether my readers love reading them is altogether another matter. If they don't, the fault is entirely mine. If they do, then I'm afraid I'm unable to take all the credit. I have been stimulated by numerous colleagues at many events in the making of this book. Dialogue at the following institutions during the years 2003–2006 was, invariably, deeply rewarding: University of Cambridge, University of Connecticut at Storrs, Korea University (Seoul), Duke University, Western Michigan University, University of Melbourne, College of the Holy Cross (Worcester, Massachusetts), Northwestern University, and Harvard University. I thank the British Academy for offering me a grant to write this book, a grant that events finally prevented me from accepting. Harvard University granted me generous periods of leave, as well as an exceptionally stimulating collegial environment, for which I offer the warmest thanks. The outside readers' reports were profoundly helpful: one encouraged the Press to publish the manuscript exactly as it was (not unwelcome advice), while the other made dozens of no less welcome suggestions for change, many of which I adopted with gratitude. I owe especial thanks to David Aers, Sarah Beckwith, Christopher Clark, Rita Copeland, Brian Cummings, Daniel Donoghue, Milad

Doueihi, Stephen Greenblatt, David Hall, Justin McDermott, Leah Price, Ramie Targoff, and (by no means least) Nicholas Watson and Frances Whistler. Each of these friends was generous. Amitav Ghosh was even more generous, reading the entire manuscript with both an eagle eye and astute receptivity.

An earlier form of Chapter 5 was published in *Medieval and Early Modern English Studies (South Korea)*, 12 (2004): 133–165; I am grateful to the editors for permission to reproduce this material.

Contents

Illustrations

Note on Citations

I have consistently modernized the spelling and punctuation of all texts cited. The argument of this book is not dependent on philological discussion of cited texts; readers unfamiliar with sixteenth-century English will find their way more easily into quotations whose spelling has been modernized. In places where I cite a text by "image," I am citing from the electronic archive Early English Books Online (EEBO). The bibliographical policy of my book is, so far as possible, light. Wherever possible and appropriate, citations from the Hebrew scriptures and from the New Testament will be drawn from Tyndale's translations, published in, respectively, 1530 and 1534.

Burning to Read

Introduction

SOMETIME IN 1971, at the age of about seventeen, I received an intellectual shock. In my final year at a Presbyterian boys' school in Melbourne, Australia, I chose a history course entitled "Renaissance and Reformation." We had a superb teacher, Mr. David Paul, but in one lesson I felt sure he'd got things wrong. He told us that Luther believed that works were utterly useless, and that Catholics, by contrast, believed that works had real purchase on God's decisions about us. This, I felt quite certain, had to be an error.

I had grown up in a minimally religious culture. Religion for me was more a social division of sorts, especially between Catholics and Protestants. I had many Jewish friends from school, but Catholics were beyond my ken; they went to different schools. In this environment, where religion played very little explicit role, I wasn't so worried about salvation. But I was worried about work. Even if my benign familial environment wasn't stridently intolerant in any way, I nevertheless felt pretty certain that we (the Protestants) were quite a bit superior. After all, we were the rational ones. We were the ones who knew what work meant, and whose entire culture was grounded in the dignity of work rationally rewarded. Catholics were still a bit medieval; they were burdened by wholly superfluous, irrational guilt.

Here, however, was my admired teacher telling me that sixteenth-century Protestants felt irredeemably guilty, regarded works as the fruit of free will with derision, and believed that God's reward was a pure gift. They also believed that this divine gift was wholly a matter of God's impenetrable decision, made without regard to the efforts of humans, which were, in any case, worthless. Even more confusingly, my respected teacher was telling me that Catholics believed that, in one way or another, God did reward the human effort of works in the world. This assertion was so patently at odds with everything I'd absorbed that it just had to be wrong.

Needless to say, my teacher was right. Discovering that truth was my first confounding yet energizing experience of the paradoxes of modernity. Modernity was, I learned then and there, darker and more paradoxical than the Protestant triumphalism by which I'd been nourished had allowed.

In this book I seek to illuminate more of the dark, energizing paradoxes of Protestant modernity, with regard to a fairly tightly defined practice and period. The practice is reading; the period is 1520 or so until 1547; and the place is England. Some of the writers concerned were in exile from England, but their work was focused on the English situation.

Why a history of evangelical reading? Modernity and reading are intimately bound; the formation of one powerful strand of modernity in the sixteenth century was, in good part, produced by a profound transformation in the way Europeans read. The simplicity and primacy of the literal sense, and the right of the individual reader to read canonical books in freedom, without reference to either history or communities—both these foundations of a liberal reading culture, each underwritten by Luther's conscience-driven and courageous stance against the might of an institution, are taken to be irreversible gains of the Protestant Reformation. Individual reading capacity, liberty, and resistance to institutional disciplines are all foundational elements of the liberal tradition's self-understanding, according to which the sixteenth-century Lutheran moment is the turning point that generates what was to become the liberal tradition.

The individual reader's freedom is so foundational, indeed, that any resistance to the idea that such freedom was a sixteenth-century gain is difficult to comprehend. Here I attempt to judge the force of these foundational claims. I also seek to understand sixteenth-century resistance to the evangelical culture of the Book, arguing that the reader's freedom is not among the gains of sixteenth-century evangelical culture. What was achieved in the sixteenth century is better characterized as the origin of fundamentalism than of the liberal tradition. Contrary to the liberal tradition's often complacent assumption that fundamentalism is reactionary and "conservative," this book will maintain that fundamentalism is a distinctively modern phenomenon, the inevitable product of newly impersonal and imperious forms of textuality, and of the application of ever fewer textual instruments to ever larger jurisdictions. Sixteenth-century resistance to fundamentalism was, by contrast, a civilized, meditated, and partially plausible alternative modernity.

In short, the liberal tradition's derivation of itself from the sixteenth-century Reformation requires careful revision. The liberal tradition damagingly traces its origin, I contend, from exactly the source that in fact produced the liberal tradition's principal enemy (that is, fundamentalism). I generate this argument not in a spirit of dismissing the liberal tradition (far from it), but rather in an attempt to provoke the liberal tradition to understand itself better and redraw its own genealogy.

Why so short a time frame and such a narrowly defined geographic limit? Revolutions do not produce great literature, since the

revolutionary moment actively eschews the indirections of literature. That moment can, however, produce great thought. The initial
shock of proposed change tends, in fact, to produce clearer thought
in powerful minds than does the secondary phase of the revolution. The clearer, more illuminating positions are the privilege of
a moment that precedes the formation of entrenched party lines.
That moment also precedes the formation of the revolution's material
institutions, with their attendant disciplines. This clarity and pre-
science of thought were evident in early sixteenth-century England,
where the first shock of the Reformation produced two writers, William Tyndale and Thomas More, who articulated exemplary accounts
of two compelling, but exclusive and entirely non-negotiable, reading cultures. This period of powerful and prescient reflection occurred in the years between 1520 (the importation of Lutheran theology into England) and 1547, when the death of Henry VIII opened
the entirely new situation of an unequivocally Protestant king.

Chapter 1 sketches the history of two hundred years of Biblical violence in Europe. In Chapter 2 I retell the stirring narrative of how
the evangelical Bible was heroically produced and disseminated under conditions of extreme danger. The rest of the chapters devoted
to evangelical reading practice tell a different, less familiar story:
each of them explores the dark and powerful paradoxes of reading
and modernity that took shape in the early sixteenth century.

Chapter 3 examines a doctrine of salvation (or soteriology)[1] that
makes peculiar demands on readers who want to be saved by their
reading: such readers had better hate texts before they love them.
Reading promises the truth about one's salvation, but that promise
can only be arrived at through detestation of oneself and the text.
God's law is found in Scripture and Scripture alone; however, the
point of that written law is to insist on the reader's inability to fulfill
it. Because human will and reason are irredeemably abject, in a Lu-

theran scheme, Biblical injunction hovers over an abyss: apparently it says "do this," but in reality it says "know that this cannot be done."

A second paradox underlies the first: evangelical reading repudiates ambiguity in its affirmation of scriptural clarity; but evangelical reading practice derives in the first place from, and only from, the recognition of verbal ambiguity.

A third paradox surfaces as well in Chapter 3: that the evangelical "faith alone" culture turns out to manifest all the signs of a "no faith" culture. A theological culture of "faith alone" that insists so relentlessly on the primacy of the written text is actually symptomatic of a culture in which faith is under intense pressure. One might expect a "faith alone" culture to treat written contracts with disdain, since such contracts are the textual instruments of those who do *not* trust each other. Evangelical culture, however, simultaneously proclaims faith alone, and yet insists that it all be written, in covenant, in black and white.

Chapter 4 explores a number of paradoxes, all dark. A reading culture with an extreme emphasis on the simplicity and legibility of the literal sense ends up producing its opposite: an extremely authoritarian account of the institutional element in reading. Such insistence on the simplicity of Scripture produces an unreadable text written in the heart of the elect. Reading might be for everyone, but predestination certainly isn't.[2] The only "good" readers of Scripture are predestined readers, readers who already belong, before they start reading, to a very select and exclusive institution. What's more, predestination turns the whole world into a very complex text, full of signs and portents by which one descries the divine decision. Thus, extreme emphasis on the simple text produces very complex, not to say unreadable, texts. Claims about pure transparency produce near total opacity.

Chapter 5 illuminates the darkness of Protestant culture with regard to the paradox of personal relations: the exaggerated emphasis on the wholly accessible and incontrovertible literal sense produces private and fragmented, if not paranoid, reading experiences. Here I focus especially on sixteenth-century reception of the Psalms. In Chapter 6 I examine another dark paradox, that of a reading culture that prizes historical integrity in so relentless a way as to produce a hollowing out and repudiation of history.

Across these chapters I present, then, an image of Biblical reading as unsettlingly recessive, always moving back across a horizon as one approaches it. In this I offer a parallel with Max Weber's arguments about Protestantism and work/s. The paradox that a theology so hostile to works should have produced a work ethic was solved by Weber in 1904: even if Lutheran (and Calvinist) works do not contribute to salvation in any way, good works are nevertheless a *sign* of God's election. Works, then, despite their uselessness as currency, become valuable as signs of a gift already bestowed. If Protestants did indeed work harder and idealize work, it was not because works had gained in theological value; it was rather because works had become a semiotic field that one must scrutinize for signs of divine approval. The uncertainty and necessity of the search produced the neurotic commitment to keep working until such a sign demonstrably appeared. A Protestant worked, and worked all the harder, precisely *because* works had become useless as currency and useful as signs.[3]

The same logic applies to the "work" of reading: because reading is itself a work, and because the works promoted by reading are, already, irredeemably useless, reading becomes necessary as a field of scrutiny, but useless as a field of directive action. One reads, to replay the paradox, and one reads all the more intensely, precisely because reading has *lost* its purchase on the world of action.

The substance of the book consists of scholarship, but its structure is shaped as an essay: it's impossible, in dealing with such fundamental issues, not to take sides. Given that the Protestant case has held near-absolute sway for so long, I attempt to right the balance a little. The book's structure reflects my attempt to understand the truly shocking reality of Protestant reading and, in part, of Protestant modernity.

In Chapter 7 I deepen the debate by examining the position of Thomas More, who also understood the shocking reality of Protestant reading. I present More's position not as a rearguard action, but rather as a plausible alternative to sixteenth-century Protestant textual modernity.[4]

Despite this partiality, I have made every effort not to be untrue to the materials. Partiality is, however, at least provisionally necessary: misunderstanding of sixteenth-century reading and its historical effects is pervasive and of long standing; the consequences of that misunderstanding are far-reaching and ongoing. What's needed now are clearly targeted studies delineating the conceptual issues and stakes of sixteenth-century cultures that have been deeply misunderstood. Such clarity of understanding is urgent at this point in the history of Western societies, as Biblical fundamentalism holds the institutions of liberal society and liberal scholarship in contempt. As long as liberals claim their descent from the very tradition that most threatens them, they are vulnerable.

Partiality does, however, have its limits. In the final chapter I step back from antagonism and describe the confrontation rather as a tragic one, in which each side is inevitably and profoundly compromised by an encounter it cannot avoid. Here I focus on the helpless and tragic transformation of the pluriform, Catholic More into his literalist enemy. We gain only a certain amount by rehearsing the agon of the Reformation; we gain more by recognizing that the agon is our own history as well, and that we can no more step onto one side or the other than travel in time. We cannot travel across temporal boundaries into the safe territory of the past, since we are ourselves the products of our whole past.[5] We are at the same time part of the problem, and part of the way forward.

Why are these matters so resonant now? Religion as a category is, happily, subject to a powerful revisionism in the academy. Few now argue from confident Enlightenment condescension to religion, as if religion can be treated as a mere allegorical reflex of, or code for, the "true" reality (usually politics or economics). Instead, the secularity of what appear to be purely secular phenomena in Western culture is increasingly seen in silent dialogue with its repressed religious counterpart. Religion is now the central arena in which all the big questions are examined: narratives of national identity and freedom; of individual liberties; of the history of scholarship; and of subjectivity. Although all of these narratives (and more) were until recently constructed from purely secular materials, each now requires an understanding of the history of religious experience.

If a powerful revisionism of religion is under way across the academy, there can be no doubt about religion's profile in the "real world": fundamentalist reading practices are, for example, becoming a legislated norm or at least a desideratum in some democratic states, while from afar (and occasionally from not so far) we distinctly hear the sounds and cries, not of the political revolutionary's, but of the religious fundamentalist's bombs. Reading and its consequences are once again becoming capable of violently changing the world. We ignore understanding our religious history, and particularly the history of religious reading, at our own peril. No attempt is made here to persuade the fundamentalist of the error of literalist reading, which, given the nature of fundamentalist conviction, is a lost cause. The book does aim at the more modest goal of setting into profile the grounds of such a reading culture and its inevitably violent results.

Some practical matters: I consistently use the word "evangelical" in this book, for want of a better term, to designate "Protestant" culture. I do so partly because the word "Protestant" is not used by any of the writers I study, and was not in use anywhere until the Holy Roman Emperor's Diet in Speyer in 1529. The word "evangelical," by contrast, would have been recognized by any of the writers treated here as signaling a set of sympathies. I imply no necessary connection with the specific sense of the word "evangelical" in contemporary religious usage, particularly in the United States.[6] I beg indulgence for the philologically unauthorized word "fundamentalism" in my subtitle: this word is of American origin and derives from early twentieth-century usage. The word does nevertheless designate a movement based on the literal inerrancy of Scripture; and many forms of that movement are vibrant in many parts of the world today. My use of the word in one high-profile place is designed to connect sixteenth-century debates with contemporary issues, a connection that will, I hope, be accepted by the time readers have finished the book.[7]

CHAPTER ONE

Two Hundred Years of Biblical Violence

BOOKS can unleash terrific energies. In this chapter I sketch some of the ways in which new forms of Bible reading produced nearly two hundred years of violence in western Europe between 1517 and 1700. I also look at the historiographical tradition in which that release of extraordinary energies has been almost universally admired.

The reign of Josiah, king of Judah (640–609 BCE), as related in the Second Book of Kings, reveals the vital yet destructive energy that books can unleash. Josiah's father, Manasseh, had so angered the God of Israel with idolatry that God threatened to annihilate Jerusalem itself: "And I will wipe out Jerusalem, as a man would wipe a dish, and when he hath wiped it turneth it upside down" (2 Kings 21:13). God nevertheless promises to leave a remnant of the faithful, which, happily, includes the boy king Josiah, who comes to the throne at the tender age of eight. Once eighteen, Josiah orders the temple rebuilt; as money is given to the "carpenters and masons" for the works, a book is found by the High Priest. The reading of the book before the young king produces an immediate and energetic penitential response: he tears his clothes, and declares that "a great wrath of the

Lord . . . is kindled upon us, that our fathers have not hearkened unto the words of this book, to do in all points as it is written therein" (2 Kings 22:13).

Josiah's recognition of the book's truth saves him: the prophetess Oldah predicts that Josiah will see none of the destruction soon to be visited on Jerusalem. His first public act is to read the book, himself, before a large assembly of all the men of Judah and all the inhabitants of Jerusalem; they jointly promise to "make good the words of the said appointment that were written in the foresaid book" (2 Kings 23:3). If divine violence is deferred by this communal assent to the written law, that assent now manifests itself, and manifests itself only, in a maelstrom of human violence.

No other acts are recorded in the reign of Josiah except his iconoclasm, destruction of pagan temples, and killing of the pagan priests. Josiah commands the priests to cleanse the temple of all the vessels made for Baal, which are promptly burned. He "puts down" the priests of the pagan gods, who burn "sacrifices unto Baal, to the sun and to the moon and to the planets" (2 Kings 23:5); he "defile[s] the hill altars," and he sacrifices "all the priests of the hill altars," stamping the broken altars to powder and burning the groves dedicated to the foreign gods (2 Kings 23). In short, Josiah puts "out of the way" all "workers with spirits, soothsayers, images of witchcraft, idols and all other abominations" in order to "make good the words of the law which were written in the book that Helkiah the priest found in the house of the Lord" (2 Kings 23:24).

This compact narrative sets one form of authorization against another: the rediscovered written document is held to constitute the Law, mainly because it's taken to be the Word of God, and because it reawakens an ethnic historical consciousness. That written Law exercises absolute sway over the places, the idols, and the persons of any alternative religious authority.

Recognition of the written law activates other struggles as well. Architecturally, temple repair involves (pagan) temple destruction. Geographically, the Law demands a reaffirmation of geographic possession, since the list of idolatrous sites reads like a map of the land of Canaan before the victories of Joshua eight centuries earlier. The altars of the goddess Astarte, chief deity of the Sidonians to the North; of Chemosh, god of the Moabites to the Southeast; and of Milcom, god of the Ammonites to the East—these "the king defiled: and brake the images and cut down the groves and filled the places with the bones of men" (2 Kings 23:14).

In Josiah's time the state of ancient Judah was extremely fragile: the kingdom of Israel had already fallen (c. 721 BCE), leaving only Judah threatened by Assyria, before its imminent demise by decisive Babylonian invasion and the destruction of the Temple (587 BCE). Josiah responds to this precarious situation not only by targeting the imported Assyrian religious practice, which is all the worse for having been practiced by Josiah's immediate ancestors; he also targets worship of the gods who inhabited Canaan before the Israelite invasion. In the previous reign, Josiah's father Manasseh had been castigated by God for reintroducing "more wickedness than did the heathen people which the Lord destroyed from before the children of Israel" (2 Kings 21:9). To practice the religion of contemporary invaders is to remind Judah of the religious practice in its territories prior to Israel's own occupation of those lands. The rediscovered book might remind Judah of its authentic past, but it equally provokes the memory of Israel's own long tradition of idolatry. Provisional pacification of a jealous God demands a clean, iconoclastic, xenophobic break with all examples of Israel's recurring acceptance both of imported religion, and of Canaanite, non-Abrahamic religions.

The story of Josiah's rediscovery of a book is an exemplary moment in the history of reading. Here reading is represented as nothing if not publicly performed ("And he [Josiah] read in the ears of them all the words of the book of the covenant" [2 Kings 23:2]), and reading is nothing if not socially oriented. Fresh recovery of a canonical book provokes a reimagination of both community and history. Those rediscoveries of indisputably authentic written law are capable of both soldering community and at the same time legitimating powerful violence against those who fall beyond the pale of the newly redefined written law.

The events of Josiah's reign were taken to have direct pertinence to mid-sixteenth-century England. William Tyndale (c. 1494–1536) was most probably the translator of the Books of Kings in the Matthew's Bible of 1537, the manuscript of which he had prepared by 1535;[1] he was also probably responsible for the marginal glosses to Kings in that edition, in which he insinuated parallels between the idolaters targeted by Josiah and his own Catholic enemies. One set of pagan priests (the Camarites) is glossed, for example, as the "black monks of Baal."[2] But the full force of the parallel between the reign of Josiah and events in Tudor England could only be exploited after 1547, with the accession of the child king Edward VI at the age of nine.

Evangelicals wasted no time in billing Edward as the new Josiah. The reign of Josiah not only provided the model of a boy king but also, with providential accuracy, portrayed a program of reform driven by recovery of the long-hidden Word of God. That rediscovery legitimated aggressive iconoclasm against a religion newly defined as foreign and superstitious. Further, as in the reign of Josiah, the ecclesiastical arm worked under the supervision of a king in the recovery of a national religion. In his coronation speech on 20 February 1547 (the first such speech before a monarch who did not recognize the authority of Rome), the reforming Archbishop Thomas

Cranmer (1489–1556) was quick to point out the parallelism. He directs Edward that his duty is

> . . . to see, with your predecessor Josiah, God truly worshipped, and idolatry destroyed, the tyranny of the bishops of Rome banished from your subjects, and images removed. These acts be signs of a second Josiah, who reformed the Church of God in his days. . . . It is written of Josiah in the book of the Kings thus: "Like unto him there was no king before him that turned to the Lord with all his heart, according to the law of Moses, neither after him arose there any like him."[3]

This is no vague exhortation but a specific, Josiah-inspired reform program: the "foreign" religion is to be banished, and its cult redefined as idolatry. These acts are grounded in recognition of the one authentic law, and inspired by the promise of renewed strength for England, for, as Tyndale had said, God "is no patcher, he cannot build on another man's foundation."[4]

Legislators enacted the Josiahan program with alacrity. Already in 1547, the Royal Injunctions (directions for ecclesiastical officials), published in the name of the boy king Edward VI, moved aggressively to the offensive. They reignited the war between the recovered divine Word and the "superstitious" past of imported, foreign, nonscriptural religious practice. Injunction 28 neatly encapsulates the battle lines, by reorganizing the interiors of churches in two ways. It begins by extending iconoclastic injunctions promulgated by Henry VIII in 1538. Church officials will

> . . . take away, utterly extinct and destroy all shrines, covering of shrines, all tables, candlesticks . . . pictures, paintings, and all other monuments of feigned miracles, pilgrimages, idolatry, and superstition: so that there remain no memory of the same in walls, glass-windows, or elsewhere within their churches or houses.[5]

This abolition of all religious pictorial memorials, and of certain forms of memory itself, makes way for the second change to church interiors in the same injunction: churchwardens, "at the common charge of the parishioners in every church, shall provide a comely and honest pulpit . . . for the preaching of God's word" (1:126). Thus, reading displaces images; the written, the unwritten; worship, idolatry; the national, the international; codified law, customary practice. As in all periods of new knowledge technologies, the winner reclassifies other, older technologies as outmoded, superstitious, or both.

The parallelism with Josiah remained a leitmotif of evangelical historiography. John Foxe, who makes the comparison between Edward and Josiah explicitly,[6] begins his account of Edward's reign in his *Actes and Monuments* (1563) with Edward implicitly following in the steps of Josiah.[7] In the upper panel of an illustration in that book we see the papists "packing away their paltrye," as the iconoclastic fires burn in the background, while in the lower panels we first see Edward distributing the Word to a respectful clergy and nobility; then the eye moves right, to the church cleansed of all images and celebrating the only two sacraments with, in the evangelical account, scriptural authority (that is, Baptism and the Eucharist) under a "comely and honest pulpit" from which that Word is preached.[8]

The energizing and violent drama of reading in the reign of Edward VI was only one scene of that same drama being enacted throughout northern Europe, from the second decade of the sixteenth century. Of course late medieval Europe had already witnessed scriptural movements that championed the authority of Scripture above "men's traditions," particularly in late fourteenth-century England and Bohemia.[9] But only the combination of mass reproduction of books (possible from the middle of the fifteenth century), and the astonishing theological and polemic force of Martin Luther (1483–1546), could produce a Josiahan drama that would envelop Europe in more than a hundred and fifty years of violent upheaval.

In fact the mass reproduction of books itself might evoke parallels with the century of Josiah, since, according to some scholars of the Hebrew scriptures, it was only in the seventh century BCE that the spread of literacy in ancient Judah provoked a specifically written tradition.[10] Clearly the advent of the book printed with movable type in Europe (c. 1455) was prompted by increasing literacy, but the new printing method in turn hugely promoted the spread of literacy and a culture of the book.[11] Both seventh-century BCE Judah and sixteenth-century Europe were periods of new literacies, which championed the authority of the book above customary practice.

The Biblical account of Josiah focuses on the destruction of objects rather than the killing of people, though it does make reference to the "sacrifice" of the priests of Baal. Other accounts of the purging of idolatrous religious practices in ancient Israel are more direct in their account of murder in the name of a divinely inspired Word. King Jehu (ruled 842–815 BCE), for example, who was anointed on the orders of the prophet Elijah, is commanded in the Second Book of Kings to initiate a coup against the house of Ahab. He orders that Ahab's Sidonian wife Jezebel be thrown to her death from her upper-story window; he arranges for the beheading of the seventy sons of Ahab; and he kills everyone else associated with the idolatrous Ahab, "all that were great with him, and his companions and his priests, until he had left him naught remain" (2 Kings 10:11).

Extinguishing all traces of the reigning royal house was, however, only half the job. Jehu acts "according to the saying of the Lord which he spoke to Elijah"; to complete the task of purification, he must also eliminate Ahab's non-Abrahamic religion. He pretends he wants to make a sacrifice to Baal, and calls for "all the prophets of Baal, and all his servants and all his priests that none be lacking. For I have a great sacrifice to do to Baal" (2 Kings 10:19). The assembled devotees do not understand that they are themselves the sacrifice: they innocently enter the temple of Baal until it is filled, wall to wall;

Jehu then orders a check that no worshipper of the Lord is in the temple, before commanding the eighty men to surround the temple, on orders not to allow anyone to escape. The building having been thoroughly surrounded, Jehu orders the guards to enter and be certain to kill all within. The purging of the temple follows, with the image of Baal thoroughly broken. God approves: "Then the Lord said to Jehu: because thou hast lustily done that [what] pleaseth me . . . therefore shall thy children in the fourth generation sit on the seat of Israel" (2 Kings 10:30).

✸ This scene of exclusivist religious violence in the reign of Jehu is not driven by the discovery of a book, as in the reign of Josiah; it is instead directed by the living word of God, in the mouth of the prophet Elijah. In sixteenth- and seventeenth-century western Europe north of the Alps, scenes like these were not unusual, whether inspired by prophetic voices or, as was much more common, by understandings of rediscovered Biblical truth.[12] Of course not all such scenes were inspired by religious convictions alone, and the violence was performed as much by Catholics as by Protestants, and often by one stripe of Protestant against another. However mixed the motives and the perpetrators may have been, parts of Europe witnessed between 150 and 200 years of violent upheaval, from the Lutheran challenge begun in 1517 until the mid- to late seventeenth century.

In 1524, only seven years after Luther's first public challenge to papal religion, the Peasants' War ("Europe's most massive and widespread popular uprising before the 1789 French Revolution")[13] erupted north of the Alps in a broad, northward-moving front from Switzerland to Hungary. By Luther's account, the peasants acted under the impulse of their own understanding of the Gospel: "They cloak this terrible and horrible sin with the gospel."[14] Luther's response was also Gospel-driven, and set the tone for the brutal repression. He was guided by Romans 13:1–2: "The powers that be, are ordained of God. Whosoever resisteth power, resisteth the ordinance of God. And they that resist, shall receive to themselves damnation." Luther exhorted those repressing the revolt "to smite, slay and stab, secretly or openly, remembering that nothing can be more poisonous, hurtful or devilish than a rebel. It is just as when one must kill a mad dog." If a man is in open rebellion, "everyone is both his judge and his executioner."[15]

That revolt was the precursor of much more organized, princely warfare within the boundaries of the Habsburg Empire into the mid-sixteenth century, as different principalities sided with or against the Lutheran, and then with or against "Reformed" Protestantism, and then chose between one or another of these now-divided evangelical camps. The Peace of Augsburg of 1555 marked an important pause to the wars in German territories since 1547, with the firm establishment of the principle of *cuius regio, eius religio* (whose region, his religion), although it left the profound and bitter divisions between Lutheran and Reformed Protestantism unrecognized.[16] Warfare in the German territories did not effectively end, however, until the Peace of Westphalia in 1648, after thirty years of war in which between 15 and 40 percent of the population of the German lands died prematurely through either fighting, famine, or disease.[17]

In France the two dozen executions of evangelicals ordered by Francis I in 1534 heralded a fierce civil war that extended throughout the sixteenth century. Full-scale civil war broke out between Catholics and Huguenots in 1562. It was conducted with an "extraordinary degree of bitterness and savagery," and reached a pause only in 1598, with the Edict of Nantes in the reign of Henry IV (1589–1610). The Edict legislated freedom for both Protestant and Catholic worship in France, and granted full civic rights to Huguenots (French Protestants). This pause was only achieved, however, after the massacre of up to 5,000 Protestants on St. Bartholomew's Day (24 August 1572), and the effective collapse of the French state under eight separate and bloody bouts of civil war. The Edict was revoked by Louis XIV in 1685, provoking the exile of more than 400,000 Huguenots.[18]

In the Low Countries the situation was complicated by foreign dominion of the Habsburg Empire. The new spiritual culture had been actively persecuted by Habsburg authorities up to the end of the 1550s, but Spanish bankruptcy and the consequent need for higher taxation provoked trouble from 1557. The Habsburg army sent in 1567 executed noble leaders along with about 1,000 others; more than 100,000 people left the Netherlands in exile.[19] By 1572 the Habsburg forces had been repelled, but that check was not only the prelude to the durable division of the Low Countries into a Catholic kingdom to the south (Belgium) and the evangelical United Provinces, or Netherlands, to the north. It also led to "a prolonged confrontation" between the Habsburg Empire and the Protestant powers of northern Europe, "which by the 1590s became a war on a global scale."[20]

In England the worst period of persecution by Catholic authorities occurred in the reign of Queen Mary (1553–1558), who attempted to reverse the Josiahan revolution set in train by her evangelical half-brother. That persecution involved the burning of nearly 300 people, "numbers unprecedented in England,"[21] but this savage repression itself heralded more of the same to come (although from different quarters), either in the Civil War of 1642–1648, or in the Cromwellian invasion of Ireland, which included, for example, the storming of Drogheda in September 1649, killing "perhaps 3000 royalist troops in hot and cold blood, [and] all the Catholic clergy and religious he [Cromwell] could identify."[22]

Earlier in his career Oliver Cromwell (1599–1658) had seen scriptural authority for the banishment of the king: meditation on Psalms

17 and 105 prompted him confidently to declare to Parliament that "they that are implacable and will not leave troubling the land may be speedily destroyed out of the land."[23] So too did Cromwell appeal to divine sanction in the case of his bloody invasion of Ireland, since one of his own justifications was religious: this was "a righteous judgment of God upon these barbarous wretches who have imbrued their hands in so much innocent blood."[24] Although Cromwell denied that he had tried to extirpate the Catholic religion from Ireland in 1650, by 1652 he might have supported the "Act of Settlement of 1652 that envisaged up to 100,000 executions, mass emigration, and ethnic cleansing on a scale unknown in western European history."[25] It was not until 1689, under William III, that the English parliament passed a limited toleration act, although Catholics, Jews, and Unitarians had to wait for legislation passed between 1778 and 1871 for full religious emancipation in England.

This somber and very selective litany of horrors and repressions sketches a history of western European religious violence and persecutions at which few contemporary readers will fail to shudder. In the seventeenth and eighteenth centuries many Europeans, exhausted as they were by long bouts of internecine viciousness, themselves began to shudder, and to formulate the ground rules for religious toleration.[26] At the beginning of the long fight, however, those with broad perspectives regarded the struggle ahead with relish. They also approached the fight with theological justification for intolerance.[27] In England, the Catholic proponent Thomas More had no desire to see toleration between opposed religious camps. He is reported to have said to his son-in-law that

> I pray God, that some of us, as high as we seem to sit upon the mountains treading heretics under our feet like ants, live not in the day that we gladly would wish to be at a league and composition with them, to

let them have their churches quietly to themselves, so that they would be content to let us have ours quietly to our selves.[28]

On the evangelical side, Luther, for example, figured the position of the True Church as a Babylonian captivity, suffering the wrath of God as a result of idolatrous deviance. Near the very beginning of his polemical career, in an open letter (1520) to Pope Leo X, he defended his polemical aggression on the model of Christ's own example: "He Himself was keenly hostile to his opponents, and called them a brood of vipers, hypocrites, blind, children of the devil."[29] A few years later, in 1524, he rebuked Erasmus for being faint of heart before the battles of liberation ahead, and for preferring "carnal peace" above "the Word of God." "Let me tell you, therefore," he goes on,

> that what I am after in this dispute is to me something serious, necessary, and indeed eternal, something of such a kind and such importance that it ought to be asserted and defended to the death, even if the whole world had not only to be thrown into strife and confusion, but actually return to chaos and reduced to nothingness.[30]

From here Luther cites Christ himself in defense of the tumultuous reception that the Gospel must inevitably provoke: it is regularly the case, he argues, that the Word of God throws the "world in a state of tumult"; this is "plainly asserted by Christ."[31] Among other citations, Luther invokes Matthew 10:34 ("Think not, that I am come to send peace into the earth. I came not to send peace, but a sword"), and Luke 12:49 ("I am come to send fire on the earth: and what is my desire but that it were already kindled?").

Not only is the need for Christian violence felt to be authorized by the Gospel, but the very simplicity and solidity of the text also evokes violence against its obverse: a whole world of once numinous objects that have become mere inert, oppressive things. As writers of different persuasions describe these mere things in lists, one can feel their desire to sweep them away violently. The longer the list, indeed, the looser the syntactic grip, and the more lightweight and ersatz the objects appear to become. In his skeptical account of pilgrimage devotion, for example, Erasmus piles up a huge list of relics whose very lack of syntactic organization itself begs for an iconoclastic response. Erasmus attacks

> the superstitious worship and false honor given to bones, heads, jaws, arms, stocks, stones, shirts, smocks, coats, caps, hats, shoes, miters, slippers, saddles, rings, beads, girdles, bowls, bells, books, gloves, ropes, . . . candles, boots, spurs (my breath was almost past me) with many other such damnable illusions of the devil to use them as gods contrary to the immaculate scripture of God.[32]

Lists of this kind are an essential and recurrent weapon in the evangelical rhetorical arsenal. The verbal junk here could go on forever (exhausting the capacities of the breath itself): it's an infinite, jumbled, unsorted pile of rubbish, the only sane response to which is hammer and broom.[33]

How has cultural history received this melancholy story of religious violence?

Faced with what was registered as an oppressive, tawdry, and finally melancholy pile of things, and with what they saw as an oppressive theology of salvation, evangelical writers of the first flush of what became the Protestant revolution hailed their own movement as one of evangelical liberty. The simplicity and clarity of the text relieved them from the oppressive weight of both things and the unending rituals that promote only anxiety. Luther's early polemical titles proclaim that message of liberty: *Von der Freiheit eines Christenmenschen* (Concerning the Liberty of a Christian, 1520); *De Captivitate Baby-*

lonica Ecclesiae (Concerning the Babylonian Captivity of the Church, 1520). That last work trumpets the theme of liberty that has become so powerful a strand in the historiography of Protestantism:

> I lift my voice simply on behalf of this liberty and conscience, and I confidently cry: No law, whether of man or of angels, may rightfully be imposed on Christians without their consent, for we are free of all laws.[34]

Modern readers of Luther, in light of the melancholy history of the sixteenth and seventeenth centuries, might see the confidence of his clarion call to liberty as rash and blithely overconfident. For Luther, we recall, was prepared to have the whole world "return[ed] to chaos and reduced to nothingness."

For all that, extremely powerful traditions of Western historiography continue to see this Lutheran moment as fundamentally positive and inspiring: the liberal tradition grounds itself in Luther's defiance as an individual against the power and threat of an institution. In the estimation of Herbert Butterfield, for example, Luther was indispensable to Whig interpreters of history: "The whig historian can draw lines through certain events, some such line as that which leads through Martin Luther and a long succession of whigs to modern liberty; . . . all demonstrating throughout the ages the workings of an obvious principle of progress, of which the Protestants and whigs have been perpetual allies, while Catholics and tories have perpetually formed obstruction."[35] The individual conscience's act of defiance against a threatening institution with the instruments of violent repression at its service has left an ineradicable distrust of institutions in the liberal tradition.

Even more profoundly, the Lutheran moment has left a deep commitment to the liberties and heroism of individual conscience informed by its *reading*. No longer blocked and oppressed by a mediating institution, the individual Christian is finally able to read the Biblical text for him- or herself. Given the intimate connection between reading and liberty, a connection that underwrites all sites of reading, both professional and private, in Western culture, the Lutheran moment is hailed as an irreversible advance in the West. Thanks to Luther's brilliant textual polemic and courageous intervention, the private reader can ever afterward read in liberty, discovering the immense liberties and pleasures of private reading unobstructed by oppressive and threatening institutional demands.

One need only look at the arguments of the lesser Catholic combatants in the sixteenth-century confrontation over the vernacular Bible to see just how untenably poor their position can appear in the light of subsequent history. In 1539, a complainant to Thomas Cromwell reported that his vicar was persecuting him for reading the Bible. The vicar described the reading of God's word as "a green learning that will fade away"; he is reported to have called the Bible "the Book of Arthur Cobbler," and readers of it heretics.[36]

Likewise, in the reign of Queen Mary, one John Standish produced a text entitled *A discourse, wherein it is debated whether it be expedient that the scripture should be in English for al men to reade* (London, 1554).[37] Standish begins tepidly by arguing that the question should be debated in Parliament, and that Scripture's translation would be appropriate if all English people were good Catholics—evidently far from being the case (images 2–3). From here on, however, the tract becomes rancorous in its hostility to vernacular translation. Things have gone badly ever since Bibles were made available in churches in 1539 (image 5); Scripture is difficult to understand, a point made often in Scripture itself (image 12); God wanted to preserve the sacred mysteries from the vulgar, and he did so through Scripture's rhetorical difficulty (image 18); Scripture is in any case very difficult to translate (image 31); and the letter kills (image 36). All those points precede the real nadir of his "argument": most people are evil and most also ignorant (image 66); besides, servants have been stubborn and recalcitrant ever since vernacular Scripture was available to them (image 73).

Given crude and meanly distrustful arguments of this kind, the judgment of history has only one choice—to dismiss Standish and his ilk into the backwaters of historical losers. In cases like this, opposition to the Bible in English is opposition to both religious and linguistic freedom. In both cases that defense of freedom is located at the fundamental and non-negotiable point of unfettered Bible reading.

Positions of the kind put forth by Standish are obviously unpersuasive and unimpressive. In contrast, the promotion of widespread literacy by evangelical writers is indisputably attractive to the intellectual cultures, of pretty well all stripes, in the West since the sixteenth century. We might disagree about what we read, but no one disputes that reading is massively desirable.

This chiaroscuro of negative and positive positions—with, thankfully, one indisputable winner—may account for why the question of reading has played so muted, not to say nonexistent, a part of the recent revisionism of the English Reformation initiated by John Scarisbrick, Christopher Haigh, and Eamon Duffy.[38] Duffy readily acknowledges a Catholic vulnerability in the revisionist flagship volume, *The Stripping of the Altars* (1992): "Fear of Bible translations was a major weakness in the educational and devotional programme of late medieval English Catholicism."[39] Thereafter the topic is given hardly any profile whatsoever, surfacing only timidly in the account of Marian spirituality. Bibles were removed from parish churches by Marian officials, to be sure, but "Bible-reading or the possession of Bibles was never condemned by the regime." Cardinal Pole, although a committed Bible reader himself, felt it was better for the people to absorb the faith through the liturgy, to find in attentive and receptive participation in the ceremonies and sacraments of the Church the grace and instruction on which to found the Christian life. This was the true Catholic way, the spirit of the *parvuli*, the "little ones" of Christ, for whom penitence, not knowledge, was the true and only way to salvation.[40]

By the 1560s, Duffy tells us, the Bible commanded a new respect, even among participants in the Northern Rebellion of 1569, and "something of the old sense of the sacred was transferring itself from the sacramentals to the scriptures."[41]

In short, Duffy leaves the subject effectively untouched, and into that space (his weakest), Duffy's most formidable evangelical opponent, David Daniell, pours all the energy of the opposite point (his strongest), hailing Tyndale as the champion of the common reader.[42] Whereas Duffy is nearly silent about Bible reading, Daniell is nearly silent about evangelical theology, beyond insistent, single-line references that imply that Daniell's own theology is the Christian norm.[43] Daniell is most certainly not silent, however, about the virtues of the common person reading the Scriptures in the vernacular, and the heroism, the scholarship, and the authorial brilliance of William Tyndale, who made that common reading possible.

Daniell is not alone in championing Tyndale as the source of liberal freedoms. Anne Richardson also sees Tyndale in this way, tracing a direct line between Tyndale and the U.S. Bill of Rights of 1791: "Such was the gospel of modernity that Tyndale brought us, his English-speaking heirs. It was from sheer pluck, based on belief in the equal standing of his people, *coram Deo*, that Tyndale made his case for a world humanized by law."[44] It is Daniell, however, through his tireless editorial work, who has provided the bibliographical basis for renewed interest in Tyndale, and it is Daniell who has promoted the idea of Tyndale as the forgotten champion of English liberties.

In Daniell's view, Tyndale plays the role to the English that Elijah played to the people of Judah. As with Tyndale under Henry VIII, only Elijah under Ahab "protested against the importation of a foreign religion."[45] Elijah "came to stand even more for the rights of ordinary people against tyranny."[46] Moses, too, provides another subtext for Daniell's narrative of Tyndale: turning the corner of the 1530s "was suddenly to be faced with a vast, sunlit territory, a land flowing with the milk and honey of new images and metaphors, and the rediscovered ancient monuments of God-given religious, political and social revelation."[47]

Daniell's position is pretty well identical not only to that of sixteenth-century reformers themselves, but also to nineteenth-century Anglican champions of the "native religion" against the "foreign" parasite.[48] In keeping with those prior movements, Daniell claims that Tyndale represents both a revolution and a recovery of "native" continuities. This double claim, often made by revolutionary proponents, also has linguistic implications which Daniell, like his nineteenth-century predecessors, is not slow to highlight. The linguistic correlative is this: that Tyndale's recovery of "Saxon" English, with its frequently monosyllabic vocabulary and straightforward syntax, is also a repudiation of enervating, foreign language (that is, French and Latin). It was "during the mid-sixteenth century," when the "English language was a poor thing indeed, almost dead at the bottom of the pond," that Tyndale revived it,[49] and so demonstrated the "continued vitality of Saxon speech. It was never lost, and no more than colored by French. It was, indeed, during the mid-sixteenth century that the older Saxon roots of the language pushed up strong, fresh shoots through the leaf-mould of the forest floor."[50]

Arguments of this kind themselves make manifest an unbroken continuity, though in this case with nationalist traditions of Protestant historiography that began in the sixteenth century and had a powerful efflorescence in the nineteenth century.[51] The manifest fragility of their linguistic evidence aside,[52] it's surprising to find arguments like these made more than a hundred years after they were first brought forth in the full flush of British imperialism, and more than seventy years after unabashed theories of Germanic national character were used with such devastating effect across Europe.

Nor is Daniell shy about claiming Tyndale as the source of liberties exported to the whole world, in the face of tyranny. Perhaps the most revealing metaphor that Daniell offers for the Tyndalian Bible is the Russian tank in the Second World War.[53] Simple in design and built in factories distant from the front with massive determination, these tanks repelled the German war machine. The story of these tanks produced "the immense national driving power that was needed."[54] The tenor of this odd metaphor would seem to be that the Catholic Church was not unlike the German army, while the simple tanks play the role of vernacular scripture. Liberation from this foreign tyrant spread liberty, via Bible reading, not only to the United States but also, as Daniell frequently reminds us (in keeping with a powerful English tradition at once nationalist and imperialist), to "the whole world."[55] Everything that English spreads to the rest of the world advances under the banner of liberty, while all that the language imports must either bear the mark of tyranny, or else be rendered thoroughly "native."

✿ Daniell's strident nationalism and unexamined imperialism should not detain us at all; any counter-offensive would produce a broad, bland, and familiar set of arguments. It remains the case, however, that many readers who would find Daniell's nationalism offensive would nonetheless be persuaded by his claims about the progressive effects of Protestant Biblical reading. What I therefore propose in this book is a meditation on the truth of deep-set claims (by no means restricted to nationalists like Daniell) regarding the un-questionably and unreservedly positive advances brought about by Protestant reading practice. Most broadly, I propose to develop an unusual suggestion: that evangelical reading did not produce either readerly liberty or freedom from institutional restraint. In particular, I underline the multiple ways in which the Biblical text can unleash different forms of violence. I'll focus especially on psychological vio-lence directed against evangelical readers themselves. Here, by way of introduction, I declare the varieties of Biblical violence baldly; fur-ther chapters will supply evidence for each of these claims.

Most obviously, as in the case of Josiah, the book's authority as written document devastates alternative forms of cultural authority. The authoritative book, read in a certain way, legitimates violence in its many instances of violent narrative or injunction, in both Hebrew and Christian scriptures.

Second, and in ways more hidden from historical purview, the Bib-lical text, read within an evangelical reading regime, is capable of ex-erting a psychological violence on its own committed readers, in the experience of reading itself. Many Biblical texts are uncompro-misingly austere, and under some conditions—with no recourse to anything but the literal sense, with the certainty that your experi-ence of reading is a sure symptom of God's decision concerning you, and with the uncertainty that you are reading as a member of God's elect—Biblical reading can easily provoke both fear and self-loathing. For the evangelical reader, the Bible was in the first place a tightrope of terror across the abyss of damnation. Better a tightrope than nothing, if that's all that's available, but few of us are built to sus-tain that kind of challenge. As Richard Hooker was to say about the *scriptura sola* position in his *Of The Laws of Ecclesiastical Polity* (1586–c. 1593): "Admit this [*scriptura sola*] and what shall the scripture be but a snare and a torment to weak consciences, filling them with infinite perplexities, scrupulosities, doubts insoluble, and extreme despairs?"[56]

Finally, and not least, the authoritative book read under these conditions also unleashes an aggression and, not infrequently, a violence between different groups of evangelical readers themselves. In the Reformation, modes of reading became the criterion of institutional inclusion and exclusion—exclusion of all the evangelical's obvious enemies, but also, more interestingly, of other evangelical readers. As in any revolutionary situation that begins, perforce, as a movement of schism, the logic of schism remains deep within the schismatic movement. Revolutionary movements that begin thus tend to replicate the schism into further splinter groups, even, or perhaps especially, after the revolutionary victory.[57]

Vulnerability to schism is particularly pronounced within the terms of an evangelical Biblical reading culture. For the evangelical reader is persuaded of the truth of his or her reading (and therefore of his or her salvation) by, and only by, what Tyndale calls a "feeling faith," an inner, passionate conviction of being chosen and forgiven. That this conviction should be authenticated by intense feeling alone proves an unsteady ground for institutional belonging and solidarity. Such movements tend to produce spectacular and heroic displays of authentication, most obviously in evangelical readiness to endure the flame.

One other spectacular display of authentication is, however, readiness to reject one's evangelical friends. A feeling faith cannot be fully trusted until it has been proved capable of striking at one's most intimate colleagues. In sixteenth-century England, evangelical culture was characterized and energized by profound personal distrust, along with its inevitable Doppelgänger—repudiation of, and attack on, former friends. A Protestant reading culture, leads, I suggest, to what a recent author has called the "persecutory imagination."[58] That desolating experience of paranoia, or at least of being surrounded by nothing but ferocious and sharp-tongued enemies, is especially resonant within the courtier's experience of the Tudor court. That lived predicament was nourished by Biblical genres that were special favorites in court, notably the Psalms.

David Daniell claims that "too much has been made of the [Protestant] factionalism."[59] One might counter that claim by reference to the many wars and bitter disputes in both Germany and England between different Protestant groups; in this book I will be countering it by reference to a more personal context: the vicious betrayals by Tudor courtier evangelicals, and the bitter disputes between Tyndale and his own colleagues.

How has cultural history received the other main player in my narrative, Thomas More? The confrontation between More and Tyndale needs to be revisited because it has always, in my view, been misunderstood, to the detriment not only of More but, more significantly, to the detriment of an alternative, nonevangelical reading culture with its own compelling force. In English cultural history the More/Tyndale confrontation has consistently been set into a single, well-scripted narrative in which both players seem to play their part to perfection: on one side is the manic, persecuting, repressive Thomas More, who has rejected the civilized humanism for which he had earlier stood, and now leads the troop of all who are hostile to the vernacular Bible. On the other side, the solitary, persecuted Tyndale leads the heroic fight for liberty of conscience nourished by liberty to read the Scriptural Word in the vernacular.

Thomas More always produces division in English cultural history. Not even his supporters, however, much want to champion More the Catholic polemicist. Certainly those of an evangelical persuasion have always repudiated him as a hateful repressor of the Word. Those who admire More as humanist are repelled by his performance as Catholic polemicist. Those who honor him as Catholic martyr and saint tend to focus on the events of 1534–1535 (imprisonment, refusal to acquiesce to royal demand, and execution bravely borne), rather than the events of 1523–1533 (anti-Lutheran polemic and legal persecution of religious opponents).[60]

The confrontation between More and Tyndale has been read within sets of simple oppositions, of the following kinds (Catholic versus evangelical position): between the Bible in Latin and the Bible in English; between those who would preserve arcane knowledge for an elite few, as against those who wanted to publish that knowledge far and wide; between those who posited that the divine and allegorical mystery of the sacred text was so deep as to be intelligible only to the expert few, as opposed to those who saw the simplicity of the literal sense offering an invitation to all; and between those who would place the institution and authority of the Church above the individual reader, and those who promoted the individual reader. From these starting places, and with these supporters, there can only be one winner in cultural history. Thomas More has to lose this fight, not only because he did so in history, but also because he looks so bad within the non-negotiable commitments that almost all of us have to the right of liberty in our reading.

These starting places are, in my view, mistaken. For to characterize the whole debate in these terms is to misunderstand it, and to miss the opportunity to understand a much more significant confrontation. The debates and struggles that took place between 1520 and 1547 are about differing definitions of self and communities that derive from different reading practices. They are not primarily debates about vernacular translation; and neither are they, therefore, primarily debates about depriving lay readers of the Bible in English. It's also a confrontation that has the dimensions of tragedy, since each of the two reading cultures becomes more rigid in the face of the other, and the Catholic side in particular contracts a kind of virus of literalism from the evangelical side, while the evangelicals contract an idolatry of the book and the written.[61] This is the kind of confrontation in which both sides are inevitably and permanently transformed from within by contact with each other.

In short, this book looks again at one of Western culture's most stable narratives. Far from seeing the evangelical reading revolution as an unqualified boon, I argue that it imposed punishing pressures on those who adopted it. Rather than being at the root of liberal values, I argue that it is at the root of fundamentalism. Instead of seeing its Catholic enemy, in its most articulate form at any rate, as either stupid or hopelessly authoritarian, I argue that we should take stock of that alternative, communitarian tradition of reading.

CHAPTER TWO

Good Bible News

THE STORY of the Bible in English between 1525 and 1547 is a stirring narrative of heroic challenge and unstoppable victory. Those who produced it did so under extremely threatening conditions; those who resisted it acted with blunt and brutal weapons; and those for whom it was destined consumed it with thirsty intensity. In this chapter I rehearse the vibrant story of the struggle for the Bible in English between these dates. Each of the four subsequent chapters is downbeat about the evangelical Bible. But before the downbeat is sounded, we do need to hear the upbeat. People were, after all, extremely eager to read this Bible and its accompanying books, and they did so with avidity.

The barest narration of the actual events concerning the introduction of the vernacular Bible into England in the 1520s and 1530s confirms the challenges at stake, challenges that evangelicals were prepared to face with extraordinary courage.[1]

William Tyndale arrived in London from Gloucestershire probably in 1523, having already suffered at the hands of a bishop's chancellor, who "threatened me grievously, and reviled me, and rated [chided] me as though I had been a dog."[2] Thinking that he would be well received by Cuthbert Tunstal, Bishop of London (and friend of Erasmus), Tyndale applied for a position in his household, but was turned down. After a year of disappointment, he recognized "at last not only that there was no room in my lord of London's palace to translate the New Testament, but also that there was no place to do it in all England."[3]

April 1524 probably marks Tyndale's exile from England. He would never return. Between 1524 and his death in 1536, Tyndale's life was wholly devoted to the translation of Scripture into English; to the defense of that translation; and to a defense of the theology by which it was underwritten. His first translation of the New Testament (the first scriptural translation into English from the original Greek) was interrupted in print, in Cologne, in 1525. Only one set of sheets up to Matthew 22 survives.

Tyndale escaped to Worms, where in 1526 he produced a full New Testament, of which only three copies, one complete, survive. This text, the first full translation of the New Testament from Greek into English, was clearly a great success among readers. It was smuggled into England and Scotland, and, if the ecclesiastical response is anything to go by, it met with keen demand. Bishop Tunstal (to whom Tyndale had applied for a position) issued an edict in October 1526 to the effect that "the evident appearance of the matter" reveals that "many children of iniquity, maintainers of Luther's sect," have "translated the new testament into our English tongue, entermedling [mixing] there with many heretical articles and erroneous opinions . . . seducing the simple people."[4] Tunstal commanded, under pain of excommunication, that all such books found be delivered to him within thirty days. On 27 October 1526, he presided at St. Paul's over a burning of the books so found, echoing the earlier London burnings of Lutheran books in 1521 and 1525.[5] In November 1526 Cardinal Wolsey's agent in the Low Countries sent two copies to his master from Antwerp (where more copies were being produced), adding that he hoped to see "a great many of them afire" within two weeks. It may be true, as the Elizabethan historian Edward Hall reports, that the authorities went further on the offensive, going so far as to buy up copies in order to destroy them.[6]

Tyndale learned Hebrew while in exile, and by 1530 he had translated and published the Pentateuch, with each of the five books supplied with a prologue. This is the first translation of the Scriptures from Hebrew into English. Possibly a year later he published his translation of the Book of Jonah. Before his likely translation, though not publication, of Joshua to 2 Chronicles by 1535, Tyndale had published the second, revised edition of his 1526 New Testament, in 1534.

Throughout this period, from 1528 to 1534, Tyndale was also occupied in producing polemical works and theological introductions to Scripture.[7] In 1528 he published both *The Parable of the Wicked Mammon*, designed primarily to define the place of works in his theology, and *The Obedience of a Christian Man*, designed to promote the supreme authority of both Scripture in the Church and the king in the state. In 1530 he attacked the prelacy in his *Practice of Prelates*, and in 1531 he produced *An Answer unto Thomas More's Dialogue*. Tyndale also wrote expositions and guides to Scripture during this period: *The Pathway to Scripture* (c. 1530), a revision of the Prologue to the 1525 New Testament; *An Exposition upon the First Epistle of John* (1531); and in 1533 *An Exposition upon the V, VI, VII Chapters of Matthew*. His *Brief Declaration of the Sacraments* was published posthumously in 1548.

In Antwerp Tyndale lived in the English House, but he was betrayed on 21 May 1535 by an English *agent provocateur*, one Henry Phillips, who lured Tyndale out of the house, whereupon he was seized by Imperial officers. Tyndale was imprisoned in Vilforde Castle for sixteen months, during which period he was tried for heresy. From prison he asked that "I . . . be allowed to have a lamp in the evening; it is indeed wearisome sitting alone in the dark." He also asked that he be allowed "the Hebrew bible, Hebrew grammar, and Hebrew dictionary that I may pass the time in that study."[8] In early August 1536 he was convicted of heresy, and in October of that same year he was strangled prior to being burned.

Between the age of 29 (and no doubt earlier) and his martyrdom at 42, then, Tyndale devoted himself utterly to the production of vernacular scriptures and to the defense of that crucial work. His devotion is consistently associated with the danger of punishment, and particularly with punishment by fire, either for his books or for himself. Sometimes the threat of punishment hangs not so much over his person as over his books, given the possibility of errors: in the Preface to the 1530 Pentateuch he humbly submits this book "and all other that I have made or translated, or shall in time to come" unto all those who give themselves to the Word of God. If, after comparison with the Hebrew, they find it wanting, and if they first publish a more accurate translation of their own, then he will allow his translation "to be corrected of [by] them, yea and moreover to be disallowed and also burnt."[9]

At other times, Tyndale offers his own body for sacrificial punishment. In 1531 a royal agent, sent to persuade Tyndale to return to England, reported the latter's response on hearing that Henry VIII would give him a compassionate reception: Tyndale was moved "to take the same very near unto his heart, in such wise that water stood in his eyes."[10] He is reported as answering that

. . . if it would stand with the king's most gracious pleasure to grant only a bare text of the scriptures to be put forth among his people . . . I shall immediately make faithful promise, never to write more . . . but immediately to repair into his realm, and there most humbly submit myself at the feet of his royal majesty, offering my body, to suffer what pain or torture, yea what death his grace will.[11]

In Foxe's rendering of Tyndale's death, even as the executioner's rope tightens around his throat, Tyndale remains intently focused on his single aim of persuading England's king to permit a vernacular scripture: the image of Tyndale's martyrdom in *Acts and Monuments* has him saying: "Lord, open the king of England's eyes."

For all the pain of Tyndale's own life, his enterprise turned out to be unstoppably triumphant. The King of England's bloated eyes were, with a good deal of prompting, opened not long after Tyndale's death. By 1530 George Joye (d. 1553) had produced a translation of the Psalms, following up with translations of Isaiah (1531) and Jeremiah and Lamentations (1534).[12] A year before Tyndale's death a full English Bible had been produced in 1535, in exile, by Miles Coverdale (1488–1569), using Tyndale for the Pentateuch and the New Testament, with the rest being supplied by Coverdale's own translations from Latin and German texts.[13] Only two years after this, Coverdale's version was drawn on by John Rogers in Antwerp for the Matthew's Bible of 1537, now including all the Tyndale material used by Coverdale, but also using Tyndale's translation from the Hebrew of Joshua to 2 Chronicles. All this occurred, however, before the really decisive event: the Great Bible of 1539, which was promoted by the full force of the state. The Injunctions of Thomas Cromwell (Henry's Vicar-General from 1535) of 1538 enjoin every parish priest as follows:

Ye shall provide . . . one book of the whole Bible of the largest volume in English, the same set up in some convenient place within the said

church that ye have cure of [responsibility for], whereas your parishioners may most commodiously resort to the same, and read it.[14]

Priests were not to discourage anyone from reading, but "shall ex-
pressly provoke, steer, and exhort every person to read the same, as
that which is the very lively word of God."[15] In November 1539
Henry VIII promulgated a patent to printers for the printing of a bible whereby he might grant to his people "the free and liberal use
of the bible in our own maternal English tongue."[16] The Bible that
Henry (or rather, perhaps, Cromwell and Cranmer) had in mind was
the revision, by Miles Coverdale, of the Matthew's Bible. In May
1541 a further royal proclamation was issued, insisting that the earlier command to place the Great Bible in every parish church be observed (apparently it hadn't been).[17]

Certainly a good deal of Biblical material was to be produced in
English before the end of the reign of Edward VI in 1553, but the
Great Bible marks the culmination of Biblical translation for the period covered by this book (the next full-scale translation of the Bible
to appear being the Geneva New Testament of 1557, followed by the
full Geneva Bible of 1560).[18] For the moment, with Scripture published in English, the by no means easy evangelical struggle was
for official acceptance and popular absorption of the theology underlying these vernacular translations. The Book of Common Prayer
(1549) is by far the most influential of these books, but evangelical
writers also produced separate catechetical materials.[19]

Although Tyndale undeniably suffered, the central aim of his project became as full a reality as he could have wished in a very short
time after his death. Still, Tyndale was far from being the only exile
and the only victim persecuted for promoting vernacular scriptures
and Lutheran theology from the 1520s to the massive Marian per-

secutions between 1553 and 1558. After imprisonment in Oxford sometime soon after 1525, John Frith (1503–1533) fled to join Tyndale in Antwerp.[20] Captured on More's orders while on a trip to England in 1531, Frith was imprisoned in the Tower. Days after his refusal to recant, Frith wrote his own memorial, *The Articles wherefore John Frith dyed*.[21] He did die in flames on 4 July 1533, at the age of 30. Robert Barnes (c. 1495–1540) was arrested after a reformist sermon in Cambridge in late 1525; he was forced to do public penance by bearing a faggot to St. Paul's Cross and abjuring his "heresy." By 1528 he had sought safety in exile in Luther's Wittenberg. Throughout the 1530s Barnes walked a dangerous path as both English royal agent and evangelical reformer, which involved a period of imprisonment in England in 1536. Caught up in the dangerous currents of Cromwell's fate in 1540, Barnes recanted his evangelical views, but then immediately withdrew the recantation. Once Cromwell had fallen, Barnes stood no chance and was sentenced to burn, which he did on 30 July 1540, along with two other evangelicals; three Catholics were hanged, drawn, and quartered on the same day.[22] Patrick Hamilton (c. 1504–1528) fled from St. Andrews to the Lutheran university of Marburg in 1527. He returned shortly to Scotland, where he was tried and convicted of heresy on 28 February 1528; he was burned on the same day.[23]

Many other names and stories could be added to these pre-Elizabethan narratives of exile, martyrdom, or both. Each life contains combinations of generally new phenomena in English cultural and legal history: exile, sustained contact with German books and German-speaking interlocutors, marriage of priests, and execution. Thomas Bilney (c. 1495–1531) recanted his recantation of 1527 in 1531, whereupon he was sentenced and burned for heresy on 19 August 1531 in Norwich.[24] John Rogers (c. 1500–1555), as Chaplain to the English House at Antwerp, came to know Tyndale; at the time of

Tyndale's arrest in 1535, Rogers appears to have collected the unpublished Old Testament translations (Joshua to 2 Chronicles) and to have been responsible for their absorption, along with Tyndale's Pentateuch and New Testament, into the so-called Matthew's Bible of 1537. Rogers did not return to England, but stayed on in Antwerp before pursuing an expatriate ecclesiastical career in evangelical Germany. He returned to England immediately after the death of Henry VIII, and suffered at the stake on 4 February 1555, the first of the almost three hundred Marian martyrs.[25] Miles Coverdale (1488–1569) died of old age, but only after a life of three exiles amounting to 20 years, two of them prior to the death of Henry VIII in 1547.[26]

The two most powerful official figures in the promotion of evangelical Biblical culture were Thomas Cromwell (c. 1485–1540) and Thomas Cranmer (1489–1556). Both were executed, Cromwell under Henry VIII and Cranmer under Mary. Although heresy was only one of the charges (the other was treason) against Thomas Cromwell that led to his execution by decapitation in 1540, Cromwell's greatest contribution to the textual enterprise of the evangelical movement was the institution of the Great Bible in 1539.[27] The high-risk quality of his contribution can be measured by the fact that his coat of arms has been airbrushed out of the second, 1540 edition of the Great Bible, leaving a white gap on the page.

Thomas Cranmer (the figure on the king's right in the Great Bible's frontispiece) was installed as Archbishop of Canterbury in December 1533; he shepherded the evangelical program throughout the reign of Henry VIII, which he survived, just. Under Edward VI (1547–1553) he produced the Book of Common Prayer in 1549, revised in 1551–52. By September of 1553, after the accession of Mary (ruled 1553–1558), Cranmer was either in prison or (in 1555) under house arrest until his death. He witnessed the burning of his fellow evangelicals Nicholas Ridley and Hugh Latimer in Broad Street, Oxford (September 1555), and in early 1556 he signed four separate submissions to papal authority. Faced with the prospect of execution in February and March 1556, he also signed two recantations. On 21 March, however, instead of rehearsing his recantations, he withdrew them; he was pulled from the pulpit as he spoke in Oxford, and taken directly to burning.[28]

🌿 This brief narrative of the evangelical push for vernacular scriptures is a story of very risky, active, and able service in treacherous territory. The story of the attempted repression of the evangelical action reveals no less active a response by individuals in positions of institutional responsibility. Two basic positions were available to those who saw it as their responsibility to repress the Lutheran challenge, and then to repress Tyndalian vernacular scriptures: either to attack fiercely with the aim of extirpation, or else to attack gently with the same aim.

Both postures are perceptible in sermons that John Fisher (c. 1469–1535), Bishop of Rochester, made at high-profile moments early in the English campaign against Lutheranism. His first sermon of May 1521 was designed to accompany the burning of Lutheran books, presided over by Cardinal Wolsey. In this sermon Fisher warms his listeners up for a murderous confrontation. While he doesn't explicitly promote violent persecution of Lutherans, he certainly does say that the Lutherans themselves have a murderous intent toward those whom Fisher calls Catholics. He cites Christ's own prophecy about the likelihood of religious persuasion producing murderous persecution: "The time shall come, that whosoever killeth you, will think that he doth God service" (John 16:2).[29] Fisher applies this murderous intent both to the Jews in the apostolic past, and to heretics throughout time. Through their misconstruction of Scripture, heretics slay the souls of men (p. 340). Given half a chance, they would also kill literally: in the late fourteenth century the Wycliffites, Fisher declares, put forward a bill in Parliament encouraging secular lords to "to slay their adversaries that resisted against them" (p. 344); if Luther had the Pope in his control, he would show "no more courtesy" to him than he'd shown to the papal books he has burned. "And so likewise I fear me that he would burn them or any other Christian man that he thought might let [hinder] his opinions to go forward" (p. 345). This sermon seems to me clearly to warn Lutherans that they will face ferocious treatment. It voices a threat that was clearly, and rightly, taken seriously by evangelicals. More's young interlocutor in the *Dialogue Concerning Heresies* (1529) expresses that fear when he says that many are now silent who would speak but for fear; any that "now hold their peace and bear them self full coldly" would "take the matter more hot save for burning of their lips."[30]

Within a few years it might have become clear to Fisher that different, more subtle tactics were necessary, and that outright aggression toward "heretics" wasn't working. Certainly the Peasants' War in Germany of 1524 had revealed the dangerously unstable potential of the situation. The subtler approach is evident in the 1526 St. Paul's sermon that Fisher delivered at the recantation of Robert Barnes. Five years after his first sermon, he was no less concerned to target and contain the Lutheran threat. All parish priests should address themselves to the problem: "It is necessary that all those that have charge of the flock of Christ [to] endeavor them self [set themselves] to gainstand [withstand] these pernicious heresies."[31] He praises Wolsey for persevering in his determination to achieve full "extirpation of the same," and insists that heresy needs to be uprooted completely, since it extinguishes the faith, and ends finally with the murder of souls.

After this aggressive thrust, however, Fisher modifies the tone and presents a very different face to covert Lutherans in his audience.[32] He makes a conciliatory offer to any Lutheran disciple:

If it may like [please] the same disciple to come unto me secretly, and break his mind at more length, I bind me by these presents [the present document], both to keep his secrecy, and also to spare a leisure for him to hear the bottom of his mind. And he shall hear mine again [in return], if it so please him. And I trust in our Lord that finally we shall so agree that either he shall make me a Lutheran, or else I shall induce him to be a Catholic and to follow the doctrine of Christ's church. (image 4)

Certainly Fisher is not proposing any doctrinal compromise: either he will become a Lutheran, or else his interlocutor will return to the Catholic fold. What he is offering, though, is space for confident discussion: the Lutheran disciple can be confident that he won't be betrayed, and Fisher is confident in his own powers of persuasion.

Two positions, then, are visible in these sermons of Fisher, one preparing for bloody confrontation, the other offering a space for discussion. Neither offers compromise. The second, more flexible position seems to have characterized Fisher's own actual practice as interrogator.[33] Thomas More, by contrast, adopted the first position from the start.[34] Indeed, even earlier, during the humanist phase of More's career, he had signaled that combating heresy wasn't worth argument. In a letter to Martin van Dorp composed in the period of Book 2 of *Utopia* (12 May–24 October 1515),[35] More runs through the two possible fates of argument in an imagined fight against heresy. Either one's heretical opponents will be ignorant, or they will be learned. If they are ignorant, they wouldn't understand scholastic terms. Learned argument with them would be as effective as delivering an oration in French to listeners whose only language was Turkish. If, on the other hand, the heretics are learned, "when will they be refuted?"

Will there be any end to disputing? For the very problems with which they are assaulted afford them no end of material with which to strike back, so that the plight of both parties is very much like that of men fighting naked between heaps of stones: neither one lacks the means to strike out; neither one has the means to defend himself.[36]

More approaches the fight with a practiced lawyer's viewpoint: he knows that the choice of argumentative weapon must be made with an eye to one's opponent's own arsenal. For all his acuity, however, the actual position points away from intellectual acuity and toward repression by force, since More recognizes that, between warring faith groups, the ground of argument is forever without purchase.

For most of the 1520s More put this perception to repressive work, but, as we shall see, there is also a historical irony to More's abjuration of argument before the decade 1523–1533. For in that decade More was to produce an avalanche of argument against those whom he labeled as heretics. The irony is all the sharper given a point that More makes later in this same letter to Dorp: that all these subtleties "slip easily away into nothing . . . and disappear like a cloud of smoke."[37] It's true that More, in this humanist period, thinks he is characterizing scholastic argument, but More's own description of theological argument as a "cloud of smoke" might have struck him as apt self-description by the early 1530s.

When More enters the fray for the first time in what is obviously his own person, he does so in bullish and bullying mode. He may well have contributed to Henry VIII's own theological tract against Lutheranism, the *Assertio Septem Sacramentorum* of 1521, but More's *Responsio ad Lutherum* of 1523 is his first clear contribution to the controversy, even if he sets up rather elaborate screens of alternative, fictional authorship in both versions.

More had entered royal service in 1518 as a member of the King's Council. When Luther responded aggressively to King Henry's anti-Lutheran tract, More was called to respond. The Latin *Responsio* is most remarkable for the purity, or perhaps I should say impurity, of its hostility. More defends the scurrility of his attack on Luther by describing how Luther gathered the material for his assault on the King. After reading the King's book, More imagines Luther shitting himself in fear, and thus depriving himself of ammunition. Buoyed up by the idea proposed by one of his drinking mates that arguments were unnecessary, given that they were only trying to foment rebellion among the mob anyway, Luther decides that muck alone would do the job. So Luther sends his ruffians off, who disperse "among the carts, carriages, boats, baths, brothels, barber shops, taverns, whorehouses, mills, privies, and stews." After months of scavenging, they assemble whatever "railings, brawlings, scurrilous scoffs, wantonness, obscenities, dirt, filth, muck, shit, all this sewage they stuff into the most foul sewer of Luther's mouth." All this refuse Luther then "vomited up into that railer's book of his."[38]

Thus the first, depressing salvo from More. He imagines his opponents in little dramatic scenarios, and builds up the background with lists. The longer the list, the more we are encouraged to dismiss the whole lot as fetid rubbish, the only decent response to which is aggressive waste disposal. More is implicitly justifying his own rhetorical level and polemical genre here (one of vituperation), but however careful and imaginative the rhetorical defense may be, this beginning does not bode well for especially illuminating discussion.

In the *Dialogue Concerning Heresies*, written in 1529, More explicitly rejects more conciliatory approaches of the kind suggested by Fisher in 1526. Toward the end of the book More argues that princes are bound to punish heretics, and that unless they do so vigorously they'll soon be faced with sedition, insurrection, and open war. Rapid and firm treatment is necessary for the first few, "which few, well repressed, or if need so require utterly pulled up, there shall far the fewer have lust to follow."[39] Soft handling will not do the job either: if heretics are "entreated, favoured, and by fair words and rewards brought home again," they'll end up prouder than ever. He cites the cases of Thomas Bilney and one other, who, treated leniently by

Wolsey, responded by becoming "worse than they were before." If the heretic confesses humbly, then he is to be treated with mercy, but the confirmed heretic deserves expulsion, as proposed by Paul. The passage to which More appeals (Titus 3:10–11) reads thus in Tyndale's New Testament: "A man that is given to heresy, after the first and second admonition, avoid, remembering that he that is such, is perverted, and sinneth, even damned by his own judgement." At the very end of the *Dialogue* More reaffirms that argument with heretics is useless: a man might just as well preach to a post as reason with a heretic.[40]

Throughout the decade of the 1520s, following the *Responsio ad Lutherum*, More followed the tactic outlined near the end of that decade in the *Dialogue*. Neither Wolsey, Fisher, nor Tunstal pursued Lutherans with much enthusiasm.[41] More, by contrast, was active, and clearly driven to be active, at the forefront of the fight against English Lutheranism and Tyndale's vernacular scriptures. High Steward of Cambridge from late 1525, More was vigorous in pursuit of Lutheranism both in that university (where Lutheran theology found the most receptive audience) and in London. In December 1525 he personally led the first of two raids on the London house of the Hanseatic merchants, seeking to enforce the ban on Lutheran books. The subsequent ceremony at St. Paul's in January 1526 was surrounded by flames, both actual and imagined: the four merchants were forced to abjure their heresies on pain of death; Lutheran books were burned. Robert Barnes, who had preached a reformist sermon in Cambridge on Christmas eve of 1525, was forced to bear a faggot. This was the standard ritual for the recanted heretic, reminding him of the punishment for failure to recant or any future changes of heart.

From 1526, however, the target of official repression was not only Lutheranism, but also, much more challengingly, vernacular scripture. Starting in 1521 itemized Lutheran opinions had been banned in England,[42] but by 1527 specific books were officially proscribed. A list of books to be handed in under pain of excommunication in 1527 included "The New Testament of Tindall," along with other polemical evangelical books by Tyndale and others.[43] Two lists of banned books, each listing *"translatio Novi Testamenti,"* were published in 1530 under More's direction as Lord Chancellor. The first of these includes "The Chapters of Moses, called Genesis," and "The Chapters of Moses, called Deuteronomy."[44]

The royal proclamation of 1530 is not just targeted to mere opinions; it has "erroneous book and Bible translations" in its sights. His Majesty, having perceived the danger posed by the devil and men of "perverse inclination and seditious disposition" who have spread "divers heresies and erroneous opinions" by "blasphemous and pestiferous English books, printed in other regions and sent into this realm, to the intent . . . to pervert and withdraw the people from the Catholic and true faith of Christ," is to legislate against them. One plank of the legislation targets the printing of Scripture: no one is to print any books in English "concerning Holy Scripture" that have not been printed in England previously, until and unless the book has been approved by a bishop. The printer will be required to set the name of the approving bishop, and his own name, in the book.[45]

The same proclamation complacently declares that the "Primates and virtuous, discreet, and well-learned personages in divinity" have advised him [the King] that

> by them all it is thought that it is not necessary the said Scripture to be in the English tongue and in the hands of the common people, but that the distribution of the said Scripture, and the permitting or denying thereof, dependeth only upon the discretion of the superiors, as they shall think it convenient.[46]

The text ends with a command that any books of the New or Old Testaments in English must be handed in to one's bishop. Anyone who fails to do so will "answer to the King's highness at their utter-most perils."[47]

More himself possibly composed this proclamation; he was one of the "virtuous, discreet, and well-learned personages in divinity" on whom Henry VIII relied. In 1528 More had been consulted for his forensic skill and, unusually for a layman, his theological knowledge to answer the Lutheran challenge in English. Bishop Tunstal promulgated a license for More to read books adjudged heretical, imported from Germany but translated into English, in order that he, More, should compose a reply for the "simple and unlearned" ("simplicibus et idiotis hominibus").[48] The result was More's *Dialogue Concerning Heresies*, which, while not opposed to vernacular scriptures in principle, vigorously attacked the particular translations by Tyndale on offer.

By 1529, however, More was Lord Chancellor, replacing the fallen Wolsey. It was More who oversaw the proclamation prohibiting erroneous books and Bible translations. It was also More who devised the procedure whereby offenders would be tried in the secular court of Star Chamber rather than before an ecclesiastical court. More imprisoned men for owning books, and he "engineered" the arrest of several book handlers; six Lutherans were burned under More's chancellorship (1529–1532).[49]

More resigned his chancellorship, on 16 May 1532, in protest over the submission of bishops in Convocation to the authority of the King. He was not, however, resigned to any failure on behalf of his polemical campaign against heretics for the Church's prerogatives. Defense of those prerogatives was now much more dangerous for More, precisely because royal policy was now itself one of More's potential targets, and More was in turn one of royal policy's targets. In 1532 he published the first part of the huge *Confutation of Tyndale's "Answer,"* which focused on the grounds of scriptural authority. The second part appeared in 1533. In December 1532 he wrote against

John Frith's Zwinglian understanding of the Eucharist, in the *Letter Against Frith* (published in late 1533). Throughout 1533 More devoted himself to rebutting the arguments of Christopher St. German in favor of making the King the Head of the English Church, in *The Apology* and *The Debellation of Salem and Bizance.* His last polemical book, also written in 1533, was *The Answer to a Poisoned Book* (published in 1534), again defending what he saw as the orthodox position on the Eucharist.

Throughout the period between 1529 and 1533, then, More was staggeringly active on a very wide front, in which the status of Scripture was but one element, however central. More fought at first as a learned layman in defense of the status quo, and in the end as a marked man in defense of what had become a treasonous position. On 17 April 1534, having refused to swear to the Act of Succession, he was imprisoned. Convicted of treason at a trial on 1 July 1535, he made a powerful speech against royal supremacy of the Church. He was beheaded on 6 July 1535.

Even if the vicious undertow of political and ecclesiological events had not swallowed More as it did, he knew that he was going to be on the losing side.[50] For all his astonishing energy and forensic creativity, More gives the impression throughout his polemical career of a man producing Herculean energies in a losing battle, of fighting naked among heaps of stones. As we have seen, he had already unwittingly predicted his own defeat in his argument against heretics in 1516. In the *Responsio* (1523), after having analyzed the slipperiness of Luther's arguments, he summons up the required energy: "We shall drag out this blind serpent, despite his resistance, from his disgusting and darksome hiding places into the light."[51] Even in that early work, however, More is already conscious that the clarity of epic victory isn't available here; rather, this is a dirty fight in which both sides are going to lose. He expresses the disgusting, demeaning nature of his fight with Luther, which befouls him even as he engages with it, by saying that he is "shamed even of this necessity, that while I clean out the fellow's shit-filled mouth I see my own fingers covered with shit."[52]

Perhaps the most pathetic expression of weariness appears in the *Confutation*, where More hankers after an age of innocence. He longs for a time past when English lay readers were unbothered either by the works of "heretics" (e.g., Tyndale) or, more revealingly, by those of their respondents (e.g., More himself).[53] This is the talk of a man who feels exhausted by having expended enormous energy in a battle that he cannot win, and that is steadily destroying him. Throughout the polemic More knows that if he wants to nail the arguments of his opponents he'll need to cite them in full; and the moment he does so, he is publishing those very arguments even as he tries to extinguish them.

Of all the arguments More produced in this period, his attack on vernacular scriptures must have seemed like the biggest loser. More himself was not opposed to vernacular scriptures; rather, he was opposed to the translations of "Wycliffe" and Tyndale,[54] which he read as prejudicial and damaging to his (More's) understanding of the Church. He was also anxious about lay reading of Scripture, unbridled by learned instruction. Above all, as we shall see, he was profoundly opposed to evangelical hermeneutics, but that question was fundamentally separate from the issue of reading Scripture in the vernacular.

Indeed, toward the end of the *Dialogue Concerning Heresies* More actively defends the notion of vernacular scriptures, revealing total agreement with many of Tyndale's own arguments. Having said why lay reading is potentially dangerous, More broaches the question of Scripture in the vernacular directly: "I never heard any reason laid why it was not convenient to have a bible translated in to the English tongue."[55] The original languages of the Bible, and of Bible translations, were themselves vulgar tongues. That English is not up to the task, More dismisses "as but a fantasy": "And if they would call it barren of words there is no doubt but it is plenteous enough to express our minds in any thing whereof one man hath used to speak with another."[56] That Scripture can't be translated at all is clearly disproved by the history of Scripture. Nothing ought to be banned simply because some might misuse it: Scripture was first written in the vulgar tongue, "such as the whole people understood not in secret ciphers but such common letters as almost every man could read."[57] So on the question of vernacular scriptures themselves, More's position overlapped, at least, with that of his enemies. Given his serious objections to the translation of certain controversial words, however, he was nonetheless obliged to fight on that front too.

If More looks like an intelligent loser (and we shall see a good deal more of his intelligence in Chapter 7), his ecclesiastical contemporaries also look like losers, though much less intelligent. In 1525 Edward Lee, for example, wrote to the King with news that a shipment of English New Testaments was about to arrive. All previous "governors of the Church of England hath with all diligence forbad and eschewed publication of English bibles," he proudly avers; he knows that Henry, too, will do the same, that is, "to undertread them that they shall not now again lift up their heads, which they endeavour now by means of English bibles."[58] One Robert Ridley, chaplain to Bishop Tunstal, wrote a letter to a fellow chaplain in 1527 in which he expresses rage in uncontained bursts of Latin amid the English: the "common and vulgar translation of the new testament in to English, done by . . . M. W. Tyndale," as shown especially by the prologues and annotations, is full of the "most poisoned and abominable heresies that can be thought, he is not *filius ecclesiae Christi* [a son of the

Church of Christ] that would receive a gospel of such damned and precised [complete] heretics."[59]

By 1530, the tone of these epistolary protests is not so much desperate as melancholic, not waving but drowning: Bishop Nix of Norwich wrote to the Archbishop of Canterbury in May 1530 that he is "accombred with such as keepith and readeth these erroneous books in English." He is on the point of giving up, since Lutheran numbers seem ready to multiply into a majority: "My Lord, I have done that lieth in me for the suppression of such parsons, but it passith my power, or any spiritual man for to do it."[60] As mentioned above, Halle's *Chronicle* (1548) records that Tunstal had "al his new Testaments which he had bought" burned at St. Paul's in May 1530.[61]

In December 1534 the Upper House of the Convocation of Canterbury, under Archbishop Cranmer, having called for the banning of books of suspect doctrine, appealed to the King to have Scripture translated into English by "certain upright and learned men."[62] Such a project was initiated, and some bishops did translate, or rather, perhaps, "correct" the portion assigned to them.[63] Others were dismissive and successfully determined to sink the enterprise. John Stokesley (1475–1539), Bishop of London from November 1530, did nothing on his section, the Acts of the Apostles. Asked why not, he replied that he wouldn't spend an hour on the task of translation, since it "abuseth the people in giving them liberty to read the scriptures, which doth nothing else but infect them with heresies"; besides, the report goes on, "it is the Acts of the Apostles, which were simple poor fellows, and therefore my lord of London disdained to have to do with any of their acts."[64] This last comment is so implausible as to render the entire story suspect, but the fact remains that Cranmer did try to initiate such a joint project, and that nothing came of it.[65]

Within official Catholic culture we might draw this depressing narrative of scriptural repression to a provisional close by citing a paragraph from the decisions of the fourth session of the first meeting of the Council of Trent, decreed on 8 April 1546. It declares that, in order to keep the unlearned within proper bounds, no one

> must, relying on his own judgement . . . dare to interpret Holy Scripture by twisting it to his own personal understanding, thereby contravening the sense which our blessed Mother Church, whose responsibility it is to establish the true interpretation of the Holy Scriptures, has and continues to hold.[66]

By 1564 the Tridentine Index stipulated that anyone wanting to read a Bible in the vernacular must obtain permission from the local bishop, and in the Roman Index of 1596 "the ban became complete and without exception."[67]

Within the newly founded religious polity of England, political attempts were made to contain the force and effect of the Biblical text; after legitimation of the Great Bible in 1539 such attempts, dressed up as they are in the garments of official, legislative rhetoric, look no less feeble than the foaming private missives cited above. In 1542–43, for example, a statute was passed entitled "An Acte for the Advancement of True Religion." The situation the act addresses is the seditious and disruptive translation of Scripture. Many "seditious" and "arrogant" people have translated and interpreted the Bible, creating schism as a result of "their perverse froward and malicious minds, wills, and intents, intending to subvert the very true and perfect exposition . . . of the said Scripture, after their perverse fantasies."[68]

The legislative response to this hermeneutic anarchy is to delimit carefully the spaces in which and the social classes by which vernacular Bible reading is permitted, and to disallow Biblical interpreta-

tion. Tyndale's translation is proscribed. All "annotations and preambles" to other translated Bibles must be cut out. Moral songs and
plays are permitted, as long as they avoid interpretations of Scripture. Detailed regulations specify which classes and which genders
within each class can read the Bible, and where. The last clause of the
Act closes any possible loopholes; it declares that, even within the
licit spaces and classes of Biblical readers, no one shall "take upon
him openly to dispute or argue, to debate or discuss or expound
Holy Scripture or any part thereof . . . upon the pains of one month's
imprisonment."[69]

Legislative documents of this kind expose a complete failure to appreciate the still-new possibilities of printed material; they express
fantasies of royal control over private and domestic spaces, as well as
royal control of how people read. Along with private responses of
the kind cited above, they also betray an English belatedness in
the wider western European context, where for a long time already
vernacular Bibles had been available in print in all the principal languages of western Europe (even if the Church had also waged a campaign from at least the late twelfth century against vernacular scriptures).[70] In 1516 Erasmus had set New Testament scholarship on a
new footing: his *Novum Instrumentum* presented a new Latin translation in parallel text with its Greek original, with a copious scholarly apparatus. By 1517 the Complutensian Bible, prepared at the
Complutensian University in Spain at Alcalá de Henares near Madrid, was ready for its subsequent publication in 1522. It was a six-
volume edition of the entire Bible, giving, as appropriate, parallel
texts in Hebrew, Greek, and Latin with the Septuagint Greek for the
Old Testament.[71] These Bibles, and especially that of Erasmus, provided the basis for new translations of the New Testament into German (Luther's 1522 New Testament), French, Dutch, Danish, Swed-
ish, and English (Tyndale's work from 1525).[72] Even earlier translations

of the entire Bible had appeared in print: in German-speaking territories the first printed Bible appeared in 1466, and went through eighteen editions before Luther's New Testament of 1522 (1534 for Luther's whole Bible). In France the story is similar: the first version of a printed New Testament may have been available as early as 1470, with the d'Etaples translation appearing in 1523 (New Testament) and 1528 (Old Testament); both were produced together in Antwerp in 1530. The first printed Italian Bible appeared in 1471.[73]

Above all, More and the bishops seem so behind the times, whether intelligently or not, whether actively or lazily, because the vernacular Bible was so unstoppably popular. The figures for its production, no less than accounts of the reading experience itself, reflect the intense demand. It's revealing that some testimonies to the intense effect of Scripture in this period are voiced (and therefore persuasively voiced) by those hostile to or skeptical about it. In 1531, for example, a text attributed to William Barlow recounts the views of a former evangelical lately returned from Germany who, having seen the results of Lutheran application of Scripture, now repudiates his former Lutheran commitment. He is shocked by the lengths to which people will go to read Lutheran material, unchecked by official sanction:

> . . . all Tyndale's books, which [are], for the manifold mortal heresies contained within the same, openly condemned and forbidden; they are, I say, yet unto those books so sore affeccionate, that neither the condemnation of them by the clergy, nor the forbidding of them by the king's highness with his open proclamations upon great pains nor the danger of open shame, nor peril of painful death can cast them out of some fond folks hands, and that folk of every sort.[74]

His interlocutor agrees that people in England are so desperate to get hold of vernacular scripture and Lutheran books "that they put them selves in no small jeopardy many times for the having of it."[75] Similarly, in More's *Dialogue Concerning Heresies* (1529), More's young interlocutor says that he's not interested in any other discipline, for "he hath no light but of holy scripture." He says he learns many passages by heart, and attempts to interpret Scripture by himself, without recourse to glosses: "he found so great sweetness in the text [it]self that he could not find in his heart to lose any time in the glosses."[76]

Personal testimonies to the intensity and sweetness of reading the Word of God survive, describing reading experiences in which, in Tyndale's words, "every syllable pertaineth to thine own self." That intensity explains why readers were prepared to suffer for their reading.[77] Thomas Bilney, for example, is reported to have recalled his moment of conversion as a reading experience produced by Erasmus's New Testament in 1516:

> I chanced upon this sentence of St. Paul in I Tim. 1. "It is a true saying, and worthy of all men to be embraced, that Christ Jesus came into the world to save sinners, of whom I am the chief and principal." This one sentence, through God's instruction and inward working, which I did not then perceive, did so exhilarate my heart, being before wounded with the guilt of my sins, and being almost in despair, that immediately I felt a marvellous comfort and quietness.[78]

The same accents of intense affect can be heard in the text of John Frith, written from the Tower as he awaited the trial that would end in his burning. Frith refuses to stay silent, driven as he is to speak by the intensity of his reading: "I neither will nor can cease to speak, for the word of God boileth in my body, like a fervent fire, and will needs have an issue and breaketh out, when occasion is given."[79]

Throughout this book we will see more such testimonies to the life-changing and life-sacrificing power of reading.[80] The sales figures alone suggest that experiences of these kinds were common: before the vernacular Bible became official in 1539, as many as fifty thousand copies, combined, of Tyndale's and of Coverdale's translations of Scripture had been produced, each copy bought under conditions of danger.[81] Before his death in 1546, Luther's German Bible had gone through more than four hundred total or partial printings.[82]

We should step back momentarily from narratives to examine the grids through which such narratives were shaped. The narrations of both evangelical activity and official repression were generated within durable, and plausible, models of representation. The evangelical script for the vibrant drama of introducing the vernacular Bible had three principal sets of players: the "people" for whom the Biblical text was designed, portrayed as canny but unlearned, and unjustly deprived of necessary spiritual sustenance; Catholic resisters of the Gospel, represented as a powerful and violent vested interest; and the evangelical promoters of Scripture, who represent themselves as heroic under all too real threats of persecution.

Such a repertoire of decisive players shapes any number of evangelical narratives; we can see all three at work in, for example, this little polemic by George Joye. In 1544, the year after repressive legislation severely restricted access to the vernacular Bible, the exiled evangelical polemicist and Biblical translator Joye (1490/95–1553) wrote a fiery exhortation: Gospel defenders were to stand firm in the face of the persecution that the Gospel inevitably provokes. Joye brilliantly manages to mimic the voice of his Catholic enemies as they try violently to repress the vernacular Bible. The official bullies excoriate "this new learning and Lutheran (for so call they God's holy word)," fearing as they do "innovation, commotions & mutations" should it be published.[83] "And therefore," Joye imagines them blustering,

tread down this blessed seed with your filthy feet, suffocate it, burn it,
thrust it from you with sword and fire, and nourish still among you
rather a legion of devils, compelling men to recant and renye [deny]
the truth openly and oft preached, or else burn them. (image 4)

If we are here invited to imagine the bishops stomping and foaming
in rage, Joye later transforms their rage into a comic theatrical spectacle, as the simple people blow their cover with mocking laughter.
The bishops "wrest the scriptures so violently"

that the very babes in the grammar schools, and the plough men, shoe-
makers and wives spinning at their rocks [distaffs] jest on them and
laugh them worthily to scorn. (image 42)

This is, however, a theater of cruelty, since the raging authorities
("these princes, magistrates," and bishops) are still capable of wield-
ing dreadful violence in pursuit of those who promote the Gospel:
"yet cruelly and violently they thrust it [the Bible] from them with
faggots, fire and sword" (image 2). The simple, even as they laugh at
the stamping, Herod-like bishops, are also the victims of spiritual
starvation. Though the bishops should be the protectors of the walls
of Jerusalem, Joye imagines them as betraying the city: they rob the
best garments, and "even the holy Bybles, Testaments, the word of
our faith and salvation, starving the poor hungry souls with famine"
(image 6).

Thus, for all its mercurial intensity, Joye's polemical narrative draws
on what was already a set of stock characters: the "people"; their
Catholic oppressors; and their evangelical liberators.

❧   Each one of the parts articulated in this tripartite drama had a
history behind it by the time Joye wrote in 1544. Already in Erasmus's introduction (called *Paraclesis*, or *Exhortation*)[84] to his New Testa-

ment of 1516, we find a moving call to spread scriptural knowledge to all, and to have this new verbal culture woven into the fabric of daily life. "I would desire that all women should read the gospel and Paul's epistles" (image 6), Erasmus declares; in addition, he wants translations made available to the Scots and Irish, and to "Turks and Saracens" (image 6). Lest anyone think he's not in earnest, Erasmus goes one step further, to imagine a populist and justly celebrated vision. Erasmus's novel understanding of the relation between our innermost selves and our daily conversation leads him to advocate a new form of conversation, inflected by Scripture. Inwardness with Scripture will be the antidote to the grinding boredom of manual or pedestrian work; quotidian chores will be transformed by the new, inner landscape of reading:

> I would to God the plowman would sing a text of the scripture at his plowbeam, and that the weaver at his loom with this would drive away the tediousness of time. I would the wayfaring man with this pastime would expel the weariness of his journey. And to be short, I would that all the communication of the Christen should be of the scripture, for in a manner such are we ourselves, as our daily tales are. (image 6)

In England, Erasmus's populist clarion call fed most immediately into William Tyndale's no less passionate pleas for a vernacular Bible. Tyndale begins his *Obedience of a Christian Man* (1528) with a volley of arguments in defense of a vernacular scripture: God gave the children of Israel the Law in their own mother tongue. The laity is no more encumbered in the world than are ecclesiastics, so want of time for proper reading can't be an argument against lay Bible reading. Nor is the argument valid that every lay person would interpret Scripture according to his own desire ("every man after his own ways").[85] For it's only a matter of decent instruction (of a kind currently not on offer, Tyndale adds) that will teach the laity to read well.

To the argument that English isn't fit for bearing the weight of a learned language, Tyndale retorts that this is nonsense: in fact English has deeper affinities with Hebrew than with Latin, an argument that few of his enemies would be in a position to counter. In any case, he asserts that earlier, pre-Conquest English kings did commission scriptural translation into English. He remembers reading as a child that "King Athelstan caused Holy Scripture to be translated into the tongue that was then in England" (p. 16). Even if, as he thinks may be the case, Tyndale's memory fails him a little here (there is no record of Athelstan [925–939] commissioning scriptural translation), the force of the argument is untouched, since translations of the Scriptures were in fact made into Anglo-Saxon between the ninth and eleventh centuries.[86] Tyndale's arguments in favor of vernacular scriptures reflect a trust in lay readers, and can be augmented: "A thousand reasons more might be made (as thou mayst see in *Paraclesi Erasmi* . . .) unto which they [repressors of vernacular scripture] should be compelled to hold their peace or to give shameful answers" (p. 25).

Tyndale's trust in lay readers survived the official acceptance of vernacular scriptures, in the Bibles themselves at any rate. The Erasmian arguments can be read in the highest-profile Biblical sites in early Tudor England. In the Prologue to the second edition of the 1539 Great Bible (1540 edition),[87] for example, Thomas Cranmer picks up the call. He evokes the Gospels by declaring that the text is designed for "publicans, fishers and shepherds" (p. 120), as well as for the learned with all their erudition. He goes on to expand on the down-to-earth, universal address of the Biblical text:

Here may all manner of persons, men, women, young, old, learned,
unlearned, rich, poor, priests, laymen, lords, ladies, officers, tenants,
and mean men, virgins, wives, widows, lawyers, merchants, artificers,
husbandmen, and all manner of persons of what estate or condition so
ever they be, may in this book learn all things what they ought to believe, what they ought to do, and what they should not do, as well
concerning almighty God as also concerning themselves and all other.
(p. 121)

The second set of players in Joye's imagined drama, the learned
ecclesiastical keepers of the Biblical text, play the obverse role to the
cruelly deprived laity. Evangelical polemicists portray papal academics and officials as self-protective and exceptionally menacing. Luther trenchantly lays out the charge in one of his critical tracts of
1520, *To the Christian Nobility of the German Nation.* The Roman Church
has built three protective and illicit walls around itself, he says, the
second of which is false jurisdiction over Scripture. Luther dismisses
this protective barrier as easily penetrated:

The Romanists want to be the only masters of Holy Scripture, although they never learn a thing from the Bible all their life long. They
assume the sole authority for themselves, and, quite unashamed, they
play about with words before our very eyes.[88]

Luther's own attack, at this early stage of the confrontation, is pitched
purely in terms of usurped, self-protective jurisdiction over Scripture.
Eight years later, in 1528, Tyndale also launched jurisdictional arguments in the *Obedience.* He too puts self-serving arguments in the
mouths of imagined academics. "Scripture is so hard," he has the
learned man saying, "that thou couldest never understand it but by
the doctors."[89] No man can in any case understand Scripture without

the aid of Aristotelian philosophy, which Tyndale pungently miscalls "Philautia" (or Self-love). In contrast to the plain simplicity of scriptural truth, Tyndale has his windy academics huffing and puffing with unintelligible academic jargon, with "predicaments, universals, second intentions, quiddities, haecceities and relatives. And whether *species fundata in chimera* be *vera species* [a kind based on nothing whatsoever be a true kind]."[90]

For Tyndale, however, these incipiently comic figures are funny only up to a point. They are also extremely dangerous. Their unsettling mixture of comedy and malice is evident in Tyndale's *Parable of the Wicked Mammon*, also published in 1528.[91] For here those who resist Tyndale's translated Scripture are pictured as the Anti-Christ, temporarily playing the parts of Catholic officials. We are not to imagine that the Anti-Christ is readily visible as a physical person; he is instead a spirit, and he plays his part like an actor. This metamorphic, spiritual quality makes him harder to spot, and also makes him indefatigable. If he's beaten once by the Word of God, his nature is "to go out of the play for a season, and to disguise himself, and then to come in again with a new name and new rayment."[92] Once the Pharisees played this part, but now the Pope, Cardinals, and Bishops "have yet gotten them new names and other garments and weeds [clothes], and are other wise disguised," but "the thing is all one" (p. 43).

The game that Catholic theologians play is not, however, in the least innocuous: like the Pharisees, these new masters of the text have hidden the key of knowledge, and command men to break divine law. Above all, they kill anyone who challenges them. They killed Christ, and now they will kill Tyndale. They act out of a "good zeal, they say. They love you so well that they had lever [rather] burn you than that you should have fellowship with Christ" (image 5). In the face of the Anti-Christ's pitiless, ahistorical, and ineradicable malevolence, Tyndale makes a moving (especially because accurate) prophecy of his own death at their hands, on account of his work as translator of Scripture:

> Some man will ask peradventure why I take the labor to make this work, in as much as they will burn it, saying they burnt the Gospel? I answer in burning the New Testament they did none other thing than that I looked for [expected], no more shall they do it [otherwise when] they burn me also. If it be Gods will it shall so be. (image 5)

✳ Tyndale's prophecy of his own martyrdom points to the third set of players in Joye's dramatic scene: the learned evangelicals, whose scholarship must be matched by unwavering courage. It is no accident that, of the Hebrew scriptures Tyndale chose to translate beyond the Pentateuch, the prophet Jonah should have been among the first.[93] For that book (published separately around 1531) offers a model for the learned evangelist bearing a divine yet dangerous message into inhospitable terrain.

In the Prologue to Jonah, Tyndale says that Scripture contains three things: the Law, Gospel, and "the stories and lives of those scholars" who learned to believe the "mercy that is promised them."[94] By "scholars" Tyndale means all Christians who have learned from their "schoolmaster" Christ, but, in the context of the story of Jonah, he is also clearly thinking of those who bear a more strictly scholarly responsibility for spreading knowledge of the Word. Jonah is "a man chosen of God to testify his name unto the world," but he's also like the young evangelical preachers whom Tyndale wishes to inspire: Jonah is "but yet a young scholar, weak and rude, after the fashion of the apostles" (p. 631). For these neophytes the story of Jonah is perfectly pitched: although Jonah is not unreasonably afraid of prophesying to a heathen people, he thinks to escape "and be no more a prophet, but live at rest and out of all cumbrance" (p. 632). Once the consequences of his absurd attempt to escape become clear to him, Jonah's conscience torments him in ways that would be replicated for the next two centuries, in a powerful evangelical tradition of autobiography. Jonah's

> . . . conscience raged no less than the waves of the sea. And then he thought that he only was a sinner, and the heathen that were in the ship none in respect of [in comparison to] him, and thought also, as verily as he was fled from God, as verily God had cast him away. (p. 633)

This period of desperation, a prelude to its metaphor in Jonah's three days in the belly of the whale, is of course followed by his "resurrection." The narrative turns on the conscience of the prophet: Jonah's conscience tells him that escape from the categorical moral responsibility of entering occupied territory is impossible, and would lead only to despair. Once resurrected from the whale's belly, he must courageously proceed to prophesy in enemy territory.

Tyndale saw himself as a prophet. Jonah's story doesn't quite match Tyndale's own mission to the English, however, since Tyndale seems never to have wavered. The fearless models of either, say, Jeremiah or Paul are better fits for Tyndale. Whether or not the Book of Jonah resonated with Tyndale's own experience of persecution and exile, he clearly intended it to resonate for any prospective evangelist to the English. For Tyndale now goes on (in this long Prologue to a very short Biblical book) to list examples of prophecy being offered to the inhabitants of the British Isles, and of "God taking cruel vengeance" when "repentance was offered and not received" (p. 634). Gildas, the fifth- or sixth-century British historian, tells us that God punished the British peoples with destruction when they refused to heed the message of repentance; Wyclif (d. 1384) preached repentance "not long since"; failure to listen to that prophet produced the murder of a rightful king (Richard II) and three successive illegitimate kings (that is, Henry IV, V, and VI), with England's nobility being destroyed in the ensuing civil wars (p. 635). All this was clearly intended as a prelude to the latest attempt to preach repentance to the English, Tyndale's own and that of his followers.

The Book of Jonah, then, is a kind of aspiring prophet's handbook, teaching constancy in the face of potentially terrifying persecution. It also teaches that this is a challenge from which one cannot swerve. The representation of the heroic evangelical prophet is ubiquitous in English evangelical writing from the 1520s, and finds its fullest expression in John Foxe's *Acts and Monuments* (1563). Preaching the Gospel is consistently associated with the threat of pain, not least because the Gospel itself says it will be. The apostolic life is dangerous, by Paul's account: he exhorts the converts at Philippi "to maintain the faith of the gospel . . . nothing fearing your adversaries . . . For unto you it is given, that not only ye should believe on Christ: but also suffer for his sake" (Philippians 1:29). Underlining Paul's point, Tyndale glosses this passage by saying: "Tribulation is a token of salvation to the true believers."[95] Evangelicals needed to present the horror of pain, and especially of death by fire, as an immolation devoutly to be wished: pain becomes consolation when it's Gospel pain. Persecution is to be welcomed, precisely as the surest sign of God's favor to his chosen saints.

Thus, as we have seen, the traditions of evangelical writing worked within a straightforward representational repertoire that contained a simple, tripartite cast of characters: innocents being deprived of Scripture at the cost of their eternal souls; murderous Catholic chancellors, theologians, and bishops bent on blocking vernacular scripture; and conscience-driven evangelical scholars equally bent on giving unlimited access to the Scriptures, and prepared to suffer martyrdom in the attempt.

Many scholars in the humanities are deeply sensitive to the power of representation, since their historiographical default position from the 1980s has been that nothing stands outside the realm of representation. Everything is "constructed." This view is not without its profound force, but we should be wary of simple application of the notion that everything in history is "constructed." We should be especially cautious about forever relocating "reality" into the field of "representation" when we are dealing with how threats to life were experienced.

I make this point here because this evangelical "representation" of history would not have looked to the writers themselves like a representation manipulated to cover other, deeper realities. On the contrary, this simple but vibrant representational repertoire would have looked very real to those many evangelical writers who were prepared to die in their attempt to produce and promote a vernacular scripture between 1520 and, say, 1558 and beyond.

The story told thus far is, then, a "narrative of heroic challenge and unstoppable victory." This is where the story usually ends. The next four chapters will be devoted to the darker side of this decisive moment in the history of reading. If the title of this chapter is "Good Bible News," the headline to the subsequent four chapters could be "Bad Bible News."

CHAPTER THREE

Salvation, Reading, and Textual Hatred

THE STORY of the struggle for the English Bible told in the previous chapter is, effectively, the story so far in historiographical terms. Scholars committed to an evangelical culture have told this story in detail and at length. Revisionist scholars of the Reformation have, by contrast, pretty well ignored it. Once the story has been told, there seems nothing else to say. What else could there be to say with regard to such an indisputably desirable historical win? Expanded possibilities for reading so obviously mark a progressive step in our cultural history; unmediated access to one of the principal texts of our culture, untrammeled by institutional authority, has to be a moment of decisive liberation; and the Bible itself is so clearly a good and edifying book to read. So once the tale of heroically forcing acceptance of the vernacular scriptures on a variously lazy, obtuse, and belligerent officialdom has been told, the story seems to be over. All that's left is to admire the translator's literary style.[1]

We should certainly thank David Daniell for bringing the crucial and triumphant Tyndalian chapter of the story into the main narrative of the history of the Bible in English. In fact we should thank him for making this the *main* chapter in that narrative. Nevertheless, there is a good deal more to say about this story. The positions I take in this and the three subsequent chapters are rather less familiar. I reflect on the consequences of this moment in the history of reading, in particular the consequences of violence unleashed, and of exhaustion, paranoia, and limitless anxiety for the evangelical reader.

In this chapter I highlight the competing claims of text and theology in the evangelical package: the text might offer a warm invitation to all, but the theology is rather more selective. The Lutheran moment unquestionably invested the act of reading with a new and unavoidable command, but the work of reading wasn't all that was required of the evangelical convert. That newly welcomed reader also had to build into the act of reading another commanding fact: God wasn't prepared to welcome everyone into heaven, and he'd made his mind up already. All works were wholly, radically inadequate before God, so the works commanded by reading, and the work of reading itself, weren't going to help.

From this point on evangelical readers knew they were either saved or damned through their reading alone, but it wasn't the work of reading that determined the salvational outcome. That had already been decided by God. Thus, although only Scripture could help them, the help it offered was no less evanescent than human works. Scripture was not useful as a source of direction about how to live in the world. For how could the injunctions of Scripture help a Christian so abject that only God's grace could do the saving work? Given the irredeemable abjection of the human will, the injunctions of Scripture were designed rather to rub this in: one can't meet those injunctions. Scripture seemed to say "do this," but it really meant "know it: you can't do this." That is, Scripture was useful in the first place by way of insisting on the reader's abjection: one had to hate the text before one could begin to love it. Scripture was useful, then, not as a source of injunction, but as a source of abject feelings, for feelings were signs: if you felt good (that is, bad) about the reading, if it was hot, that was a sign that God's election had gone your way. If the reading was cold, then things looked bad. God's selectivity bit aggressively into the welcome offered to newly converted readers. The evidence for this aggressive bite will be drawn in the first instance from very high-profile sites of welcome: the prologues to evangelical Bibles.

This is the major paradox explored in this chapter: that in order to love the text of Scripture, the evangelical reader must hate it. I also develop two other paradoxes. The first of these concerns textual ambiguity: evangelicals insist that Scripture is everywhere unambiguous and wholly open, but evangelical reading can start only by recognizing textual ambiguity. The second paradox, which will reappear across these four chapters, concerns faith: although evangelicals insist on "faith alone," a culture that insists on written and only written contracts is, historically, a culture in which faith can no longer be taken for granted. If faith could be assumed, then there would be no reason for the written document. Thus, evangelical "faith alone" culture, in its relentless insistence on the written and only the written, manifests signs of a "no faith" culture.

In the Prologue to the 1535 Bible, Miles Coverdale imagines the vernacular Bible being gratefully received by a calm and meditative public. He runs down a list of figures from different social levels and with different functions, and he encourages each in turn to apply the scriptural text to their respective positions in the world. If the reader is a judge or "ruler of the people," then "let not the book of this law depart out of thy mouth, but exercise thyself therein both day and night, and be ever reading in it as long as thou livest."[2] If the reader is a preacher, then

. . . be ever reading, exhorting, and teaching in God's word, that the
people of God run not unto other doctrines and lest thou thy self
(when thou shouldest teach other) be found ignorant therein. And
rather than thou wouldest teach the people any other thing than God's
word, take the book in thyne hand, and read the words even as they
stand therein (for it is no shame so to do; it is more shame to make a
lye). (image 7)

Male householders are encouraged to love their wives as Christ
loved the "congregation," and to raise their children "in the nurture
and information of the Lord," by which Coverdale clearly means
scriptural information, since he goes straight on to direct illiterate or
over-busy fathers to hire a master for their children. The reading
master to the child is, he says, as important as the mother. Whoever
the reader, let him (Coverdale seems to be addressing males) take
"these words of scripture in to thy heart, and be not only an outward
hearer, but a doer thereafter, and practice thyself therein: that thou
mayest feel in thine heart, the sweet promises thereof for thy consolation in all trouble, and for the sure stablishing of thy hope in
Christ." Those who do so will have the skill to judge all "spirits," and
be free from all error, "to the utter destruction of all seditious sects
and strange doctrines" (image 7).

Coverdale imagines a book informing a whole society, producing
justice, doctrinal unity, and familial coherence. Everything follows
from assiduous Biblical reading, day and night: the judge's mouth
should voice nothing but these words; the priest should not be embarrassed to have his own voice usurped by that of the book, since it's
better simply to read from the book than to stray into error by *viva
voce* performance; the induction of children into this reading culture
is no less important than the training they receive from their mother.
Like Erasmus in the *Paraclesis,* Coverdale imagines a society in which
the daily life of people is informed at every turn by their Bible knowl-

edge and reading: "Sit thee down at the Lord's feet and read his words," he exhorts,

> when thou sittest in thyne house, or goest by the way, when thou liest down, and when thou riseth up. And above all things fashion thy life, and conversation according to the doctrine of the Holy Ghost therein, that thou mayest be partaker of the good promises of God in the Bible. (image 6)

Above all, the Biblical reader will be endowed with a wholly new and deeply pleasurable perception of the world: "Thou shalt find sweetness therein, and spy wondrous things, to thy understanding, to the avoiding of all seditious sects, to the abhorring of thy old sinful life, & to the stablishing of thy godly conversation" (image 6).

Coverdale's imagined society of the book is all unity, pleasure, and calm. The book has flowed into every interstice of social relations, expelling both rebellion and division. Coverdale doesn't provide much actual doctrinal instruction here; there is certainly no Lutheran fear and trembling before the terror of God's fierce judgment.

That fear and judgment are, however, visible just below the surface. Coverdale provides a brief and generally anodyne account of the relation of the Old and New Testaments: the New makes clear how God carries out the promises he made in the Old Testament; it is declared and included in the Old (the one distinctively evangelical accent here); and it fulfills and verifies the Old (image 6). Of actual salvation theology (known as "soteriology"), though, we hear nothing.

Or almost nothing. Soteriological issues have, however, arisen obliquely a moment earlier, in Coverdale's discussion of translation choices. Coverdale draws attention to the translation of one word ("penance") that had particularly inflamed Catholic readers of Tyndale's New Testament. In this apparently philological discussion (and

Coverdale tries to keep it philological as far as he can), potentially more unsettling accounts of evangelical theology and reading are just visible.

Coverdale has this to say about his choices as translator of words related to the concepts of penance and repentance:

> And this manner have I used in my translation, calling it in some place penance, that in another place I call repentance, and that not only because the interpreters have done so before me, but that the adversaries of the truth may see, how that we abhor not this word penance. (image 7)

A small philological digression is necessary to explain why Coverdale should take care to isolate this one word in his Prologue. For translation of the word "penance" is one of the apparently small philological fault lines on which a good deal of the edifice of the Catholic Church would tremble and, in much of Europe, collapse within short order.

The Greek word *metanoia* appears frequently in the Greek New Testament. *Metanoia* means, literally, "after thought," and its figural sense is "repentance." Tyndale had taken issue with the standard Latin Vulgate translation of this word as *penitentia* (penitence). The word is used, for example, in Matthew 3:2. John the Baptist's announcement of the coming of Christ reads thus in the Vulgate: "'Poenitentiam agite; adpropinquavit enim regnum caelorum'" ("Repent / Do penance, for the kingdom of heaven has come near").[3] The Wycliffite Bible, in the 1380s, had translated the passage thus: "Do ye penance, for the kingdom of heavens shall neighe."[4] Tyndale, however, translated it in 1526 in this way: "Repent, the kingdom of heaven is at hand."[5] What had happened between the Wycliffite "Do ye penance" and the Tyndale "Repent"?

The simple answer is Erasmus's *Novum Instrumentum* of 1516. The actual text of Erasmus's Latin translation of the Greek New Testament changes the Latin Vulgate only slightly. Instead of "Poenitentiam agite," as in the Vulgate, Erasmus's text reads: "Poeniteat vos," an impersonal and subjunctive construction whose translation might be rendered "May you feel penitence."[6] Now that seems a slight enough change, but the ample notes that accompanied Erasmus's text opened up what would become an institutional crevasse.

Erasmus begins by justifying his change on philological grounds: the Vulgate reading seems like bad Latin to him.[7] He then explains the Vulgate reading by reference to a historical understanding that the public repayment, "the satisfaction or suffering" (the "satisfactio sive poena") for sin committed began, at some unspecified, though post-Augustine, stage in Christian history, to be called "poenitentia." He goes on to say that various theologians then twisted that public satisfaction to a new sense, one of "grief of soul, which they call contrition" ("ad animi dolorem, quam contritionem vocant"). From here he suggests that another sense, and therefore another translation of the term, would be better: "By my judgement it would be more properly translated 'recover one's senses,' or 'reflect'" ("meo iudicio commode verti poterat, Resipiscite, sive ad mentem reddite").

"Penitence" versus "repentance" is one of the translational choices over which More and Tyndale came to blows in the years between 1529 and 1533. Tyndale capitalized on the availability of Erasmus's Greek, but pushed much further into possible meanings of *metanoia* than Erasmus was prepared or inclined to do. In Erasmus's notes to the *Novum Instrumentum*, as we have seen, the discussion is for the most part philological, with only passing reference to the way in which theologians had "twisted" the sense of *penitentia*. In both *An Answere unto Sir Thomas More's Dialogue* (1531) and the *Confutation of Tyndale's Answer* (1532–33), Tyndale and More, respectively, state what Erasmus must have known but did not make explicit: that this philological discussion has profound institutional consequences.

Tyndale certainly doesn't neglect to make the philological point (for him cardinal, since institutional authority flows from the words themselves). He says this: "As for their [that is, Catholic theologians'] penance, the scripture knoweth not of. The Greek hath Metanoia and metanoite, repentance and repent, or forthinking [regretting] and forthink [regret]."[8] This philological point is made, however, only after the institutional and theological implications have been aggressively targeted: "By this word penance they [Catholic theologians] make the people understand holy deeds of their enjoyning, with which they must make satisfaction unto Godward for their sins. When al the scripture preacheth that Christ hath made full satisfaction for our sins to Godward."[9]

More is no less explicit about the institutional and theological implications of this philological fight. In his polemical works against Tyndale's scriptural translations, More had consistently focused on what he saw as Tyndale's prejudicial translation of certain key words, one of which is the latter's choice of "repentance" over "penance." In the *Confutation*, More shifts the ground from philology to theology straightaway: in using "repentance," Tyndale is "not angry with the word but because of the matter." If the word "repentance" had the semantic value of "penance," More argues, then Tyndale would be just as angry with that word too, because it's the "matter," not the word, that drives evangelical rejection of "penance." The "matter" is both institutional and theological: Luther and Tyndale are angry because the orthodox understand by the word "penance" "not a bare repenting or forthinking only, but also every part of the sacrament of penance, confession of mouth, contrition of heart, and satisfaction by good deeds."[10]

The profound significance of the translation issue is now clear: one of the sacraments of the Church is, for More, threatened by any variation from "penitence." Discussion of philology, or the meaning of words, takes us quickly into nonphilological territory, because so much is at stake in the choice of one translation over another. In this case, the cornerstone of the pre-Reformation Church's sacrament of penance was being pushed out from under a weighty sacramental edifice. From the Fourth Lateran Council of 1215, annual confession for each Christian who had reached the age of reason became compulsory. That legislation marked a decisive new step in the history of both self-analysis and ethics: Christians were expected to be able to locate sin within a quite complex penitential map; to feel contrition for the identified sins; to articulate their failings; and to perform some deed ("satisfaction") to repay for sins committed. This is the basis of the three parts of the sacrament as listed by More: contrition of heart, confession of mouth, and satisfaction, or repayment for sins committed. A vast penitential literature developed as a result of this legislation, and that literature was itself part of a mighty pastoral program, designed to instruct the laity in the basics of the faith, from the beginning of the thirteenth century.[11] One crucial part of that entire edifice (devoted to the sacrament of penance) now balanced uneasily over a crevasse opened up by the translation of a single word.

❧   We can now return to the Coverdale Bible and its Prologue with a sharper sense of the fraught issues involved in the choice of specific words. Coverdale himself translates Matthew 3:1–2 thus: "In those days John the Baptist came and preached in the wilderness of Iury, saying: Amend yourselves, the kingdom of heaven is at hand."[12] Coverdale clearly tried to avoid reigniting the dynamite of the very hot verbal choices on offer to date: by using the word "amend," he cannily avoids both "penance" and "repent."

That choice looks emollient. So too does his discussion in the Preface to the 1535 Bible about how he chose translations in the contentious semantic field of grief for sin. There he initially smoothes over the fierce asperities of the More/Tyndale dispute by leading us back into the domain of learned philology. As we saw earlier, he says that he sometimes uses the word "penance" in his translation, sometimes "repentance." He has done so not only because there is historical precedent for this, but also in order to advertise to his adversaries that he has no prejudicial hatred of the word "penance": "We abhor not this word penance (as they untruly report of us) no more then the interpreters of Latin abhor *penitere*, when they read *resipiscere.*" With this discussion we are back in the Erasmian study, mulling over different senses of words, recalling ancient usage, evoking the very choices Erasmus himself proposes (for example, *resipiscere*, "to come to one's senses"). In this irenic mode, the choice of one translation is often as good as another.

At this Erasmian moment in Coverdale's apparently moderate Biblical welcome, however, he strikes a different and wholly anti-Erasmian note. He goes on immediately to underline the non-negotiable theological persuasion that undergirds his translation, regardless of the particular word chosen:

> Only our heart's desire unto God is, that his people be not blinded in their understanding, lest they believe penance to be ought save a very repentance, amendment, or conversion unto God, and to be an unfeigned new creature in Christ, and to live according to his law. For else shall they fall in to the old blasphemy of Christ's blood, and believe, that they themselves are able to make satisfaction unto God for their own sins, from the which error God of his mercy and plenteous goodness preserve all his. (image 7)

That is, as long as his readers understand the meaning of "penance" (as having nothing to do with the Catholic sacrament), Coverdale is, in sum, perfectly happy to use it.[13] As long as his readers understand the Lutheran theology of penance, then one word will serve as well as another.[14]

The language of this non-Erasmian statement in Coverdale's Preface now suggests the fire behind the issues: the people are not to be "blinded"; they are to believe in the power of "conversion"; and if they don't, they will "fall into" the "old blasphemy" of believing in the sacrament of penance. Reflection on the theological backgrounds to this discussion of penance reveals the hotter intensity awaiting the evangelical reader.

Three penitential and spiritual cultures are visible in this Preface. Coverdale's "old blasphemy" here signals the Catholic sacrament of penance, which comprises a negotiated process whereby the sinner resituates him- or herself within the strictures of God's justice and within the Christian community. The premise of the sacrament is that the Christian's works can, within the gracefully mediated terms of God's justice, change the sinner's situation: one can persuade God, through verbally articulated contrition for sin committed and social repayment for that sin, to readmit one into the company of the absolved. The institution of the Church is the indispensable channel through which the negotiation is made, via a priest. Individual initiative is a *sine qua non* of the process, but so too is the institution's treatment of that initiative.

The second penitential culture is Erasmian. When Coverdale says that "we abhor not this word penance (as they untruly report of us) no more then the interpreters of Latin abhor *penitere*, when they read *resipiscere*," he is evoking an Erasmian model of penitence. Despite the fact that Erasmus certainly never repudiated the sacrament of penance, he did cultivate a much more personal sense of contrition that had its own integrity outside the institution of the Church. The very word for penitence that Coverdale uses here (*resipiscere*, drawn directly from Erasmus's notes to his *Novum Instrumentum*) itself evokes Erasmian sweet reasonableness: it means "to recover one's senses," to "come to oneself again." It implies a spiritual culture of confidence in the Christian's independent movements of his soul, and confidence in the possibility of recovery of a desirable, prior state.[15] Erasmus says that some major theologians twist (*detorquent*) what Augustine meant by *penitentia*, by applying the word to private contrition. In making this point he is clearly opening, though not himself taking, an opportunity to use philological knowledge to criticize the sacrament of penance.

Both Erasmus's Christian humanism and Catholic sacramentalism stand in the starkest contrast to the third, Lutheran penitential culture visible in Coverdale's Preface. This third, evangelical conception of penitence expresses a radically different conception of the psychology and institutional treatment of contrition. On 31 October 1517 Luther had attacked the abuse of the sacrament of penance with both courageous daring and polemical skill when he posted his brilliant, provocative, and mercurial 95 theses on the door of the Castle Church in Wittenberg. Number 50, for example, expresses an intensely compressed, poetic appreciation of the relation between magnificent ecclesiastical architecture and the intense but hidden human suffering upon which its magnificence arose: Christians are to be taught that the Pope would prefer that "the basilica of St. Peter's were burned to ashes than built up with the skin, flesh, and bones of his sheep."[16]

While most of the theses that address the sacrament of penance restrict themselves to the question of indulgences, the first two signal a much more radical critique of the sacrament of penance itself. I cite them in order:

1. When our Lord and Master Jesus Christ said, "Repent" [Matthew 4:17], he willed that the entire life of believers to be one of repentance.
2. The word cannot be understood as referring to the sacrament of penance, that is, confession and satisfaction, as administered by the clergy.[17]

Luther's Latin here cites the standard Vulgate reading of "Penitentiam agite," no doubt because he is not yet using Erasmus's text.[18] Despite that citation, he is clearly poised to push into the radical institutional implications of the translation issue, even if he does not here take the philological perception to a full critique of the sacrament of penance.

Luther moved closer to a full critique three years later in *The Babylonian Captivity of the Church*, published in October 1520. In this text Luther consigns four of the Church's seven sacraments to the dustbin of human traditions without scriptural foundation. Baptism, the Eucharist, and penance survive. By penance, however, Luther means something entirely opposed to the sacrament of penance as promulgated by the traditional Church. His expansion here is consistent with what he had said in the first of the 95 theses. The papal Church has placed contrition above faith; Luther responds that faith drives contrition. With "faith and its work destroyed, we go on secure in the doctrines and opinions of men, or rather we perish in them."[19]

Although Luther preserves the sacrament of penance, and the practice of confession, he transforms the first and relocates the second. For Luther, repentance is the product of faith. Emotionally it is the painful part of the dialectic of the faithful life, whose upside is consolation. In this emotional dialectic we hear nothing of the gradual, accretive steps of the Catholic sacrament of penance; nor do we hear Erasmian accents on inward reflection. Instead we hear a more sublime echo of the turbulent inner life of the convinced evangelical sinner. This turbulent spiritual life is marked by sudden moments of personal conversion, just as the evangelical sense of history is marked by sudden, chiaroscuro shifts from old and dark to new and bright. Faith is found only in the promises and threats of God; such faith,

> intent on the immutable truth of God, makes the conscience tremble, terrifies it and bruises it; and afterwards, when it is contrite, raises it up, consoles it, and preserves it. Thus the truth of God's threat is the cause

of contrition and the truth of his promise the cause of consolation, if it
is believed. By such faith a man "merits" the forgiveness of sins.[20]

Here we can clearly hear the *Sturm und Drang* of the Lutheran spiritual life that is only just audible in Coverdale's Preface. The soul
imagined by Luther in this short passage confronts the terror of
God's judgment alone and without mediation. The terrified Christian
can have recourse to none of the obvious resources for placating an
angry God: not the sacramental steps of penance, nor any work or
deed that might mollify God. Above all, the Christian must have no
confidence in any human resource whatsoever. The only available resource amid the terror is faith in God's own initiative.

Why should Luther dispose of works and human initiative, especially when such disposal leaves the Christian in so exposed a position? Luther does not answer that question in the *Babylonian Captivity*,
which provides scriptural, but not full theological, grounding for the
demolition of so many of the sacraments. By November of the same
year, however, Luther was to supply a much clearer statement of the
theology that underwrote this more turbulent and exposed spiritual
experience of repentance. In *The Freedom of a Christian* (November
1520) we enter more directly into the energizing, unstable intellectual structure of Lutheran paradox. The work begins, indeed, with a
paradox of Lutheran freedom, simultaneously promising and denying
freedom:

A Christian is a perfectly free lord of all things, subject to
    none;
A Christian is a perfectly dutiful servant of all, subject to all.[21]

The rest of the treatise reflects on and expands this irresolvable, Pauline paradox of the Christian life in which Christians are both free
and enslaved. Christians have, by Paul's account, both inner and

outer selves: selves free from the Law by God's promises, and selves subject to the Law through original sin. Liberation from the Law is beyond human capacity for Luther, precisely because humans have fallen into a condition so irredeemably sinful that any initiative of their own is hopelessly flawed. Above all, works are of no value whatsoever. The only human exercise that can save is a faith derived from the Biblical text. This point is cardinal in the Lutheran system, as the following quotation attests:

> This faith cannot exist in connection with works—that is to say, if you at the same time claim to be justified by works, whatever their character . . . Therefore the moment you begin to have faith you learn that all things in you are altogether blameworthy, sinful and damnable, as the Apostle says . . . "There is none righteous, no not one . . . they are all gone out of the way, they are all made unprofitable" [Rom. 3:10–12, citing Psalm 14:1–3]. When you have learned this you will know that, if you believe in him, you may through this faith become a new man in so far as your sins are forgiven and you are justified by the merits of another, namely of Christ alone.[22]

This passage compresses the essence of the Lutheran system into short compass: humans share an irredeemable abjection before God; they can do nothing to escape from that abjection; only a psychological conviction, or faith, in God's promise of salvation will serve to relieve the despair of one's abject condition; the grounds of that promise of salvation have been laid by the works of God alone, in Christ.[23]

Many consequences, momentous for the formation of early modernity, flow from this reaffirmation of Pauline spirituality. Above all, spiritual experience is relocated from action in the world, and placed instead in a psychological act of faith alone. Action in the world, invested with the dignity of labor, and performed in the hope of reward, is dismissed as already flawed and utterly inadequate. If action in the world is useless, then so too is the sacrament of penance as understood by the Catholic Church, since that requires works of satisfaction for sins committed. The Christian faces an angry God alone. In this newly defined spirituality, the spiritual life is essentially an emotional life, informed as it is by the emotional content of both terror and overflowing gratitude.

Further forms of Lutheran and early modern equality, individuality, and liberty, new and strangely dark, all rise rapidly from this moment.

Christians are equalized, yes, in a de-hierarchized sacramental system, stripped of mediating levels. They discover their equality, however, only in horizontal abjection. They also discover it through vertical distance from a newly transcendent God. This God has been reinstated in his due position of being wholly unshackled by human mediation, human justice, and human intervention. This God, that is, has spectacularly broken through the constraining dialectic of absolute and agreed jurisdictions to which the late medieval Christian God had willingly submitted himself.[24]

Late medieval Christian theologians had constructed a theology that gave full recognition to two opposed traditions: the positivist, Hebraic tradition of God's absolute justice, and the Greco-Roman notion of a divine reliability and rationality, perceptible to humans. Luther demolishes that elaborate structure and leaves only the positivist notion in place. What God decides is right because God decides it, and God decides everything. So a Lutheran equality can only be measured in relation to an external, fixed point, and in this case the fixed point is a good deal further away; there are few recognizable paths to it; and its justice is all its own.

Christians are individualized, yes, but this individualization does not belong to the history of the secular subject's freedom, so much as the reverse: a sense of individuality rises dramatically in profile precisely because self-consciousness is enlarged as it confronts a single and menacing source of absolute power. Confronted directly with a punishing God, Christian subjectivity is suddenly magnified to itself in its terror.[25]

Christians are liberated, yes, from the constraints of a material regime of ritual observance, but they are simultaneously enslaved to a demanding psychic regime.

The other immediate consequence of this diminution of human powers and initiative concerns justice and textuality. Writing, in the form of sacred Scripture, occupies an entirely new centrality as the ineluctable site of both law and promise. The new prominence of the written is, however, gained at the expense of many·consolations of writing. For this scriptural culture prizes the written status of the Law in a wholly new way, without precedent, I contend, in Western history: it prizes the written status of the Law precisely by insisting on the incapacity of readers to apply the lessons of such writing. This remarkable novelty leads, that is, less to the Enlightenment and more to Kafka's story *Before the Law*.

Luther explicitly affirms both the ineluctability of the written statement of the Law, and its uselessness as a model for action, in *The Freedom of a Christian*. How do we derive this faith in God? Certainly not through the material Church, and neither through direct inspiration, both of which Luther repeatedly dismisses very aggressively elsewhere.[26] We derive this faith only through a particular textual kinesis, or movement. We derive it through Scripture itself, through the documentary testimony to both divine threat and promise: "Faith alone is the saving and efficacious use of the Word of God."[27]

So "faith alone," or *sola fides*, paradoxically produces another "alone" argument of *scriptura sola*, Scripture alone. One "alone" would normally exclude another, but this is not, perhaps, a deep paradox: the documentary form of the promise is the sole ground of believing the promise.

A moment's reflection reveals, however, a deeper, truer, more unsettling paradox. In Western cultural history, writing is usually *opposed* to faith, or at least is a compensation for want of faith: one writes the contract down precisely because there's a shortfall of faith. Oral culture relies primarily on witnesses, while literate culture gives primacy to documents. True faith would dispense with the written document. In the Lutheran system, by contrast, the book has become the repository of faith, unsustained by any surrounding structure. We must have faith alone, but at the same time we must see the small print, in black and white. This is, as we shall see, an extremely testing and difficult position to maintain with any consistency.

Scriptura sola bears the even more startling surprise of a grander, darker paradox embedded within it. For what, in the Lutheran system, is the function of read Scripture? If the Bible is indeed an edifying book, the ground for that claim would presumably be the models of action provided by the book. If, however, one's theological premise is that righteous works are simply out of fallen human reach, then what purpose can be served by the Bible's promotion of good works? There is a very long history of reading in the West that defends the reading of books by accentuating the way in which books provide ethical models.[28] When Luther places the Bible in so central a position, we might expect him to be subscribing to that tradition. After all, not only is the Bible taken to furnish many models of ethical behavior, but it unquestionably prescribes ethical behavior with a certain frequency and force.

If we expect Luther to enlist himself in this tradition, we will be badly disappointed. For, on the contrary, Luther explicitly *denies* that the works promoted by the Bible serve any function but that of threatening readers with powerlessness, and provoking despair at that powerlessness. The very point of the prescription is to insist that the reader can't fulfill it. For Luther, the power to change oneself, or the world, through the models provided by one's Biblical reading is a receding horizon: the model for change only reveals one's incapacity to imitate that model. The model, that is, can only provoke despair at the reader's impuissance to base action on the model. Luther underlines this point explicitly in *The Freedom of a Christian*, and he would make it more forcefully within a few years, in his fierce debate with Erasmus about reading, moral effort, and predestination. This is what he says in *The Freedom of a Christian*:

> Should you ask how it happens that faith alone justifies and offers us such a treasure of great benefits without works in view of the fact that so many works, ceremonies, and laws are prescribed in the Scriptures, I answer: First of all, remember what has been said, namely, that faith alone, without works, justifies, frees, and saves . . . Here we must point out that the entire Scripture of God is divided into two parts: commandments and promises. Although the commandments teach things that are good, the things taught are not done as soon as they are taught, for the commandments show us what we ought to do, but do not give us the power to do it. They are intended to teach man to know himself, that through them he may recognize his inability to do good and may despair of his own ability.[29]

Lutheran reading is, by this account, a permanent experience of recession, a Tantalus-like situation of reaching out to something that is inevitably beyond one's grasp. The point of the reading is not to offer the model, but to underline that the reader is too sinful to profit from the model. That is, the immediate point of reading (and only reading will save) is to provoke despair. That despair is part of the emotional dialectic of salvation.

What, we might ask, is the condition of language in these circumstances? Under the regime of evangelical theology, language always falls short of its own enterprise; it's a kind of shadow play, gesturing to a situation in which language might, but cannot, be activated. Language stands at an extremity, on the abyss, meaning an opposite of what it enjoins. Readers, presumably, become the terrified witnesses to their own incapacity. Promise and threat share a strange and menacing proximity in the Lutheran system: written words are our sole source of consolation, but those words torment us even as we commit ourselves to them.

I used the phrase "Lutheran system" in the previous section because it seems to me that a core set of positions on both salvation and Scripture, all radically new, were available to Luther pretty much as soon as his voice was publicly heard in 1517. So far the account of these core positions in this chapter has been abstract, if anything in Luther can be said to be abstract: his writing takes us so directly into a world of dark paradoxes, which curiously energize even as they crush, that we are never far away from intense experience. Nonetheless, we do have one account of Luther's actual experience from his own hand. We should look at this moment before we return to the prologues of the English Lutheran Bible, since it reveals ambiguity to be the very motor of Lutheran reading.

The actual date of Luther's moment of conversion is uncertain (is it before or after the 95 theses of October 1517?);[30] for our purposes the important thing is not the date but the representation of the experience. That representation, by Luther himself, was made very much later, in the preface to Luther's Latin works, published in Wittenberg in 1545. In it Luther presents an extraordinarily intense personal experience that is centered, indivisibly, on both reading and justice.

Luther tells us that he was about to interpret the Psalter afresh, having first delivered university lectures on Romans, Galatians, and

Hebrews.[31] He emphasizes both his passionate captivation by ("ardore captus") and his profound trouble with Paul, and he underlines his difficulty with one word in particular. The passage stresses both reading and salvation. It reads thus:

> For I am not ashamed of the gospel of Christ, because it is the power of God unto salvation to all that believe, namely to the Jew, and also to the gentile. For by it the righteousness which cometh of God, is opened, from faith to faith. As it is written, the just shall live by faith. (Romans 1:16–17)

The one word that had obstructed Luther was "righteousness," in the phrase "righteousness of God." The Latin, Vulgate reading of the phrase with which Luther was grappling is "iustitia Dei," the "justice of the God." Luther says he hated that word ("Oderam enim vocabulum"), since despite his living a blameless monastic life, he nevertheless felt that he was a "sinner with an extremely disturbed conscience." He finds himself secretly hating the God who punishes sinners, since he feels sure that God could not be placated by his (Luther's) "satisfaction," or deeds of penance. He feels that God is rubbing the Christian reader's nose in the mire of his or her own damnation. For isn't it enough, he had rebelliously murmured, that the Christian reader is damned by the Law of the Decalogue, without God adding insult to injury in the Gospel ("per evangelium dolorem dolori adderet") by threatening us with righteousness and wrath there too?

Out of this experience of self-loathing and hatred of God, Luther's breakthrough comes with a *grammatical* understanding.[32] This understanding resolves *both* the question of how Luther might still be saved, *and* his angry doubts about the Gospel itself as a text that seems to deny salvation even as it promises salvation. Genitive phrases are ambiguous: "the justice of God" can mean either "the [recognized, common standard of] justice that God practices," or it can mean "the justice that belongs wholly to God." This second kind of genitive suddenly evacuates a word (here "justice") of any of its familiar meanings.[33] Luther's conversion occurs when he suddenly realizes that the genitive phrase should be interpreted in that second way. The word should, that is, be understood wholly outside of its customary usage. From that single interpretive act—the semantic evacuation of the word "justice"—flows a corrosive for all human standards and initiative. Evacuation of human standards, in order to make way for the alien standard of the divine, is, indeed, the essence of Lutheran theology. God is reinvested with his full and wholly unintelligible, inscrutable divine prerogatives. The text holds out just one human rope, of faith, to this newly estranged God: "As it is written, the just shall live by faith."

A grammatical ambiguity suddenly opens up a new world: "Here I felt that I was altogether born again [*renatum esse sensi*] and had entered paradise through its open gates." Luther rereads the whole of Scripture (which he knows from memory) with a new and entirely fresh perception. He moves from a state of hostile fury ("Furebam ita saeva et perturbata conscientia") to one of immense, joyful relief. The hatred he had felt for the word *iustitia* is transformed into its exact opposite of sweetness ("tanto amore dulcissimum mihi vocabulum extollebam").

Luther's grammatical perception opened, by this account, a new personal world for Luther, and that sudden conversion also serves to articulate one world from another. Simultaneously, a new order of reading and spirituality is born of this moment: a world is born of a word. In light of the darker accents underlined in this chapter thus far, I end this discussion of Luther's exhilarating reading lesson with some reflections on the surprising relation between what produces the conversion and what the conversion, in turn, itself produces.

In the first place, self-loathing, feelings of profound inadequacy, and hatred of God produce the conversion experience. The feelings that the conversion resolve into are, in turn, feelings of self-loathing, profound inadequacy and, possibly, gratitude to God.

Second, the reading experience that produced the conversion was one of textual hatred ("Oderam enim vocabulum istud 'Iustitia Dei'"): the Gospel, as long as it was read as a threat, had seemed to add pain to preexisting pain: "dolorem dolori adderet." Interestingly, however, the state of mind that the conversion resolves into is, as we have seen, one in which the converted reader feels textual hatred for the prescriptions of the Biblical text: "The commandments show us what we ought to do but do not give us the power to do it. They are intended to teach man to know himself, that through them he may recognize his inability to do good and may despair of his own ability."[34] So the converted state is itself one that I will continue throughout this book to call "textual hatred."

Finally, it is an intense struggle with textual ambiguity that produces the conversion experience. Luther had to work at interpreting the hated word day and night with unrelenting intensity: "meditabundus dies et noctes connexionem verborum attenderem."[35] The conversion experience is nothing if not textual at every point: it turns on a grammatical ambiguity; it requires intense interpretive effort; once resolved, the faith by which we are justified is only legible, and legible only, through the Gospel text. The location of ambiguity is itself coincident with the theological point: just as the resolution of the lexical ambiguity reinstates alien, divine meaning (by expelling customary meaning), so too the resolution of the theological anxiety reinstates alien, divine prerogative.

For all the intensity and ambiguity of this reading experience, the converted reader must, however, simultaneously become a tireless reader, and yet deny the possibility of ambiguity in scriptural reading. The plain, evident simplicity of Scripture is perhaps the most insistent theme of evangelical polemic in this period (a topic to be taken up in the following chapter). Tyndale, for example, castigates his Catholic opponents who dream up new meanings for scriptural words: "Therefore they ever think that it hath some other meaning than as the words sound, and that no man understandeth it or [has] understood it since the time of the apostles."[36] Unless evangelical polemic commits itself to the incontrovertible plainness of the literal sense, it's lost. Evangelical writers must make this commitment for many reasons, not least because, if a movement is to ground itself on a text, the text must be unambiguous. If evangelical polemic must insist on the plainness and easy legibility of the literal sense, however, it must also strenuously repress its moment of origin in the reading of ambiguity. (Tyndale himself represses the ambiguity of the genitive phrase here with his formulation "righteousness which cometh of God.")[37] For Luther does exactly what Tyndale condemns his enemies for doing: he understands a word in a way that "no man understandeth it or [has] understood it since the time of the apostles."

🐝 I return one last time to the Preface to the Coverdale Bible. To be sure, the tone of that preface remains calm and inviting, unheated except in the one passage I have cited in which Coverdale warns his readers not to be "blinded in their understanding," and not to return to the "old blasphemy" of believing "that they themselves are able to make satisfaction unto God for their own sins." Despite that evenness of tone, and despite, indeed, its sweetness of temper, we are now in a position to see the jolting, stark paradoxes behind that single paragraph about penance. For in declaring that the only true penance is a "very repentance, amendment, or conversion unto God," without any confidence in the works of penance, Coverdale is evidently subscrib-

ing to the fundamental article of Lutheran belief, that works are useless.

In the light of that evident commitment, the rest of the Preface
starts to look different. The rest of the Preface, that is, encourages
works. We have seen that different potential readers (judges, priests,
fathers) are encouraged to speak and spread the Gospel. The Preface
ends with a call to works:

> Finally, who so ever thou be, take these words of scripture in to thy
> heart, and be not only an outward hearer, but a doer thereafter, and
> practice thyself therein: that thou mayest feel in thine heart, the sweet
> promises thereof for thy consolation in all trouble, & for the sure
> stablishing of thy hope in Christ. (image 7)

Being not merely a hearer, but also a doer of Scripture sounds clear
enough, but in the context of Lutheran reading practice, this injunction is not at all straightforward. Indeed, what it might be translated
as saying is that the reader is to be a doer by recognizing inability to
"do." The "sweet promises" of the Gospel consist in a promise of salvation *despite* one's inability to be a doer of the Gospel.

So echoes of darker reading practices can be heard even in Coverdale's Preface. Lutheran self-loathing and what I have called "textual
hatred" are not so far away. Are these echoes heard, and heard more
stridently, in other English evangelical Bible prologues? We might
expect unauthorized texts, written as part of an underground Lutheran program, to be less embarrassed about bringing the dark if dynamic aspects of this reading culture to the fore. In fact, however,
even the authorized Great Bible (first published in 1539), read within
the Lutheran optic, turns out to shock its readers even as it welcomes
them. Accordingly, I will examine three examples, the first two unauthorized and the third an official text: Tyndale's Prologues to his
1525 and 1534 New Testaments and (in the final section of this chap-

ter) Cranmer's 1540 Preface to the Great Bible. As we shall see, these highest-profile welcomes, and particularly those by Tyndale, turn out to be decorated with a good deal of barbed wire: "do" means "can't do."

The Prologue to Tyndale's 1525 New Testament is a cardinal document, standing as the very first welcome to the printed vernacular scriptures in English. A short introductory section is a translation of the Preface to Luther's 1522 New Testament; the rest, apparently, is Tyndale's own work.[38] The short section drawn from Luther offers, as we might expect, a warm welcome. "Evangelion," we are told, is a Greek word meaning "good merry, glad and joyful tidings, that maketh a man's heart glad, and maketh him sing, dance, and leap for joy" (p. 9). This good news is, however, soon subject to less uplifting intelligence. In the section for which no Lutheran source has been located, Tyndale expatiates on Luther's valuation of human worth, and here the news is very bad indeed. By Adam's fall we are "children of wrath and heirs of the vengeance of God by birth." We have

> our fellowship with the damned devils . . . while we are yet in our mother's wombs; and though we show not forth the fruits of sin [as soon as we are born], yet are we full of the natural poison, whereof all sinful deeds spring, and cannot but sin outwards (be we never so young) [as soon as we are able to work] if occasion be given. (p. 14)[39]

Of course this (and there is a good deal more of it) is part of the Lutheran emotional dialectic: one must, in faith, recognize one's utter abjection before God, by way of activating God's grace. "By grace . . . we are plucked out of Adam, the ground of all evil, and grafted in Christ, the root of all goodness" (p. 14). Tyndale makes the emotional pattern clear: the situation is not unlike that of the sentenced criminal who sees nothing before him but "present death," at which point a charter from the king arrives to deliver him (p. 16):

Likewise, when God's law hath brought the sinner into knowledge of himself, and hath confounded his conscience and opened unto him the wrath and vengeance of God; then cometh good tidings. The Evangelion sheweth unto him the promises of God in Christ, and how that Christ hath purchased pardon for him, hath satisfied the law for him, and hath appeased the wrath of God. (p. 17)

Tyndale's welcome to this text, then, includes the standard Lutheran theology of salvation: out of a faithful self-loathing, and an accurate estimation of total incapacity, arises an overwhelming sense of gratitude to a God who takes all initiative into his own hands and works everything by grace. The text of Scripture here is no mere bearer of the story, since, as with the letter borne to the criminal awaiting execution, it plays a crucial part in the story. From this welcome to Scripture we learn not only that we will appreciate our abjection only by reading Scripture; we also learn that the same Scripture will bring the necessary letter of release. Reading is an indispensable element in this soteriology, a bringer of good news that will not arrive if Scripture is not also read as bad news.

Tyndale is not prepared to leave the "welcome" there, however, and goes on to summarize and develop all that's been said. Our will "is locked and knit faster unto the will of the devil, than could an hundred thousand chains bind a man unto a post" (p. 17). This submission to the devil is itself a textual phenomenon, as "the law and will of the devil is written as well in our hearts as in our members, and we run headlong after the devil with full zeal, and the whole swing of all the power we have" (p. 17).

The textual experience, with the devil's text written onto our hearts, is the full-blown Lutheran experience of what I have called "textual hatred." It is impossible for a natural man to consent to the law or to believe that the God who made the law is just. Such a law "only setteth man at variance with God,"

... and provoketh him to and stirreth him to rail on God, and to blaspheme him as a cruel tyrant. For it is not possible for a man, till he be born again, to think that God is righteous to make him of so poison a nature . . . and to give him a law that is impossible for him to do, or to consent to; his wit, reason and will being so fast glued, yea, and chained unto the will of the devil. (p. 18; a passage added in the 1530 version)

This is obviously (to my mind) a pretty complex reading program, prescribing that the reader must read the same text in a double fashion: only if the textual hatred is experienced can the faithful reader read through to the promise embedded in the same text.

This reading program might look complex to us; Tyndale insists, by contrast, that Scripture is simple and plain. He makes this point as he closes the Prologue. Even as he affirms the simplicity of Scripture, however, he takes care to say that it has to be read in a certain optic. If, he concludes, one attempts to read Scripture outside this (Lutheran) understanding of law and grace, then the reader will be able to read, but will understand nothing. So reading itself is not a guarantee of salvation:

In these things to be ignorant, is to have all the scripture locked up; so that the more thou readest it, the blinder thou art, and the more contrariety thou findest in it, and the more tangled art thou therein, and canst nowhere through. (p. 27)

Reading can, or rather must be, a dangerous business, especially for the sincere seeker after truth.

So the welcome offered by Tyndale in this first Prologue is not unqualified. David Daniell is clearly taken aback by this passage, and goes out of his way to blame it on someone else. At first it's "a dark cloud of St. Augustine"; this then gives way to something that (impossibly) "has the feel of older, more scholastic, even monkish, writing"; and then we hear that these pages "smell strongly of Luther."[40] Daniell's next shot is that the passage is a translation of "some writing by Luther not yet identified," somehow tacked on to Tyndale's Prologue. All this has an air of panicky desperation, but Daniell has one further villain up his sleeve beyond the malodorous Luther: he suggests that this was the work of William Roy, one of Tyndale's assistants. The work is crude, and there is nothing in it "which quite sings in Tyndale's voice."[41] The fact that Daniell rushes to give so many explanations of this shocking passage weakens the force of any single explanation. For the present purposes, it is only necessary to repeat that, whoever wrote it (and Tyndale obviously approved of it), this is the first welcome to the first printed English vernacular text of Scripture.

If the 1525 Prologue does not quite "sing in Tyndale's voice," what of the Prologue to the revised 1534 New Testament? How sweet is the welcome there? Already in the third paragraph it's clear that not everyone is welcome:

> Moreover, because the kingdom of heaven, which is the scripture and the word of God, may be so locked up, that he which readeth or heareth it, cannot understand it: as Christ testifieth how that the scribes and the Pharisees had so shut it up and had taken away the key of knowledge that their Jews which thought themselves within, were yet so locked out, and are to this day that they can understand no sentence of the scripture unto their salvation, though they can rehearse the texts everywhere and dispute thereof as subtly as the popish doctors of dunce's dark learning, with their sophistry, served us.[42]

Tyndale is clearly facing powerful enemies, and it is no surprise that he should contrast his hermeneutic openness with the practice of his competitors, both Jewish and scholastic scholars who thought that they had control and possession of the Scriptures. Tyndale takes an absolutely routine position of evangelical polemics here, by describ-

ing Hebraic custom so as to suggest Catholic custom. Of course that
is not merely a matter of historical analogy, since the Jews, by Tyndale's account, remain locked out of Scripture "to this day." In a single
move (indeed in a single sentence), Tyndale excludes two sets of
readers, Jewish and scholastic theologians, from understanding the
text with which they had seemed to enjoy such intimacy. These
guides "make us put our trust in those things that profit their bellies
only and slay our souls" (p. 4).

Once he has aggressively rejected these blind readers as treacherous guides to Scripture, Tyndale proceeds to open the text to his own
liberated readers. Scripture is simple; there is a right way, "yea, and
the only way to understand the scripture unto our salvation," and
that is by searching out the explicit covenants between God and us.
Scripture interprets itself; Scripture is, as Luther often says, its own
interpreter, *sui ipsius interpres,* wholly removed from the messy negotiations of history in which other texts must find their meaning.[43]

Salvation, then, is a matter of reading and recognizing our abjection in the face of that reading of covenant. As the Prologue continues, however, the simplicity and openness diminish rapidly. We
might be unsurprised to find nonevangelical readers irredeemably excluded from Tyndale's imagined readership. Much more surprisingly,
however, Tyndale now threatens his ideal, evangelical readership, his
"most dear reader," with rejection. Those "most dear readers" might
say that they have Scripture "in our hands, in our eyes, in our ears, in
our mouths, but most of all, in our hearts," but that very incorporation of Scripture will be a source of acute discomfort.[44] They might
be faced with an entirely textualized domestic space, as in Thomas
Becon's *A Christmas Banquet* (1542), in which every item of furniture
and every utensil speaks Scripture: "here nothing is dumb, all things
speak"; but as each object utters its injunction, the evangelical reader
knows that these injunctions cannot be met.[45]

Tyndale's sectarian habit of thought is characteristically tertiary:

he makes promises to friends; he threatens enemies; and then he threatens false friends. (Readers trained in a Leavisite tradition will recognize the pattern.) Here Tyndale promises salvation to his evangelical readers, damnation to those who resist, and then, often, damnation to those who erroneously *think* they understand. Thus, in the Prologue to the New Testament, the promises we've already observed are followed by threats to Jews and scholastics, and those threats in turn are followed by threats to a committed, evangelical readership. Having said earlier that a contract pertains between God and Christians, Tyndale now proceeds to undo any sense of contract. "Two things are required to begin a Christian man," he declares, and the first of these is faith: a faith "to obtain all the mercy that he hath promised us, through the deserving and merits of Christ's blood only, without all respect to our own works" (p. 5). Tyndale's theology oscillates uneasily (much more uneasily than Luther's) on the question of works.[46] We can see the oscillation in this very prologue: having begun by affirming the value of works, Tyndale now withdraws that, and reverts to the standard Lutheran position that works are entirely useless, given our irredeemable abjection before God. Interestingly, this affirmation of predestination has immediate implications for reading practice, since reading, too, is after all a work. Biblical reading now looks much less straightforward, much less securely available in the open, literal sense of Scripture:

> This I have said (most dear reader) to warn thee, lest thou shouldest be deceived, and shouldest not only read the scriptures in vain and to no profit, but also to thy greater damnation. For the nature of God's word is, that whosoever read it or hear it . . . it will begin immediately to make him every day better and better, till he be grown into a perfect man in the knowledge of Christ . . . or else make him worse and worse, till he be hardened that he openly resist the spirit of God, and then blaspheme, after the example of Pharaoh. (p. 5)

This passage emphasizes the exceptionally high, salvational stakes in reading, but it doesn't clarify exactly how the damned reader differs from the saved reader. It does insist that there will be a discrimination between good and bad, and that that discrimination will be immediate.

The next paragraph expands on the point that the effect of bad reading will be absolute and instantaneous: the reader who reads the text and has no "love thereto, to fashion his life thereafter . . . then beginneth his just damnation immediately, and he is henceforth without excuse" (p. 5). The immediacy of the required response is unsettling enough, but even more disturbing is the lack of a clear account of why one reader immediately grows to perfection through reading, while another "waxeth [becomes] worse and worse." The bad reader is, indeed, actually damaged, *immediately*, by his scriptural reading. Tyndale doesn't, however, tell him how or why he's a bad reader.

Erroneous reading, then, is either the result of God's prior election, or else it's the result of a badly disposed will. Either way, the error of misreading leads directly to the terror of damnation. This applies to evangelical readers themselves: they too will incur the Pharaoh treatment. God will scourge "any that favoureth the word of God" and is yet unresponsive, "every day sharper and sharper, with tribulation and misfortune, that nothing shall prosper with him but all shall go against him, whatsoever he taketh in hand . . . and shall plague him with plague upon plague, each more loathsome, terrible and fearful than other, till he be at utter defiance with his flesh" (p. 7).

Further investigation of the "Pharaoh treatment" only serves to underline the inscrutable opacity of why one reader should profit from Scripture while another feels the plagues of doubt. By 1524 the uneasy standoff between Erasmus and Luther had become unsustainable; in that year Erasmus came out into open disagreement with Lutheran soteriology in his *De libero arbitrio*. This text is a defense of modified free will as against the extreme form of determinism proposed by Luther. In his defense of free will, Erasmus isolates passages of Scripture that seem to deny it. One of these is Exodus 9:12. As the sores of plague appear on the Egyptians, the Egyptian sorcerers lose the power to stand before Moses, an evident sign of their weakness. The obdurate Pharaoh, however, ignores the writing on the wall, as it were. The text of Exodus 9:12 puts it thus: "But the Lord hardened the heart of Pharaoh, that he hearkened not unto them."

Does this text mean what it says? Erasmus resists the notion, absurd to his eyes, that "God, who is not only just but good also, should be said to have hardened the heart of a man, so that by the man's misdeeds He might display His own power."[47] This being unthinkable, Erasmus, citing Origen, goes on to argue that what is really being said here is that God, having given Pharaoh an opportunity to relent and having been disappointed, punished Pharaoh. After reconceptualizing the passage within the terms of his theology, Erasmus solves the textual obstruction by recourse to rhetorical practice. Scripture is using a standard rhetorical figure here, whereby "he is described as the agent who merely provides an opportunity."[48] Thus God didn't harden Pharaoh's heart; free-willed Pharaoh hardened it himself.

This is neat and professional work: Erasmus first subjects the text to theological persuasion; then, when the text resists the theology, he uses the solvent of rhetoric to dissolve textual resistance. Luther replied to Erasmus's defense of free will in the following year, in his *De servo arbitrio* (1525).[49] Specifically addressing Erasmus's arguments concerning Exodus 9:12, Luther will have none of Erasmian sweet reason and subtle rhetoric concerning Pharaoh. Luther begins by acknowledging the existence of the rhetorical trope, and acknowledging that some readers of Scripture take the passage in the way proposed by Erasmus. That, however, isn't the point. The real question is one of intention: what did the writer mean by it? For Luther, the guide here will be the meaning of the words used: "By what authority, for what reason, with what necessity is the natural meaning of the word thus twisted for me? What if the reader or interpreter should be wrong?"[50] Having asked this rhetorical question, Luther goes for the jugular, by dismissing "this miserable refuge of tropes": what "God says must be taken quite simply at its face value."

Luther then rapidly reviews a wide range of Biblical passages in which God punishes. He subjects each to Erasmus's rhetorical softening, by way of making the latter's position look absurd. The real problem, he concludes, is that human reason is offended by the passage, human reason which, "although she is blind, deaf, stupid, impious and sacrilegious with regard to the words and works of God, is brought in at this point as a judge of the words and works of God."[51] The passage about God hardening Pharaoh's heart should be taken literally, for faith believes that "God is good even if he should send all men to perdition."[52] Luther's understanding of the Pharaoh treatment is driven both by his commitment to the literal sense, and by his determinist theology, both of which coincide here: God hardened Pharaoh's heart, precisely *in order* "that many wonders may be wrought in the land of Egypt" (Exodus 11:9). The deliberate hardening of Pharaoh's heart is, by this account, part of a divine spectacle, but wholly opaque to human standards of justice or merit.[53]

✤   David Daniell describes the turn into the 1530s for "English readers" in terms both poetic and Biblical: "Turning that corner was suddenly to be faced with a vast, rich sunlit territory, a land flowing with milk and honey of new images and metaphors, and the rediscovered ancient monuments of God-given religious, political and social revelation." Embedded in this rich passage is the venerable notion of the English as a chosen people, recovering ancient monuments that are simultaneously theirs and granted by God.

One might probe that parallel in various ways. One might, for example, reflect on the nationalist conception of the English as a chosen race embedded in the parallel. Or one might ask about the land of milk and honey as witnessed by Moses; the Hebrew scriptures make no effort to disguise that it belonged to someone else first. God himself, addressing Moses, says as much: "But I have said unto you that ye shall enjoy their land, and that I will give it unto you to possess it: even a land that floweth with milk and honey."[54] In the optic of the present chapter, however, we can simply say that the new landscape might not have looked quite so sunny to all "English readers." To the many Catholics and the few Jewish English readers, the new scriptures would, predictably, have cast shadows, since they were the current "owners" of Scripture about to be cast out of their inheritance.

More surprisingly, however, the translations did not present all *evangelical* readers with new, rich territories, ripe for possession. On the contrary, all were required to experience textual hatred, and some of these would find him- or herself "at utter defiance with his flesh," back with Pharaoh in the land of Egypt, and altogether uncertain why.

Before we leave evangelical Bible prologues, we should look at the highest-profile prologue of all, that of the Great Bible, first published in 1539. The committed evangelical and Lutheran Tyndale, writing from exile to a committed readership, had espoused a purer form of the Lutheran reading experience. What about Archbishop Cranmer, writing as the second in command of an Anglican Church (Henry VIII now being in command), for every parish church in England, in 1540? (The Prologue did not appear in the first, 1539 edition.) One might expect the darker accents of Lutheran reading to be played down in this very public, very official document. For the most part they are. Still, surprisingly dark warnings about the dangers of Biblical reading nonetheless surface, even here.

Cranmer opens by distinguishing two kinds of scriptural readers in need of guidance: there are those who need a spur, and those who need a bridle. Those who need the spur are readers mired in custom who resist Scripture in English. Those who need a bridle are those who "by their inordinate reading, undiscreet speaking, contentious disputing, or otherwise . . . slander and hinder the word of God most of all other, whereof they would seem to be the greatest furtherers."[55] The first category (Catholic resisters of vernacular scripture) are dismissed as not only "foolish, forward, and obstinate, but also peevish, perverse and indurate" (p. 119). A good part of the Prologue is devoted to persuading them that vernacular scriptures have historical precedent in England (namely, the Wycliffite Bible and the Anglo-Saxon scriptures), and that they are useful, in particular by promoting "obedience, love and dread to . . . princes" among the king's subjects (p. 121).

The second part of the Prologue is devoted to bridling over-active, evangelical readers. Cranmer cites from a previous period of scriptural controversy related by Gregory Nazianzene (d. 389): overzealous readers, "subverting the order of all godliness, have respect only to this thing, how they may bind and loose subtle questions, so that now every market-place, every ale-house and tavern, every feast-house, briefly, every company of men, every assembly of women, is filled with such talk" (p. 122). As Cranmer addresses this group, all the advantages promised in the first section of the Prologue seem now to be withdrawn. The first section says that anyone can understand the scriptural text. This section denies that, still citing Gregory Nazianzene:

First, it is not for every man, but it is for such as be of exact and exquisite judgment, and such as have spent their time before in study and contemplation; and such as have cleansed themselves as well in soul and body, or at the least, endeavored themselves to be made clean. For it is dangerous, saith he, for the unclean to touch that thing that is most clean; like as the sore eye taketh harm by looking upon the sun. (pp. 122–123)

Further, those whose wits are not up to it may soon find themselves "oppressed with over-hard questions" (p. 123). Whereas the first section denies that busyness is an excuse for not reading Scripture, this section demands that the fit reader be "reposed and at rest from all outward dregs and trouble" (p. 123). In sum, Cranmer cites Gregory thus: "I forbid not to read, but I forbid to reason." In all this Cranmer has a particular eye to the very people whom he might otherwise see as his evangelical supporters. He forbids "contention and debate about scriptures," especially because those who "pretend to be the favorers and students thereof cannot agree within themselves." These, subject as they are to "tongue-itch" (p. 124), are the very ones who most damage "the cause . . . that we would have furthered" (p. 123).

In short, the Prologue of the Great Bible is full of contradictions. The welcome broadly offered in the first section is, effectively, withdrawn in the second. The unclean should beware of touching Scripture. If Coverdale imagines society becoming calm by scriptural reading, Cranmer clearly knows better: this prologue positively trembles before the prospect of endless schism opening up among evangelical readers. If the legislation of 1542 is anything to go by,[56] then Cranmer's premonition of fractious and dangerous dispute opening up around this Bible was, from an official perspective, well founded.

While Cranmer's admonitions here are politically motivated, one may still sense his awareness of the dangers, both political and spiritual, of scriptural reading. If the unclean should not approach Scripture, the one thing that any evangelical reader knows is that we are all unclean; in that culture we are all, in the words of Tyndale's 1525 Prologue, "full of the natural poison" of original sin, and unless we read with an acute consciousness of that abjection, our reading will be quite useless. That Cranmer believed this theology we can assume from his life's work; that he was prepared to make it explicit even in texts designed for the simple, we can see from a fascinating passage of his *Catechism* of 1548.[57]

This text, designed for basic instruction in matters of the (evangelical) faith, spends 130 or so pages outlining the Ten Commandments. Discussion of the Creed follows, after which, immediately, the entire, long discussion of the Commandments is put into serious doubt. For, unsettlingly, we now learn that our chances of fulfilling them stand at zero. Their whole *raison d'être* is to inflict a sense of due humiliation upon us:

> For you have heard that without it [grace] there is nothing able to reconcile us to God the father, to pacify his wrath and to bring us to the life everlasting. For although the Ten Commandments are an excellent godly and heavenly doctrine, yet we can not be saved or justified by them. For we be not able of our own strength and power to fulfill the law and God's holy commandments. But by them, we only do learn what God requireth of us, and so be brought to the knowledge of our sin. For this is the office of the law (as Saint Paul sayeth) to teach us our offences and to set before our eyes the great fear of God and the indignation which we have deserved by breaking his commandments, to the intent, that we acknowledging our own weakness, should fly to God's grace and mercy.[58]

Textual hatred is, in short, not far behind the scenes in the Prologue to the Great Bible.

Thus four paradoxes of Lutheran reading so far: to love the text, one must hate it; "do it" means "you can't do it"; faith alone means no faith; and the plain text is premised on the ambiguous text. The next chapter reveals more surprising and dark paradoxes embedded in that last one.

CHAPTER FOUR

The Literal Sense and Predestination

READING Scripture under an evangelical program, then, is accompanied by fear and loathing of two kinds. In the first place, the theological premise of the evangelical reader is that human worthlessness cannot hope to satisfy the demands of God's justice. The promise of God's saving grace, merited solely through Christ's saving action, will be recognized only by the sinner who acknowledges his or her utter abjection in faithful trust that God will save. In the second place, that promise is made available only in Scripture. By reading Scripture, therefore, one replays the dialectic of loathing and gratitude. The prescriptions of Scripture are not designed to promote reformed action in the world. On the contrary, they are designed only to promote the reader's humiliated recognition that satisfactory works are quite beyond the reader's grasp. Readers become witnesses to a world of command and obedience in which they, impotent, cannot participate except through the grief and humiliation of their exclusion. Only by passing faithfully through the humiliating portal of Law-Beyond-Reach will the reader pass through the Gate of Gospel; only via textual hatred will the reader reach textual gratitude.

That challenge cannot be described as good news to all readers, or, at the very least, not to any as "a land of milk and honey." The news, however, gets considerably worse, in a variety of ways. In this chapter I look at the ways in which evangelical emphasis on the literal sense leads directly to a despotic institutional account of textual authority.

Put that way, my contention flies in the face of at least two fundamental convictions of cultural history. Cultural historians are for the most part convinced that evangelical emphasis on the literal sense is simultaneously commonsensical and liberating. To champion the literal sense was to place commonsense readings of Scripture above the deceptive veils of medieval allegorical interpretation. The literal sense was, therefore, common sense, and to privilege the literal sense was to reclaim interpretive authority from the institution of the Church, whose possessive gatekeepers were academic schoolmen. These academics had selfishly reserved the power of interpretation for themselves, in order to protect their vested interests. Proclamation of the literal sense was, therefore, liberating: now the evangelical reader could read as an individual; his or her reading was unmediated and unoppressed by the institution of the Church.

This chapter will reveal the fragility of these standard persuasions. In any reading culture, the literal sense is only ever a fairly tenuous fiction. Any reading culture that proposes that the meaning of the words is wholly contained in the words themselves, unaided by the interpretive, unwritten assumptions of the interpretive community, will end up with authoritarian versions of interpretive authority.

Why? Since the literal sense alone turns out to be fragile, disagreements about its meaning inevitably arise. These disagreements need to be resolved somehow, and in the sixteenth century they could only be resolved by affirmations of institutional power, whether by conciliar decision or absolutist fiat. The need for authoritative mediation was true of evangelical culture no less than of the Catholic Church. The institution that exercised that power among evangelicals was the True Church of the Elect, who alone constituted the body of reliable readers. Biblical meaning was validated in this culture less by the meaning of words and more by what the True Church understood by those words. The difficulty lay, though, in communally validating what the invisible True Church, itself a creation of faith alone, actually did believe. There were further difficulties, too: who represented this Church, and where was it?

Cultural history is mistaken in thinking that evangelical reading abolished the institutions of reading. On the contrary, evangelical writers placed an extremely demanding, because invisible, institution at the very heart of their account of interpretation. One became a trustworthy reader by first becoming a member of that demanding institution. The institution was demanding both because it was invisible and because membership lay outside the initiative of the reader: one became a member of that institution, and thus a good reader, only by predestination. Lection presupposes election.

✼   John Foxe narrated the life and death of William Tyndale, an "Apostle of England," in his *Actes and Monuments* (1570 edition; first published in 1563).[1] After relating Tyndale's strangulation and burning, Foxe says that it would take too long to recite "the worthy virtues and doings of this blessed Martyr," but he does permit himself one "miracle" narrative. Resident in Antwerp, Tyndale was invited to a dinner party at which a conjuror had been employed to perform tricks; "through his diabolical enchantments or art magical," this magician "would fetch all kinds of viands, and wine from any place they would, and set it upon the table . . . before them." In the presence of Tyndale, however, the juggler's tricks fail:

> At the last, with his labor sweating and toiling, when he saw that nothing would go forward, but that all his enchantments were void, he was

compelled openly to confess that there was some man present at supper, which disturbed and letted [hindered] all his doings.[2]

Immediately after this miracle story, Foxe turns to Tyndale's books, and especially his translation of the New Testament. In answer to his many enemies with their "slanderous tongues and lying lips," Tyndale responded with "faithful dealing and sincere conscience." He declares, for example, that he never altered "one syllable of Gods word against my conscience."[3] The books are no less sincere and straight-dealing than the man: Tyndale's translated Bible disables the juggling enchantments of the Popish clergy, the story implies, just as the very presence and unfeigned simplicity of his person undid the conjuror's "diabolical enchantments." As a simple, entirely readable man, Tyndale produced a simple, entirely readable text.

Simplicity, indeed, is the leitmotif of Foxe's entire account of Tyndale. In his early career Tyndale attempted to persuade his patrons and their clerical guests "simply and plainly." When resisted, "he would show them in the book, and lay plainly before them the open and manifest places of the Scriptures, to confute their errors."[4] By the premature end of his career he had lost none of this simplicity: even the imperial soldiers commissioned to arrest Tyndale "pitied to see his simplicity when they took him."[5]

Above all, the texts that Tyndale translated and wrote were themselves simple texts designed for simple people. Whereas, in the manner of the hapless conjuror, the "pharisaical clergy" exercised all their skill to blind simple readers to Biblical truth, Tyndale opened up the plain text. The clergy would, by "juggling with the text,"

darken the right sense with the mist of their sophistry, and so entangle them which rebuked or despised their abominations, with arguments of philosophy . . . and with wresting the Scripture unto their own purpose, contrary unto the process, order, and meaning of the text, would so delude them in descanting upon it with allegories, and amaze them, expounding it in many senses laid before the unlearned lay people, that though thou felt in thy heart, and were sure that all were false that they said, yet couldest not thou solve their subtle riddles.[6]

Tyndale cuts through this web of deceit by turning Scripture "into the vulgar speech, that the poor people might also read and see the simple plain word of God."

✦ Why should Foxe have put so much emphasis on Tyndale's simplicity, both personal and textual? I suggest that simplicity, of words, style, and interpretation, is less a description of early Protestant textual practice and more an indispensable weapon in its polemical self-advertisement.[7] I begin with the claims to simplicity made by Luther and Tyndale.

Luther repeatedly insists that Scripture is an open text. The idea that everything is not plain in Scripture is, he says in his opening salvo against Erasmus in *De servo arbitrio* (1525), a notion put about by "ungodly sophists." Of course there are many abstruse scriptural texts, but now that the seals have been broken and the door of the sepulcher rolled back with the coming of Christ, then nothing in Scripture can remain hidden. So "the subject matter of the Scriptures . . . is all quite accessible," even if "some texts are still obscure owing to our ignorance of their terms." The only problem, that is, is a philological one concerning a few words, but the fundamental message of the Scriptures is absolutely plain: "Truly it is stupid and impious, when we know that the subject matter of Scripture has all been placed in the clearest light, to call it obscure on account of a few obscure words."[8]

Tyndale, in line with the entire Lutheran movement, also champions the plain literal sense. Foxe's account of clerical sophists "descanting upon [Scripture] with allegories" was in fact drawn from Tyndale's own prose, in a passage where Tyndale had insisted that Scripture "hath but one simple, literal sense, whose light the owls cannot abide."[9] Promotion of that simple, literal sense required strenuous repudiation of its competitor, allegory. Throughout his prefaces Tyndale warns his reader to "beware of subtle allegories,"[10] since allegory is the surest tool the clergy can wield to preserve their own power over and possession of Scripture. "Here a man had need to put on all his spectacles, and to arm himself against invisible spirits," he says about "false allegories": they can prove nothing, and are useful only as a teaching device, used to "declare and open a text" by the use of analogy.[11] Tyndale expands on the interpretive opportunity of the literal sense in *The Obedience of a Christian Man;* he tells his reader that "the scripture hath but one sense which is the literal sense. That literal sense is the root and ground of all, and the anchor that never faileth whereunto if thou cleave thou canst never err or go out of the way."[12]

In the history of Biblical interpretation, the "literal sense" has, of course, a large and not so simple history, extending for a long way behind and a long way ahead of this first moment of the European Reformation.[13] At present, however, we need only say that Tyndale is in fact relying (although of course he never says so) on a scholastic maxim, that arguments can be drawn only from the literal sense.[14]

Pre-Reformation Biblical interpretation proposed four senses of Scripture: the literal (that designated by the meaning of the words); the allegorical (meanings of events and things in the Old Testament revealed by their fulfillment in the New); the tropological (ethical prescriptions that derive from a Biblical passage); and the anagogical (heavenly, eternal things designated by a given passage).[15] These analytical words express a simple and dynamic concept: that scriptural sense is applicable across time. It describes the past of the Hebrew scriptures (the literal sense); bears the seeds of the New Testament future (allegory); applies to the present (the moral sense); and points to the end of time (anagogy).

Scholastic theologians, especially in the intensely academic environment of thirteenth-century Paris, devised ground rules for establishing the limits of Biblical prescription. As academic theorists tend to, they limited unbreakable authority to explicit statements, in this case made by the literal sense of the Scriptures. This academic rule was received without acknowledgment from one academic culture (that of scholasticism) by another (that of evangelical theorists).

Evangelical writers before and after Tyndale extended this academic definition of the literal sense in various ways. Precisely because the literal was an insufficient basis for explaining huge swaths of narrative in the Hebrew scriptures, evangelical writers needed simultaneously to insist that all was contained in the literal sense, and to incorporate other levels of nonliteral meaning. Thus, for example, Biblical scholars in the seventeenth century reformulated the limited Lutheran account of the literal sense in order to render it more flexible, and capable of sustaining some of the functions of pre-Reformation four-fold exegesis.[16] Even Saint Paul, after all, had used allegory in Galatians 4:22–31. Despite that apostolic precedent, Tyndale treats allegory with extremely fine kid gloves. It is symptomatic of his wariness about the word that, in his New Testament, he refuses to translate the Greek *allegoroumena* from Galatians as "allegories"; he uses the word "mysteries" instead.[17]

Tyndale gives his fullest exposition of the case against allegory and for the literal sense in the *Obedience* (1528). He begins by inaccurately summarizing the four-fold scheme, and mocking it with the word "chopological" (p. 156). That allegorical "trash and baggage stuff" swept away,[18] he proclaims his central conviction: the literal sense is the "root and ground of all" (p. 156).

Tyndale immediately goes on to make a standard scholastic point (made by Thomas Aquinas, for example), though obviously not acknowledged as such here: that of course Scripture uses figurative language, but the meaning is clear, and that meaning *is* the literal sense.[19] If a preacher allegorizes, it's for purely pedagogic ends, designed to "paint" the truth better. Thus the sword of Peter cutting the ear of Malchus (John 18:10) is like the Law, whereas Christ's healing is like the delivered promise of the Gospel. It is only a question of likeness, not, we might say, of ontology: "the allegory proveth nothing neither can do" (p. 158); it's used only for the psychological effect of impressing truth on the hearer, "to root it and grave it in the heart" (p. 159). So allegory is to be used with sobriety, rarely, and only "where the text offereth thee an allegory."

Of course, at this point Tyndale is required to address the fact that Paul himself uses allegory in describing the wives of Abraham as "an allegory." The wives are, says Paul, the two covenants (Galatians 4:24). It is only, however, a likeness, and it's the kind of likeness that permits Tyndale to use what look like allegories for a polemical purpose: Paul uses allegory here as "likewise do we borrow likenesses or allegories of the scripture, as of Pharaoh and Herod . . . to express our miserable captivity and persecution under Antichrist the Pope" (p. 159).

Once he has defined acceptable, duly chastened forms of allegory, Tyndale proceeds to encourage utter revulsion at any form of allegory that makes stronger than pedagogic claims: he teaches his reader how blind the proponents of allegory are, "that thou mayest abhor them and spew them out of thy stomach forever" (p. 160). He does this by explication of the Lutheran concepts of Law and Gospel, where he must immediately address another potential weakness in his argument, Paul's contention that we have trust in God

> not that we are sufficient of ourselves to think anything as it were of ourselves: but our ableness cometh of God, which hath made us able to

minister the new testament, not of the letter, but of the spirit. For the letter killeth, but the spirit giveth life [2 Corinthians 3:5–6].

The last sentence of this passage had been used as the bedrock of allegorical readings for more than a millennium before Tyndale's time. Because the "letter" had traditionally been identified with the literal sense, Tyndale needs rapidly to instruct his reader on the difference between the deadly "letter" and the life-giving literal sense. He does so by relocating the letter not to the text written with ink, and not engraved in tables of Mosaic stone; rather, following Paul (2 Corinthians 3:3), the true text of the life-giving literal sense is written "in the fleshly tables of the heart":

> . . . as who should say, we write not a dead law with ink and parchment, nor grave that which damned you in tables of stone: but preach you that which bringeth the spirit unto your breasts, which spirit writeth and graveth the law of love in your hearts and giveth you lust to do the will of God. (p. 161)[20]

This heart writing can be pretty painful. Luther expands on this bodily textuality in revealing ways, saying that God's word "must be in us like a . . . brand mark, burned in, not touching the heart lightly, as foam on water or spittle on the tongue which we want to spit out, but pressed onto the heart to remain there as a distinguishing sign which no one can remove from us."[21] Indeed, as the *Book of Homilies* (1547) puts it, "that thing which by the perpetual use of reading Holy Scripture . . . is deeply printed and graven in the heart at length turneth almost into nature."[22] This corporal inscription of both Law and Gospel leads more to Kafka's brilliant, excruciating *In the Penal Colony* than to the American Constitution.

Already it will be clear that the simplicity of Tyndale's position is starting to look fragile. He wants to say that the literal sense, the words themselves, of Scripture are the simply accessible location of truth, without need for allegorical interpretation. Faced with the actual text of Paul that seems to say the opposite, Tyndale relocates the text itself to the true text written in the heart: this is the one whose literal sense gives life, even if the letter written in books or graven in stone should kill.

✣ Because they are so wary of allegory, and so committed to the literal sense, both Luther and Tyndale prefer explicit Biblical discourse to Biblical narrative. They prefer, that is, explicit statements of the Law to stories. In his Preface or *Vorrhede* to his New Testament of 1522 (an introduction that was to be omitted from complete editions of the Lutheran Bible by 1534), Luther isolates the essential books ("the true kernel and marrow") of the New Testament.[23] These books are as follows: the Gospel of John, the Epistles of Paul, and the first Epistle of Peter. These are superior precisely because they're explicitly theological, and short on narrative: in them the reader doesn't find the works or miracles of Christ, but instead "depicted in masterly fashion how faith in Christ triumphs over sin, death and hell, and gives life, righteousness and salvation. This is the real nature of the Gospel."[24] It would be much better, says Luther, to be without the works of Christ than to be without his preaching. For this reason he feels the Gospel of John is far superior to the other three Gospels, which are more committed to narrative.[25]

Tyndale likewise insists on the superior force of explicit Biblical statement in the 1534 New Testament Preface. Scripture is simple, he says; there is a right way, "yea, and the only way to understand the scripture unto our salvation," and that is by searching out the explicit covenants between God and us. Scripture is no longer a code whose sense unfolds and clarifies through the passage of history. Scriptural meaning is instead concentrated in this redefined account of the literal sense.

Once Tyndale has proffered this scriptural key, he gives it one or two turns in the lock, by way of showing how the door of salvation swings easily open by it. He defines the most general covenant of all, that "if we meek ourselves to God, to keep all his laws . . . then God hath bound himself to keep us and make good all the mercies promised in Christ, throughout all scripture" (p. 4). It's true that, in Tyndale's Lutheran universe, a reader's actions will never be able to meet these covenants; that inability will force on the good reader an awareness of his or her own utter abjection. The covenants do, however, define the Law, and any spiritual understanding begins from them. The covenants create an allegory-free zone. Hermeneutic opacity and the unfolding of time cede to contractual legibility, which is wholly intelligible, as contract is, within any historical moment. Tyndale's editorial hand underlines, as it were, these key explicit statements: "I have ever noted the covenants in the margins" (p. 5).

Luther and Tyndale go so far in their championing of the limpid literal sense as to deny the need for interpretation in Scripture at all. Scripture, Luther does not tire of repeating, is its own interpreter. The sacred text, that is, is so straightforward and simple that it needs no interpretation whatsoever; or rather it does the work of interpretation itself. Scripture cannot be subject to the messy negotiations of history, and must stand untouched by human institutions. It must, in short, claim the prerogatives of surrounding interpretive institutions for itself.

In a work of 1520 designed to repudiate the papal bull against him, for example, Luther says that Scripture is "entirely secure, easy, and open through itself; it interprets itself, testing, judging and illuminating everything."[26] Scripture is the active agent here, untouched by the interpretive constructions of its readers; this is also true of Tyndale's account of how Scripture will not only tell the truth, but also cast out falsity. In the Prologue to the 1534 New Testament, he attacks the corrupting work of his erstwhile colleague George Joye by saying that "if the text be left uncorrupt, it will purge herself of all manner false glosses, how subtle soever they be feigned, as a seething [boiling] pot casteth up her scum" (p. 14).

❦ In short, for the promoters of the evangelical Bible, the Bible was easy, down to earth, and required no interpretive effort, since it did all the work. In recent studies of Tyndale some scholars have tended, I think, to take this triumph of textual simplicity rather at face value, without reflecting very deeply, if at all, on either its truth content or on what other claims may be embedded in the insistence on simplicity.

David Daniell, for example, says almost nothing about interpretation in either of his major contributions to Tyndale scholarship, and the little he does say reveals a very shaky understanding of the basics of Biblical hermeneutics.[27] What we find instead is a lexical and stylistic development of Foxe's position concerning Tyndale's simplicity. Daniell repeats one point many times about Tyndale's lexical and stylistic choices: Tyndale prized linguistic simplicity and directness. Daniell's word for this practice, both lexical and syntactic, is "Saxon."

Daniell thus emphasizes Tyndale's use of "Saxon" monosyllables and his repudiation of French and Latin vocabulary, along with his direct, "Saxon" syntax, at extraordinary length. The English language, no less than English religion, was, by Daniell's account, saved by Tyndale's simple "language of ordinary expressiveness."[28] Both the pre-Conquest religion and the "older Saxon roots" of the language had been drained of life by foreign, continental parasites, in this case by Latin and French influences.[29] As with Daniell's account of Tyndale's 1526 Prologue, there is an element of odd excess in this argument, which leads Daniell to expose his ignorance of the history of the language;[30] to make elementary errors in the description of the origins of words;[31] and to make frankly silly claims for Tyndale's influence on the history of scientific prose.[32]

The main point I wish to make here is that Daniell buys wholly into the argument that with Tyndale, Scripture became simple and straightforward. It is absolutely true that Tyndale cultivated a plain style with exceptional skill; it is also doubtless true that part of the reason for that style was to allow a much wider access to Scripture— a Scripture not only in English, but in a wonderfully supple, readable, plain English to boot. Nevertheless, Daniell understands this simplicity as purely descriptive, without thinking to ask if it had more complex cultural functions.

Why was it so important to Luther and Tyndale that Scripture should be simple, unambiguous, and wholly beyond the need of interpretation? The obvious answer is that for polemical reasons alone (not to speak for the moment of theological reasons), evangelical theorists absolutely needed Scripture to be clear. This was a non-negotiable claim. Anyone claiming to reform an institution on the basis of textual authority needed that text to be prior to the institution. They needed the text to be unambiguous. They also needed to be able to claim that everyone could see the force of that unambiguous reading. The essential polemical claim made by evangelical writers in the early sixteenth century was that Scripture preceded the Church. The only verities were written verities, declared in Scripture. As Tyndale says, it is as difficult to answer the question of which came first, Scripture or Church, as to answer the question of which came first, father or son: "For the whole scripture and all believing hearts testify that we are begotten through the Word. Wherefore if the Word is the begetter of the congregation . . . then is the gospel before the church."[33] Without that claim of absolute, non-negotiable scriptural priority, evangelicals were vulnerable to the authority of the institution they challenged, an institution that claimed legitimacy from unwritten traditions.

This insistence on the identification of truth with written documents is, of course, part of the larger drama of modernity, a drama that is legal, commercial, and cultural as well as spiritual. As societies extend and simplify their legal and spiritual jurisdictions (as western European societies did in the sixteenth century), so too must written authority make new claims, demolishing local custom and unwritten usage in the process.[34] Similarly, in societies experiencing rapidly rising populations, impersonal written forms of authority must replace the charismatic, personal force that the presence of the ruler had assumed in smaller jurisdictions. In any society undergoing profound social mobility, written authority will replace the intuitive praxis of smaller ruling elites; the new social forces habitually demand that the rules be clear (or "transparent") and explicit. They demand, in short, that the rules be written, and written in the clearest possible prose. Finally, powerful new forms of textual reproduction understandably mesmerize users of the new technology, who tend to fetishize it. Energized by the extraordinary new possibilities of printed books, sixteenth-century evangelical readers affirmed written authority at the expense of both visual and non-written forms of cultural authority.[35]

Many of these phenomena will be readily intelligible to people in the early twenty-first century. We are ourselves undergoing rapid social mobility that demands increasingly contractual, explicit, written, and "transparent" forms of cultural authority; and we are likewise experiencing breathtaking new forms of textual reproduction that are at the same time exhilarating and potentially punishing.

In the Lutheran moment of great polemical tension, however, it was necessary to focus insistently on the literal sense in a more restricted, literal way: Scripture could only provide an unbreakable plank of authority on which to stand against the Church if Scripture was absolutely clear and explicit. Not only did truth have to be located in Scripture, but that scriptural truth had to be incontrovertible. Nonscriptural claims to truth had to be rejected, and the entire machine of academic scriptural reading had to be disabled in favor of a Scripture so limpid that it interpreted itself. All forms of human interpretation were subject to academic manipulation of the kind practiced by Catholic teachers, who, in Tyndale's colorful prose, have "nailed a veil of false glosses on Moses' face."[36] No less important than the emphasis on Scripture's clarity was the emphasis on the idea that interpretation is itself wholly unnecessary as applied to Scripture: both positions were crucial weapons in the evangelical armory.

This literalism is a matter of game theory as much as anything else: without incontrovertible authority limpidly announced in Scripture, evangelicals had no sure base from which to attack the Church. This strategy was all evangelical theorists had to work with as long as they did not have the machinery of an alternative church. Luther, nothing if not an astute and courageous games player, played this card for all it was worth (as he had to if he were to win) in his celebrated speech at Worms before the Emperor in April 1521. He says that he's prepared to throw his books in the fire if anyone can prove him wrong by scriptural authority.[37] Even if bearing witness to Scripture should cause upheaval, so be it; Christ himself came to provoke internal dissension: "Think not, that I am come to send peace into the earth. I came not to send peace, but a sword. For I am come to set a man at variance against his father" (Matthew 10:34).[38] In his peroration Luther stands famously by Scripture, or rather Scripture holds him fast. He won't recant unless he be proven wrong either by the testimony of the Scriptures or by evident reason ("testimoniis scripturarum aut ratione evidente"), since he grants no authority either to the Pope or to the Councils of the Church. If no one can prove him wrong in that way, then he's a prisoner of Scripture and his conscience is captured by the word of God: "victus sum scripturis a me adductis et capta conscientia in verbis dei." Compelled by that authority, he is helpless: "I cannot do otherwise, here I stand, may God help me, Amen."[39] Modernity of a powerful kind is born in this moment of textual defeat and imprisonment (Luther's metaphors, not mine).

With this sharp and unavoidable textual weapon, Luther had already launched his attack on the Church in his astonishing series of polemical and theological treatises written in 1520. In each the message is the same: almost all the machinery of the Catholic Church was rejectable rubbish because it had no scriptural foundation. It was, instead, the product of mere "human traditions." All but three of the sacraments (Baptism, the Eucharist, and Penance) had to go, and those three needed to be reformed (Luther later rejected Penance too).[40] The priesthood should be extended to include all believers, since it has no scriptural foundation. Fraternities should likewise be rejected for the same reason (another human tradition).[41] Scripturally unfounded things pile up very quickly into lists of Lutheran junk: Penance, he says in the *Babylonian Captivity*, "has given rise to those endless burdens of vows, religious orders, works, satisfactions, pilgrimages, indulgences, and monastic sects, and from them in turn has arisen that flood of books, questions, opinions and man-made ordinances which the whole world cannot contain."[42]

Scripture becomes a great razor, then, for a revolutionary diminution and transformation of the Church. Tyndale likewise performs his no less thoroughgoing surgery on the Church into which he was born, with the same scriptural scalpel. We "ought to believe nothing without a reason of the Scripture and authority of God's word . . . Without God's word do nothing. And to his word add nothing" (p. 179). He asks readers of the *Obedience* in its Prologue to test his critique of the Church by reference to Scripture: when he alleges Scripture, "look thou to the text, whether I interpret it right which thou shalt easily perceive . . . if thou make Christ the foundation and ground and build all on him and referrest all to him" (p. 30).

A whole apparatus of numinous objects and actions are, in Tyndale's eyes, transformed into trash at best, damnable idolatry at worst, by this scriptural scrutiny. Ritual actions without scriptural foundation suddenly become absurd, divested of their symbolic force: the blessing of the bishop in absolution becomes "the wagging of the bishop's hand" (p. 137). Tyndale is not shy in listing, with relish, all those things that must go (Purgatory, most of the sacraments, pilgrimages, most images, the Pope, for example),[43] but perhaps we should hear the list from the voice of the potential victim. Thomas More expresses his astonishment in the *Dialogue Concerning Heresies* that practices that have been in use "so many hundred years" should now all suddenly be abolished on scriptural grounds:

> . . . as fasting, prayer, and almouse [almsgiving] . . . ; God and his saints worshipped; his sacraments had in reverence; Christian souls tenderly prayed for; holy vows kept and observed; virginity preached and praised; pilgrimages devoutly visited; every kind of good works commended.[44]

A whole set of religious and social practices, underwritten by an entire symbolic system, stands vulnerable before the scriptural surgery. And there can be no avoiding the surgery, given the total clarity, simplicity, and incontrovertible diagnosis of Scripture.

❧   At the very least, those who would describe Scripture as simple might concede that there were very powerful reasons why evangelical writers had to make it prior to the Church, incontrovertible, simple, and unambiguous. Of course, such a person might also add that Scripture was indeed all those things.

Was it, though, so simple and unambiguous? A number of symptoms suggest that evangelicals themselves felt very uneasy about leaving Scripture to speak for itself.[45] I begin by pointing to all those who read Scripture without, apparently, reading it properly. This reading failure, so insistently pointed to by evangelicals themselves, implies that reading the literal sense isn't sufficient: one clearly needs to do that in the right spirit. Moreover, Luther and Tyndale supplied many aids to make sure that readers did read in the right spirit. They certainly weren't prepared to leave it to the literal sense.

Since the sixteenth century, under both philological and evangelical pressure, we have come to regard the literal sense as common sense. Textual communities that insist that meaning is wholly contained in the letter of the text must, however, one way or another, give that unsustainable game away. For whatever the literal sense is, it certainly isn't a common sense, since literalism claims to do away with the need for common, implicit reading protocols. Textual communities that insist on the letter, and the letter alone, must very quickly recognize the fragility and brittleness of the literal sense alone.

How did early sixteenth-century evangelicals give the "literal sense" game away? Cultures based on correct reading need to isolate bad readers. Christians had always done this by pointing to the "carnal," often Jewish, reader who didn't see through to the deeper, allegorical sense of Scripture.[46] One of the commonest and bitterest complaints in evangelical polemic is against readers who "don't get it." Now this is, as I say, part of a long tradition, but in the case of evangelicals the situation is a little more complicated. In a reading culture that asserts deeper mysteries hidden by allegory, it is not difficult to say why one reader might miss that deeper sense, precisely because it's hidden. But in a reading culture where Scripture interprets itself through its plain simplicity, then it should be impossible to miss the point; there should be no deeper, allegorical meaning to be missed. So what about all those who read but don't understand? How could they miss the point?

Tyndale is especially hard on bad readers. He gives the impression that he is surrounded by them. As we saw in the last chapter, not everyone is welcome to the New Testament. Jews and Catholic readers are locked out, despite the fact that they know Scripture well:

> Jews which thought themselves within, were yet so locked out, and are to this day that they can understand no sentence of the scripture unto their salvation, though they can rehearse the texts everywhere and dispute thereof as subtly as the popish doctors of dunce's dark learning, with their sophistry, served us. (p. 3)

As we saw earlier, though, Tyndale's rejection of some readers who miss the obvious unsettlingly extends into his own readers—the reader, that is, who "favoureth the word of God" (p. 7).

That same shift is visible in his *Exposition on . . . chapters of Matthew* (first published in Antwerp in 1533), because the simple, literal sense turns out to be so easily mistaken by so many readers.[47] Tyndale begins with an attack on the Catholic doctors for having acted like the scribes and Pharisees: Christ is the spiritual Isaac who digs the wells of Abraham that have been "stopped and filled up with earth of their false expositions" (image 2). After a passage stressing our inability to perform the Law and our hatred of the Law for that reason (image 3), Tyndale emphasizes the importance of having the Law written on the heart first. The promises are made, however, on condition that we love the Law, and we love it only if we have it written on our hearts: "Whosoever hath not the law of God written in his heart, that he love it, have his lust [desire] in it and record therein night and day, understanding it as God hath given it . . . the same hath no part in the promises, or can have any true faith in the blood of Christ" (image 5) (see Jeremiah 31:33, cited in Hebrews 8:10; also Hebrews 10:16).

Tyndale recognizes that this precept sets the bar pretty high: loving the Law that one must hate, and being able to love it only if it's first written in the heart.[48] It is already clear that the literal sense is insufficient: if the text of Scripture can be properly understood only if it is first written on the heart, there is obviously a pre-textual event that has happened before the literal sense is read and understood. If the reader should not love the damning Law, then to "all such is the Scripture locked up and made impossible to understand. They may read it and rehearse the stories thereof, and dispute of it, as the Turks may" (image 6). Their reading profits them, however, not a whit.

This image of reading intensely without profit (in fact with damage to oneself) evokes a kind of nightmare of reading, even for the sincere reader. In literary history, it evokes Bunyan's image of poor Ignorance, who, sincere and trusting Christian though he be, terrifyingly can't find his passport to heaven when he arrives. He foolishly thought he could come in without fear of the Law, and so he is swept down the slippery route to damnation, even at the very door of paradise.

Tyndale is sensitive to the possibility of a reading nightmare, for he goes on immediately in the *Exposition* to recognize that we need to be patient with those who may have difficulty with this kind of reading. There are many degrees of those who believe in Christ's remission of sin; the stronger should help the weaker along, not calling them "heretics at the first chop," not threatening them with fire and faggot, not frightening them "with shadows and bugs" (image 6). The spiritual struggle can be like a nightmare. If the flesh should gain governance of our spirit until the promises of God do their work, it is "as though she had a mountain upon her back, and as we sometime in our dreams think we bear heavier than a millstone on our breasts, or when we would run away for fear, our legs seem heavier than lead" (image 7). All this applies to the evangelical reader; as for the Catholic reader, the literal sense will do nothing: even if men can "rehearse all the scripture without book," they are nonetheless "members of Satan" if they still preach the doctrine of works.

This discussion of the psychic distress of evangelical reading forms the Prologue of the *Exposition*. The text itself begins by warning against overmuch sorrow, lest "overmuch heaviness swallow . . . a man clean up" (image 13). Throughout this exceptionally revealing text, however, the nightmare of reading without purchase recurs. Later, for example, Tyndale makes the same point about the Jews' simultaneous knowledge of and total ignorance of Scripture. He makes it in such a way, however, as to suggest that evangelical readers may share the same condition. Tyndale says that one can never please God by doing good deeds of any kind,

> except [unless] thou have the true knowledge of God's Word to season thy deeds withal. For God hath put a rule in the scripture without which thou canst not move an hair of thine head but that it is damnable in the sight of God. As it is of the Jews, though . . . they have a fervent zeal to God, yea and have the scriptures thereto, yet because they have not the understanding, all is damnable that they do. (image 77)

So the literal sense isn't enough. Before one reads the literal sense, one must have a true knowledge; and one derives that true knowledge from another, invisible yet burning text, the one written on the heart. This is another way of saying that the literal sense is not simple: it needs to be interpreted. Erasmus understood this cardinal point in his dispute with Luther: "The authority of the Scripture is not here in dispute. The same Scriptures are acknowledged and venerated by either side. Our battle is about the meaning of Scripture."[49]

❧   Evangelical writers frequently acknowledge, then, that Scripture is not incontrovertible, since they so often insist that people are reading it incorrectly. These bad readers are not only Catholics and Jews, but evangelical readers themselves. With their frequent insistence that the truest text of Scripture is the one written on the heart, they give their game away: for if the literal sense were indeed "the root and ground of all," then there would be no need to appeal to an even more authoritative, metaphorical "literal" sense written on the heart.

In the next section I show how evangelical insistence on the literal sense alone leads in fact directly to an intensely institutional account of textual meaning, via predestination. Here I will note some other signs that Luther and Tyndale are unwilling to let the simple literal sense do all the talking. If the literal sense were so plain and incontrovertible, we might expect a reading culture free of textual apparatus, such as introductions, scriptural guides, and marginalia. We might expect, that is, that Scripture would be allowed to do the talking. In fact such is not the case: both Luther and Tyndale do a good deal of talking themselves, in telling us how we should read Scripture. These features of textual apparatus are also powerful symptoms of the weakness of any position that claims a text will interpret itself, that Scripture should be *sui ipsius interpres*. Neither Luther nor Tyndale leaves Scripture to do all the interpreting; both do quite a bit themselves.

Luther and Tyndale frequently make the point that Scripture is to be taken whole. They follow Deuteronomy 4:2, "ye shall put nothing unto the word which I command you, neither do ought therefrom," and apply this to Scripture: it is not to be broken up or selected from at will. "Without God's word do nothing. And to his word add nothing, neither pull anything therefrom," says Tyndale in the *Obedience* (p. 179), and "add nothing unto God's word or take ought therefrom" in the Prologue to Exodus (p. 85).[50] This may be a convenient maxim for the scriptural polemicist, giving him ammunition to attack his enemies when they cite Scripture partially to their own advantage. A moment's reflection will reveal, however, that no reading community can sustain the wholeness of the canon. Discussion, let alone basic thinking about reading experience, requires us to break up the text in various ways. Every textual community invents ways of abbreviating its corpus.[51] The very word *legere* (Latin, "to read") means, after all, to select.

Luther and Tyndale are no exception to this ineluctable rule of book history. They say which texts are most important; Luther rejects texts that don't suit his theology from the canon; they supply abundant prologues; they supply marginalia; Luther wrote catechisms; and they both give interpretive keys that unlock the whole of Scripture. All this should be unnecessary given the simplicity of the literal sense, and it all flies in the face of their insistence that nothing be added.

Tyndale and Luther both make a separation at the heart of Scripture by privileging certain books above others. In the Preface to his 1522 New Testament Luther distinguishes, as we have seen, some books of the New Testament as "the very kernel and marrow of all the other books."[52] These include the Epistles of Saint Paul. In his Preface to Paul's Epistle to the Romans, Luther is more selective still: he opens by saying that "this epistle is really the chief part of the New Testament, and truly the purest gospel."[53] Tyndale, translating from Luther in his Preface to Romans, declares that the Epistle to the Romans is "the principal and most excellent part of the new testament, and most pure evangelion . . . and also a light and a way in unto the whole scripture" (p. 207). In the Hebrew scriptures, Deuteronomy (because it's the most explicit of the books of Moses, offering a statement of the Law in non-narrative form) is to be preferred: "It is the most excellent book of all the books of Moses."[54] Luther and Tyndale both single out Paul because his letters, especially his letter to the Romans, articulate the doctrine of faith alone, the uselessness of works, and predestination. For similar reasons, Luther ejects the Epistle of James from the canon, since James gives him real difficulty. The

Epistle of James contains the claims that "faith, if it have no deeds, is dead in itself" and "of deeds a man is justified" (James 2:17 and 2:24). Luther's response is simple, but it breaks the rule that one should not subtract from Scripture: he dismisses and downgrades James as "an epistle of straw . . . for it has nothing of the nature of the gospel about it."[55]

Even setting aside this startlingly opportunistic rejection of James (an act of scriptural subtraction that Tyndale does not replicate),[56] Luther and Tyndale both establish a hierarchy within Scripture by their privileging of Paul. They create a conceptual key by which the rest of Scripture can be opened. They establish, in short, an intra-scriptural distinction between text and gloss: Paul is the kernel for which the rest of the text serves as gloss, or vice versa. Tyndale recognizes that Paul, however blindingly clear, might have been obscured: although Romans, he says, has been "darkened with glosses and wonderful dreams of sophisters, that no man could spy out the intent and meaning of it," in fact that meaning is "a bright light and sufficient to give light unto all scripture" (p. 207).

If it were so bright a light, one might expect it to speak for itself. In fact, and unsurprisingly, Tyndale goes on to give a very long and detailed account of Lutheran theology (in fact his explanatory prologue is translated from Luther). Of course, any committed reader wants to persuade others, but Tyndale and Luther are, it might be noticed, uneasy about such introductions, for obvious reasons. Both frequently say, in keeping with their ideology of simplicity, that no introduction is necessary; and yet, in keeping with the need to promote a certain way of reading, they will in any case provide one. So the prologues are simultaneously unnecessary and necessary; that is, they are not unlike Lutheran Christians themselves: *simul iustus et peccator* (simultaneously justified and a sinner).[57] Herewith Luther in his Preface, or *Vorrhede*, to the New Testament of 1522:

It would be right and proper for this book to go forth without any prefaces or extraneous names attached and simply have its own say under its own name. However, many unfounded interpretations and prefaces have scattered the thought of Christians to a point where no one any longer knows what is gospel or law, New Testament or Old. Necessity demands, therefore, that there should be a notice or preface, by which the ordinary man can be rescued from his former delusions, [and] set on the right track.[58]

So Luther says that although the text should be allowed to speak clearly in its own voice, without preface, the existence of the preface is nevertheless justified by virtue of preexistent confusion. Once again, the literal sense can't do its work alone, because understandings preexist and determine the literal sense.

Lutheran reading depends, as we saw in the previous chapter, on very specific and wholly new definitions of terms such as "Law," "Gospel," and so on. By "new testament", for example, Luther does not mean the books of the New Testament; he means instead the promises that are everywhere in Scripture.[59] Of course Luther would deny that these are new meanings: these are, by his account, Paul's meanings. Given Luther's conception of God as a *deus alienus*, wholly unintelligible in human categories, it's unsurprising that he should posit meanings of words that break free of human custom, as he does very explicitly in the account of his conversion.[60] In the history of Christian theology, a theologically transcendent God always exerts pressure on the meanings of words;[61] the fierce Lutheran assertion of a God wholly unconstrained by human justice or human convention is no exception to this rule.

Tyndale, translating Luther, recognizes the novelty of the meaning given to key words: in his preface to Romans, he says that "this word law may not be understood here after the common manner, and to use Paul's term, after the manner of men or after man's ways" (p. 207). So in his prefaces, Luther needs to give quick, or not so quick, tutorials, by way of training readerly predisposition. Every reading culture does this; only a reading culture that makes totalizing claims for the self-sufficiency of the literal sense will feel any awkwardness about doing it.

Tyndale also addresses readerly predisposition; he justifies doing so on the grounds that people have been confused for too long. In the Lutheran Preface to Romans in the 1534 New Testament, for example, after privileging the letter to the Romans and calling it a bright light "of itself," he justifies the need for the very long prologue (almost identical in length to Romans itself). The text has been "evil darkened with glosses and wonderful dreams," and thus needs an explanatory preface, in which Tyndale gives a long induction to evangelical vocabulary by explicating various buzz words. He does not, of course, put it like that; he will clarify "what Paul meaneth" by these words: "the law, sin, grace, faith, righteousness, flesh, spirit, and such like." Without understanding the true meaning of these words (a meaning not "after the common manner"), one can read the literal sense as often as one likes, but without profit: "or else thou read it never so oft, thou shalt but lose thy labour" (p. 207). Tyndale does not go so far as to replace the words of Scripture with his own words entirely, as Thomas Becon does in his *News out of Heaven* (1541),[62] but he makes absolutely sure that readers won't go astray as a result of reading without very specific directions.

Once again, we come to the dead end of claims that meaning is wholly contained in the literal sense. Even from within evangelical practice, we can see the ideological force of that claim. The incontrovertible simplicity of the literal sense serves well as a polemical weapon, but it turns out to be far from simple. Although both Luther and Tyndale claim to offer truth derived from the literal sense, their readings are, evidently, driven by theological presuppositions, not "after the common manner."[63]

※ At this point we could turn to book history to see the many other reading aids that Luther and Tyndale, and their evangelical followers, offered readers who needed no help but who yet needed help: to marginalia and catechisms, for example.[64] A central contention of this chapter has, however, already been demonstrated: from the evidence of evangelical practice itself, it is clear that the self-presentation of simplicity is anything but simple. The literal text is unsustainable from within its own terms: it needs authentication from a prior text, the text written on the heart; and it needs a good deal of backup from the apparatus of the new Bibles.

What are the institutional consequences of there being an incontrovertible text written on the heart? For who is to judge between different readings made by different evangelical readers? "This is my body" (for example, Matthew 26:26) is, after all, an exceptionally simple statement, but one that produced profound and bitter differences between evangelical camps.[65] What are the resources for conflict resolution when readers disagree?

To cool minds in the sixteenth century, the issues were already perfectly clear: any claim to absolute Biblical truth would lead to violence. Erasmus states the case best. He frames the evangelical question: "What need is there of an interpreter when the scripture itself is crystal clear?" and begins to answer it thus:

> But if it is so clear, why have so many outstanding men in so many centuries been blind, and in a matter of such importance, as these would appear? . . . How, then, shall we prove the spirit? By learning? On both

sides there are scholars. By holiness of life? On both sides there are sinners. . . . You say "what has an assembled synod to do with the understanding of Scripture, in which it may be that there is nobody who has the spirit?" I reply, "What, then, of private conventicles of the few, of whom it is much more likely that none has the Spirit?"[66]

Erasmus is here working around to the recognition that institutions of one kind or another will always need to be invoked in matters of canonical interpretation, for reasons of conflict resolution if nothing else. Neither philology (that is, linguistic expertise) nor virtue will answer to the case, as they will inevitably be evenly divided among opposed camps.

Erasmus's implicit recognition of the need for some social mechanism to deal with conflicts arising out of scriptural disagreement is not in itself authoritarian. It is instead born of the recognition that reading of canonical texts is a fundamentally social and historical activity, in which agreed meanings precede understanding of the literal sense; it's premised on the profound fragility of the literal sense. Erasmus pictures himself playing the role of the Pharisee Gamaliel in Acts, when the other Pharisees are bent on killing Peter and his fellow apostles. Gamaliel stays their hand: he argues against persecution on the grounds that if the apostles are truly from God, nothing can stop them; if they are not divinely sanctioned, then they will come to nothing (Acts 5:27–39).[67] Who can mediate in cases of interpretive disagreement?

In answering this urgent question, Luther and Tyndale had three available options. One might appeal to philological expertise: only the translator who knows Hebrew and Greek can judge; it's primarily a linguistic question. Or one might appeal to the councils of the learned. Finally, one might permit individual interpretation. Luther and Tyndale use the first possibility only against learned opponents, as we shall see in the following chapter. They unequivocally rejected both of the other possibilities.

Whenever Tyndale discusses councils, whether secular or spiritual, he expresses his disgust for them. In his *Answer unto Sir Thomas More's Dialogue* (1531), for example, he says that the "general councils of the spirituality are of no other manner since the pope was a god than the general parliaments of the temporality. Where no man dare say his mind freely and liberally for fear of someone and of his flatterers." Both royal and papal councils are dominated by "one two or three wily foxes that have all other in subjection."[68] Because councils are above all human institutions, embedded in the material actualities of history, Tyndale rejects them as nothing before the authority of Scripture.[69]

What then of private interpretation, unchecked by institutional mediation? Although standard narratives of cultural history assume that this was the Lutheran and Tyndalian position, nothing could be further from the truth. Leaving the Bible to individual readers, on the understanding that one reader's interpretation was as good as another's, was not an option for Luther and Tyndale, just as it wasn't for More either. Such a proposition would have been no more acceptable to them than would be the notion to contemporary Americans that anyone's interpretation and application of the U.S. Constitution was as good as anyone else's. In literate societies, the interpretation and application of canonical texts that really matter is never without an institutional element. When sixteenth-century conservatives feared that "each one man to be a church alone" if free interpretation were permitted,[70] we tend to pigeonhole that attitude as the untrusting, illiberal Catholic response to the call for interpretive freedom made by evangelicals. David Daniell, for example, champions Tyndale as standing at the head of a "cherished and English individualism which spread worldwide";[71] he avers that the Protestantism in

England was dependent on "free discussion at all levels."[72] Now every reader—man, woman, and child—"could receive this highly sacred . . . text with no one in hierarchical authority to interpret and guide."[73]

It may well have been the case that people *did* read without guidance, but this wasn't what Tyndale had in mind. On the contrary, he consistently rejects the possibility, and certainly the desirability, of "private interpretation." In the Prologue to the Epistle of Peter in the 1534 New Testament, for example, he affirms that Peter prohibits "prophetical scripture by the will of man"; neither "is any scripture of private interpretation: that is to say, may be otherwise expounded than agreeing to the open places and general articles and to the covenants of God and all the rest of scripture" (p. 332). Elsewhere he chides the "ignorant and the weak," who use the "uttermost of their liberty" with Scripture, "interpreting it after the largest fashion and most favor of the flesh."[74]

How then does Tyndale answer the question about interpretive authority? I maintain that he appealed to an institutional concept, that of the True Church, and that appeal involved an acceptance of predestination. It's true that Tyndale was much more equivocal about works than Luther, but in the earlier, purely Lutheran phase of his career he certainly believed Paul literally (that "which he appointed before, them he also called. And which he called, them also he justified" [Romans 8:30]).[75] Throughout his career, Tyndale never explicitly repudiated predestination, and once very explicitly promoted it, without ever reconciling his later commitment to works with that doctrine.[76] Above all, his position on true reading remained steady: the authority of the true reader derived from that reader's election to the True Church. Lection, that is, presupposed election.

In Matthew, the disciples ask Christ why he speaks in parables. Christ responds:

> It is given unto you [the disciples] to know the secrets of the kingdom
> of heaven, but to them it is not given . . . Therefore I speak to them in
> similitudes: for though they see, they see not: and hearing they hear
> not: neither understand . . . For this people's hearts are waxed [be-
> come] gross, and their ears were dull of hearing, and their eyes have
> they closed, lest they . . . should turn, that I might heal them. (Matt.
> 13:12–15)

This passage is signaled in the margins by Tyndale thus: "A covenant
to them that love the word of God to further it, that they shall in-
crease therein, and another that they that love it not, shall lose it
again, and wax blind." Christ's defense of opacity in parables is obviously a tricky passage for Tyndale, who has proclaimed the simplicity
and openness of Scripture so forcefully; thus it's unsurprising that he
should hasten to gloss it as a reading covenant: if you love the word
of God, you will understand it better, and vice versa.

Before we accept the openness of the text as Tyndale would have
us read it, let's look more closely at what Christ says. For Christ himself is not at all open, in this passage at least. Instead of defending
parables by invoking their pedagogic effectiveness (as Tyndale does),
Christ says something very different: he uses parables, he says, in order to speak to those who *already* know. There's a *pre-textual* event that
guarantees understanding of the text in Christ's account: "For whosoever hath, to him shall be given: and he shall have in abundance"
(Matthew 13:12). Tyndale's gloss marks the same pre-textual event,
less clearly: those who love the word of God shall further it, and vice
versa. At the very least, there's an extra- or pre-textual love here that
is not generated from the text itself. Instead, that pre-textual event of
"having" is what generates understanding of the text. The reader either has or doesn't have it.

Literalist communities must acknowledge, in one way or another,
that the reader comes to the text with a great deal *not* given by the

text, whether that disposition be trained or inspired. Christ himself is not committed to a defense of the literal sense in this passage, but Tyndale is. Yet despite that commitment, Tyndale quietly allows that something has happened *prior* to the event of reading Scripture. Does he make that allowance more explicitly elsewhere? This is a crucial question, for if he does, then we must ask how that readerly disposition is formed.

Is that readerly disposition formed against the institution of the Church, or must the good evangelical reader rather *represent* the institution of the (True) Church? In other words, does the evangelical reader resist or represent an institution? As we have seen, Tyndale valiantly attempts to sustain the primacy of Scripture, but frequently is forced onto the back foot by acknowledging a prior disposition to read Scripture correctly, guaranteed by having Scripture written on one's heart. Where does that prior disposition come from?

Tyndale frequently declares that the true interpreter of Scripture is the elect reader, just as the one who recognizes the elect reader is also one of the elect. In the Prologue to the 1525 New Testament, for example, we hear that "in Christ God loved us, his elect and chosen, before the world began, and reserved us unto the knowledge of his Son and of his holy Gospel."[77] In the *Parable of the Wicked Mammon* (1528), Tyndale defines a prophet as one who "interpreteth the hard places of scripture, as [well as] him that prophesieth things to come." Whoever receives a prophet shall have the same reward as the prophet: "For except thou were elect to the same eternal life, and hadst the same faith and trust in God . . . thou couldst never consent to their deeds and help them."[78] In the 1530 Pentateuch, the Prologue to Exodus declares that the Christian who is capable of sustaining faith in the promises, even under competing temptation, has a good sign, an "earnest that God hath elect and chosen him" (p. 85).

As Tyndale was pressed on the issue of how we can recognize the authority of the true reader, he began to explicate the institutional grounds of this conviction. He was pressed, that is, to articulate the institutional element that must inevitably form part of any programmatic reading culture. In his *Answer to More's Dialogue* (1531), for example, he affirms the primacy of Scripture: what purpose would Scripture serve, if the Christian were required to believe unwritten verities? No sooner has he made this routine claim for written verities and only written verities, however, than he shifts his ground. Even if no scriptures existed prior to Moses, "God wrote his testament unto them always, both to do and to believe, even in the sacraments . . . And in them they read the word of God, as we do in books."[79] The shift to a metaphorical scripture is revealing, but here it's restricted to pre-scriptural times. What, though, of post-scriptural times? Or what of Tyndale's own time, when he found himself in furious disagreement over scriptural meaning not only with Catholic opponents, but also, as we shall see, with his own most intimate fellow-translators?

Tyndale comes out explicitly to declare a prior, institutional basis for scriptural knowledge. In his definition of the True Church, he circumscribes the elect by virtue of the text of Scripture written on their heart. Just as we believe, he says, that the fire is hot through experience, so too do the elect have the Law of God written in their hearts, and they know it because it's hot.

> Now, therefore, when they ask us how we know it is the scripture of God; ask them how John the Baptist knew, and other prophets, when God stirred up in all such times as the scripture was in like captivity under hypocrites? Did John believe that the scribes, Pharisees, and high priests, were the true church of God, and had his spirit, and could not err? Who taught the eagles to spy out their prey? Even so the children of God spy out their Father; and Christ's elect spy out their Lord, and trace out the paths of his feet, and follow; yea, though he go upon the plain and liquid water, which will receive no step, and yet there

they will find out his foot: his elect know him, but the world knoweth him not.[80]

Tyndale deploys a beautiful (perhaps strategically beautiful) rhetorical style here to make what is for him a very difficult leap from the strict, literal sense of Scripture into a prior text, and an institutional text.[81] There is a True Church, membership of which is guaranteed by God's word being "written on the heart." That prior writing on the hearts of God's elect itself guarantees, in its turn, a true knowledge of scriptural meaning. Prior to the literal sense of the text is an anterior text, written in and on the heart itself.

"God," says Tyndale of the elect's possession of Scripture, "shall write it in their hearts with his Holy Spirit." If the evangelical is asked why he believes he shall be saved, he should answer that he "fele[th] that it be true." When asked how he knows it's true, he should answer: "because it is written in [m]ine heart." Who wrote it? Answer: "the spirit of God." How did it arise? (Tyndale is clearly preparing a kind of game plan for the persecuted acolyte): by reading Scripture or preaching, but inwardly. In actual practice, the elected Christian simply affirms that he's certain because he feels certain. Moral authoritarianism, underwritten by membership of an invisible institution, replaces the material institution.

At the heart of this reading praxis is a profound paradox: while ostensibly highlighting the covenantal force of the literal sense, Tyndale must make urgent appeal to the unwritten law of faith that precedes and makes sense of the literal. Both contradictory appeals are made stridently, which serves to disguise their opposition. Lection, that is, does indeed presuppose election.

So Tyndale does recognize the institutional basis of scriptural reading. Before one can read Scripture properly, one must be a member of the True Church. Membership of that True Church is guaranteed by what Tyndale calls "feeling faith," and "feeling faith" derives from the Scripture that is written on the heart of the elect. Thus, even as Tyndale rejects the Church's priority over Scripture, he acknowledges it, by instituting the True Church. Biblical reading implies, as it always must, the existence of the Church, but Tyndale's church is an invisible one, a Church of the elect. The elect constitute the True Church, and the experience of the elect authenticates scriptural truth. Predestination determines the membership of the True Church: those readers who are not counted among the elect face damnation. The elect only know they are elect by "feeling" in their reading of Scripture.

True evangelical reading of Scripture is not, however, without its terrors: one can only be a true reader by first belonging to the True Church, but one can never be sure of one's membership, and one can only check one's election in agony, by applying the "corrosive" of the Law not to heal sin, but "to stir it up and make the disease alive."[82] Thus the experience of evangelical reading could be a lonely business; this was certainly how Stephen Gardiner (d. 1555) imagined it in his tract against George Joye: every man would be his own church under the evangelical regime, and "each one man to pray alone . . . without days or hours, appointed for the whole body to pray together, and so all to be alone, alone, alone, mine own self all alone, and then to be devoured of the devil alone, without comfort in the wilderness alone."[83] Evangelical reading is underwritten by very tight, exhausting, exclusionary, and institutional protocols that are discovered through the painful and lonely experience of reading.

The simple plainness of the literal sense produces, indeed, an even stranger paradox: in this reading culture, Scripture, precisely because it is said to be so clear, finally displaces hermeneutic complexity to the entire life of the Christian. For the Christian living under the dispensation of predestination, everything has been decided before one acts. What remains for the Christian is to search for signs of election:

all of life, that is, becomes an opaque book, full of doubtful signs.[84] Tyndale describes this search for verification of election in hermeneutic terms. In the *Parable of the Wicked Mammon*, for example, he says that if the spirit gladly accepts scriptural prescription, then take this as "a sign and evident token thereby that the spirit of life is in thee, and that thou art elect to life everlasting by Christ's blood, whose gift and purchase is thy faith and that spirit that worketh the will of God in thee."[85] The "simple" text of Scripture produces another simple text written on the heart, but at the same time it transforms the world into a very complex and finally unreadable text that is incapable of answering the question: am I saved?[86] Thus the "simple" text of Scripture is surrounded on either side by complex, opaque texts.

Interpretive systems are not unlike hydraulic systems: there's a certain amount of pressure that must be registered somewhere. If pressure in the system is depressed in one place, it will resurface in another. Removing the institutional element from the reading of canonical texts is easier said than done: repress the material institution and you will end up with an ideational institution. Given the quirkiness of the human psyche, ideational institutions can be, and usually are, more punishing than material ones.

CHAPTER FIVE

Bible Reading, Persecution, and Paranoia

SINGLE-MINDED concentration on the simplicity of the literal sense, then, produced a much less simple multiplication of texts. The single, self-sufficient literal sense gave way in the first place to an anterior text, painfully written onto the heart. That text itself required an institution, the True Church, to underwrite it. Membership of the True Church was guaranteed by God's predestination, by which the Christian is written into another book, the Book of Life. Predestination also worked, however, to rewrite the world as an impenetrable and therefore unending text. Evangelical Christians could never be assured of their own salvation; all they could do was look for signs of divine approbation, signs that the decision already taken had gone in their favor. Affirmations of complete linguistic simplicity produced the endless work of reading opaque texts.

Thus the entire world became pregnant with signs and portents, traces in which God's inscrutable decision might be legible. The experience of reading (inspired or cold?) was itself one of those portents. Evangelical insistence on the simplicity of the literal sense paradoxically produced fathomless, unnerving, and ubiquitous textual complexity. This has historically been characteristic of such cultures: Biblical simplicity is surrounded by the illegible density of the world's signs and portents; the allegorical mysteries of the text do not disappear, but resurface in the text of the world.

In this chapter I take up the social consequences of such a complex textual culture. In particular, I highlight the frequency with which evangelical readers describe themselves as surrounded by enemies. Schism and factionalism are structurally built into this culture for many convergent reasons. In the first place, paranoia is the predictable characteristic of a literalist culture, since, however necessary the literalism, it tries to do away with intuited understandings grounded in usage. Literalism, as a cultural phenomenon, is always the child of mistrust; and literalism must likewise become the parent of mistrust. The words on the page inevitably produce division, but the literalist can only appeal to the words on the page or written on the heart. In any case, a literalist culture produces, as we have seen, a world of signs and portents, which itself is a fertile ground for paranoia, in the weaker spirits at least. A world pregnant with illegible signs of one's fate makes people start to hear voices.

Second, the *scriptura sola* position, taken seriously, leaves a reader isolated, since not all Biblical texts are good news. If the literal sense of the Law must provoke, by the Lutheran account, an intense experience of abjection and worthlessness, and if the literal sense is all one has to go on, that literal sense is often threatening.

Third, the *scriptura sola* position demands spectacular demonstrations of readerly conviction, by way of authenticating the Scripture on the heart. One way in which readers in such a culture demonstrate that conviction is to affirm exceptionally close associations with fellow evangelicals. Another is to repudiate fellow evangelicals. This social pattern is also historically characteristic of evangelical culture: tightly bound groupings, united by a common understanding of the literal sense, disagree about the literal sense, and split into bitter factions.

So in this chapter I look at some evangelical readers and writers who feel cut off, isolated, and betrayed by enemies. Does Scripture relieve their isolation, or provoke it? I focus principally on the psalm translations of Henry Howard, Earl of Surrey, which he wrote in prison while awaiting execution. In his psalm paraphrases we do not see psalm consolation; we read instead the expression of psalm anxiety. For the already betrayed and doomed Surrey, the psalms voice more betrayal and doom. Later in the chapter I examine the frequency with which William Tyndale bitterly repudiated his collaborators.

🦋 Henry Howard, Earl of Surrey (1516/17–1547), fell victim to former friends and family having turned witness, often demonstrably false witness, against him, beginning in December 1546. Scion of England's premier noble house, Surrey was first arrested on 2 December on the accusation of Richard Southwell, Surrey's childhood friend who had been raised in the Howard household. On 15 December the Privy Council cited two unnamed "witnesses" to treasonable words by Surrey, to the effect that he had confessed to a plan to overthrow both Henry VIII and Prince Edward. In the actual trial on heraldic charges, both this initial charge and the two witnesses to the treasonous words were nowhere mentioned.[1] In preparation for this trial, depositions were taken from at least twenty-two witnesses.[2] Gawain Carew and Edward Rogers had, like Southwell, served with Surrey in France; both testified against him. George Blage had been a friend; he also testified against Surrey. To Edward Warner, who testified against him, Surrey had dedicated a poem. Edmund Knyvet, his cousin, offered testimony against him. Surrey's sister testified most actively to damn him.[3]

The heraldic charges against Surrey were, as Peter Moore has recently argued, wholly spurious; Moore surmises that the plot against the Howards was generated by fear of a council dominated by anti-evangelicals after the death of the King, and argues that Surrey was "killed as a precaution."[4] Susan Brigden further suggests that the Howard lands provided powerful incentive for the campaign against them: "Many of those who had made the condemnation of Surrey possible—Blage, Southwell, Knyvet, Warner, Devereux, Barker, Hussey, Bellingham, Fulmerston—joined the gadarene rush for grants and offices at the turn of the year."[5] Surrey was thus the victim of a swarm of false witnesses—a victim, in the words of a translation of Proverbs printed in 1550, of

> A witness false that doth his lips deceitfully apply
> And covertly his neighbor grieve with some new forged lie.[6]

The narrative of Surrey's sudden and brutal downfall lends itself readily to a familiar pattern of malevolent courtly intrigue. Does this story of murderous and wholly distrustful courtly relations, however, have anything to do with evangelical religion?

❧   The Hebrew scriptures, in their broadest outlines, tell a single story of territorial occupation, defense, and loss. Unlike the Homeric narratives, the Hebrew scriptures repeatedly demand that an absolute distinction of culture be made between the parties warring over that territory. Between the people of Abraham and their enemies, there can, in God's view, be no cultural commerce. Both the Egyptians and the peoples who must be displaced from Canaan practice wholly different and, in Hebrew eyes, idolatrous religions. This absolute distinction is written into the initial promise of territory. In Genesis 12:1 God commands Abraham to leave his own country; God will make of Abraham "a mighty people," and "I will bless them that bless thee, and curse them that curse thee."

From this moment, the logic of cultural distinction unrolls across the history of the Israelite people for the next twelve hundred years, until the fall of Jerusalem in 587 BCE and the ensuing Babylonian captivity. The Egyptians suffer God's curse, no less than the peoples of Canaan who inhabit the land prior to the divinely appointed invasion led by Joshua. Just before Moses writes all the words of the Lord after receiving the Commandments (Exodus 24), God assures him of victory over the many peoples of the land that will become Israel: "When mine angel goeth before thee and hath brought thee in unto the Amorites, Hethites, Pherezites, Cananites, Hevites and Jebusites and I shall have destroyed them: see thou worship not their gods neither serve them, neither do after the works of them . . . Neither shall they dwell in thy land, lest they make thee sin against me: for if thou serve their gods, it will surely be thy decay" (Exodus 23:23–33).

One of the many extraordinary and valuable features of the Hebrew scriptures is that they do not varnish history. In this case, they do not hide the fact that the people of Israel, and then of Judah, persistently fail to respect the cultural distinction demanded of them by God. Even as Moses, having received the specifications of ritual worship on Mount Sinai, descends with the tables of law written by the finger of God, the recalcitrant Israelites have already cast the image of a calf to which they have made sacrifice (Exodus 31–32). The Biblical history of Israel is a never-ending story of persistent backsliding into idolatrous worship of the gods of surrounding peoples, and of intermarriage with those peoples.

The Book of Kings, for example, reports, much later in the history of Israel, an unceasing pattern of cultural promiscuity with neighboring religion, followed by periods of cultural revolution in which foreign practice is repudiated. I discussed some of these moments of repudiation (the reigns of Jehu and Josiah) in Chapter 1. The reign of the last king of Israel, Hoshea (732–721 BCE), offers another example. Here the Israelites have been successfully invaded by the Assyrians, and the text is in no doubt about why they fell:

For the children of Israel had sinned against the Lord their God which brought them out of the land of Egypt . . . and feared other gods. And they walked in the ordinance of the heathen which the Lord cast out before the children of Israel . . . They refused his ordinances and his appointment that he had made with their fathers . . . and followed vanity and became vain, like to the heathen that were round about them. (2 Kings 17:7–15)

This account of the causality of historical catastrophe is very consistent throughout Kings and into the period of captivity. Major and minor prophets sing variations on the same theme of lusting after strange gods, and so producing the disaster that befell both Israel and Judah.[7]

The experience of being intimately surrounded by threat is most graphically expressed in the Psalms. These lyric poems make a personal expression of what is related historically in the Books of Kings. Often in the Psalms the voice of the complainant articulates loneliness, universal threat, and the complete evanescence of human forms of consolation. Sometimes the threat is located in the enemies of Israel; the psalm voices the fear and trust of a nation: "Consider how many are my foes, / And with what violent hatred they hate me. / Oh guard my life, and deliver me; do not let me be put to shame, / for I take refuge in you . . . redeem Israel, O God, / Out of all its troubles" (Psalm 24:19).[8] At other times the complainant is a single individual, caught among threatening enemies *within* the legal system of Israel itself: "Do not give me up to the will of my adversaries, / For false witnesses have risen up against me, / and they are breathing out violence. I believe I shall see the goodness of the Lord / in the land of the living" (Psalm 26:12); "All who hate me whisper together about me; / They imagine the worst for me" (40:8).[9]

The voice of those surrounded by foreign foes, militarily weakened by obeisance to foreign gods, was picked up by English evangelical writers in the sixteenth century. Sometimes, as in the Psalms, that voice claims to speak for all England, surrounded by foes and enfeebled by old idolatry. Thus Thomas Becon's *Policy of War* (1542), for example, addresses his country in explicitly patriotic terms of a kind not found in pre-Reformation English writing: "O England, England, mine own native country," Becon writes, as he encourages English soldiers to read the Scriptures for Israelite victories.[10] Idolatry; strange worshipping of God (which amounts to worshipping strange gods); despising God's Word—all these (drawn, clearly enough, from the model of the Book of Kings) are the cause of English military decadence.[11] England will recover her military strength should she accept the pure word of God in the Gospel.

At other times, the new gospel voice expresses not the predicament of England surrounded by foreign enemies, but that of the courtier in the court of King Henry VIII, surrounded by enemies. The Biblical text of choice for these figures was the Psalms. In a very long tradition accepted by both pre- and post-Reformation scholars of the Bible, the psalms were thought to have been composed by King David. David the singer perfectly expresses the plight of both the warrior pitted against imminent foreign threat, and the courtier pitted against treacherous courtly intrigue. As related in the two Books of Samuel, David is involved in murderous relations both with his father-in-law, King Saul, and later with his son Absalom (both of them wish to kill David). The easy part of David's career is the early part, when he is pitted against unmissable, straightforward foreign enemies such as the Philistine giant Goliath. The more difficult part by far is his fight for survival in the royal household, where he is first persecuted and threatened with murder by the paranoid King Saul, and then threatened by the insurrection of his incestuous son Absalom. The psalms are imagined to have been composed by David throughout his tumultuous life, but the penitential psalms (6, 31, 37, 50, 101, 129, 142) in particular are seen as being voiced by a penitent

David grieving over his murder of Uriah the Hittite, whose death was devised by David in order that David might take possession of Uriah's wife Bathsheba (2 Samuel 11).

The psalms, then, were read as expressions of courtly intrigue and threat. They lyrically voice the pain, danger, and isolation of court that the books of Samuel narrate more in the manner of a novel. They express the predicament of encirclement by menacing courtly enemies that mirrors the larger, national predicament of Israel, also surrounded by menacing enemies. In sixteenth-century England, these texts perfectly suited the position of Henrician courtly readers, who themselves were simultaneously fighting or negotiating for the very king who threatened to consume them.

Thomas Becon's evangelical *Policy of War* was dedicated to Thomas Wyatt (d. 1542). Wyatt himself wrote a version of the penitential psalms that expresses the peculiar knife-edge on which the Henrician courtier's life was conducted.[12] Wyatt's text marshals all its energy even to address a God from whom all prerogative, even the prerogative to speak in the first place, derives. Above all, the penitential psalms are deployed here for ends wholly at odds with the usual function of those psalms. Whereas the penitential psalms had been used within the sacrament of penance, evangelical theology neutralized, as we have seen, the main functions of the sacrament. By the terms of evangelical theology, the works of penitence are impossible, given the depth of human abjection.[13] As Thomas More says in his *Apology*, the evangelicals think the "seven Psalms" "long enough without the litany."[14]

Writing between 1534 and 1542, Wyatt followed his Italian source in imagining a biographical context for King David's inspired composition of the penitential psalms. David falls in love with Bathsheba, conspires in the death of her husband, is reproached by the prophet Nathan, and immediately withdraws "into a dark cave / Within the ground, wherein he might him hide" (lines 60–61).[15] Here David is imagined singing psalms of repentance to an injured, omnipotent, and entirely silent God.

Of course all acts of repentance evoke the past in order to delete it, and so penitence is ideally a kind of self-consuming autobiography. David's sins are indeed entirely consumed, but so too, in the process, is King David himself. The unspecified narrator declares that none of the king's meritorious deeds has any bearing whatsoever on the recompense that he receives from God:

> But when he weigh'th the fault and recompense,
> He damn'th his deed and findeth plain
> Atween them two no whit equivalence;
> Whereby he takes all outward deed in vain
> To bear the name of rightful penitence,
> Which is alone the heart returned again
> And sore contrite that doth his fault bemoan,
> And outward deed the sign or fruit alone.
> (648–655)

In this poem the asymmetries between God and the sinner are so great and unmediated as to render the king's own "outward deeds" wholly insignificant. Far from having any power to persuade the "perfect intelligence" (222) of God, good deeds become, in this theology, mere signs of decisions having already been taken, the fruits of God's prior election; the conversion of the single life is itself converted into God's own initiative: "all the glory of his forgiven fault / To God alone he doth it whole convert" (658–659).

While the narrative apparently marks a moment of conversion in history from one kind of life to another, in a deeper sense the individual's history is preempted by the sheer concentration of power and initiative in God's hands. It is God who gives the sinner power and voice to declare his unworthiness in the first place: "Of thyself, O God, this operation / It must proceed by purging me from blood" (490–491). In addition, God's power beggars the civil processes of law whereby an accused person might justify himself before a judge:

> ... And after thy justice   [according to]
>   Perform, O Lord, the thing that I require;
> But not of law after the form and guise
>   To enter judgement with thy thrall bondslave
>   To plead his right, for in such manner wise
> Before thy sight no man his right shall save.
>   (731–736)

King David's isolation, then, is not merely physical; he is also cut off from the assurances of prior virtue, just as he can make no appeal to the insurance of due legal process. In the face of God's inscrutable presence and power, the purchase of individual biography on God is invoked only to be dismissed: even virtuous "outward deeds" are taken by God "as sacrifice [his] pleasure to fulfil" (507). Nothing but grace, or God's unprovoked, unmerited gift, defines the relation between sinner and God, as David unhesitatingly recognizes: "For on thy grace I wholly do depend" (758). Grace, in this account, renders the virtuous accretions of the individual life entirely redundant, or at best a "sacrifice."

🌾   Why might Henrician courtiers have adopted a theology that mirrors so clearly the oppressive experience of serving a mercurial and brutal king like Henry VIII? In both cases (that is, the political and the theological), all grace derives from a single source of unpredictable power. That Henrician courtiers did actively embrace this religion appears certain not only from Wyatt's Psalms, whose evangelical accents are, in my view, unmistakable, but also from the psalm translations of Henry Howard, Earl of Surrey.

A story concerning the courtier George Zouche provides a glimpse of how it was that the evangelical religion entered the circulation of court life so readily. As recorded in the reminiscences of one John Louthe (sent to John Foxe in 1579),[16] Zouche came across a copy of Tyndale's *Obedience* from one of Anne Boleyn's gentlewomen. Zouche, it is reported, was "so ravished with the spirit of God, speaking now as well in the heart of the reader as first in the heart of the maker of the book, that he was never well but when he was reading of that book." In this account, a most intimate bond is formed between God, the author, and the reader of the book; the narrative has all the hallmarks of a new reading experience that provokes thirsty and continued reading during a period of conversion.

At this point the ambit of the book's circulation in court widens. Zouche is so taken with Tyndale's book that he refuses to return it. From being a secret book hidden by a servant, the book now suddenly enters the central and public space of court: Anne Boleyn goes to the king, and successfully applies pressure for Zouche to be ordered to return the book. On the way back to its rightful owner, however, it must pass through the hand of a curious king. Henry VIII also thinks it's a great read: "The king read and delighted in the book, for (sayth he) this book is for me and for all kings to read." In Louthe's narrative, this is the foundational moment of the English Reformation; he says that, by Anne Boleyn's offices, the eyes of the king were opened, and he decided from that moment to repudiate the Pope and to deliver his subjects from the "Egyptian darkness" and the "Babylonian bondage" to which the Pope had subjected him.

So the samizdat book quickly becomes the trigger for the English Reformation. The rapidity of the sequence has obvious affinities with the evangelical historiographical tradition of a quick, eagerly accepted Reformation. We should of course exercise caution with a story told by a proponent of the Reformation, so long after the event. The narrative does, however, persuasively convey a highly charged situation that plausibly accounts for the kind of satisfactions a text such as Tyndale's may have offered.

Certainly the king might have been impressed with Tyndale's insistence on obedience to kings. In *The Obedience of a Christian Man* Tyndale argues (from Romans 13:2) that there can be no distinction between judgment of the king and God: "He that judgeth the king judgeth God; and he that layeth hands on the king layeth hand on God; and he that resisteth the king resisteth God, and damneth God's law and ordinance."[17] The duty of obedience extends to tyrants, since the tyrant has been appointed by God, and is better in any case than a weak and effeminate king:

> . . . though he be the greatest tyrant in the world, yet is he unto thee a great benefit of God, and a thing wherefore thou oughtest to thank God highly. For it is better to have somewhat, than to be clean stripped out of all together . . . Yea, and it is better to have a tyrant unto thy king than a shadow . . . A king that is soft as silk, and effeminate . . . shall be much more grievous unto the realm than a right tyrant.[18]

In subjection to tyrants, Tyndale goes on to argue, Christians should not be like the child who, "as long as he seeketh to avenge himself upon the rod, hath an evil heart." On the contrary, Tyndale enjoins submission: "If we . . . meekly knowledge our sins for which we are scourged, and kiss the rod, and amend our living: then will God take the rod away, that is, he will give the rulers a better heart."[19]

Political strategy may explain this astonishing promotion of servility, but we should note in passing that Tyndale's little narrative of kissing the rod of the tyrant so as to mollify him bears exact correspondence with Tyndale's theological narrative of submission to the hateful Law. The structure of this mini-narrative may suggest why Zouche, for his part, also found such consolation in this text: for, like the Henrician courtier, the evangelical sinner could find immense relief only in submission to the punishing rod of the Law. Thus evangelicals and Henrician courtiers both found consolation through abjection. That structural identity between politics and theology may partly explain why some of the courtiers became evangelicals.[20]

🎋 Let us now return to one Henrician courtier, Henry Howard, Earl of Surrey, to see how he used the Psalms in times of crisis. Surrey composed searing psalm paraphrases in prison, while awaiting execution, after he had been betrayed by a long list of those whom he might have trusted. We see in these texts the same homology between the predicament of the evangelical reader and that of the Henrician courtier.

Surrey was beheaded for treason on 19 January 1547. He had been convicted on charges of having treasonously displayed royal arms in his own coat of arms. Surrey spent most of the period between the date of his final arrest on 2 December 1546 and his execution, almost seven weeks later, in the Tower.[21] The works that Surrey seems certainly to have written during this period of imprisonment are those of a person who feels himself to be an evangelical victim. Those works are as follows: Psalms 54, 72, and 87 (Vulgate numbering).[22] There is circumstantial evidence that he also translated Psalms 30 and 50.[23] Shortly before this final imprisonment, possibly in the spring of 1546 after his return from France in military disgrace, Surrey had produced paraphrases of Ecclesiastes, chapters 1–5 inclusive.[24] At least one of these works appears to have been drawn upon by another Protestant prisoner. Other Tudor courtiers, who presented themselves as evangelical martyrs, also wrote paraphrases of some of the same psalms.

Given that Surrey was writing in prison as he awaited execution, we might expect his paraphrases to be highly personal, speaking for his own specific and deeply painful circumstances at the turn of 1546 into 1547. These paraphrases do indeed carry a highly personal charge, but this derives precisely from the *inability* of these psalms to speak for Surrey. The chosen psalms, like many others, are themselves the monologic expression of a paranoid voice: a voice that is alone, surrounded by enemies, and calling for succor from the single source of an entirely silent, unresponsive, and transcendent power. Whereas the psalms have always been a source of strength for those in dire straits, speaking as they often do with the voice of lonely and penitent suffering, Surrey's paraphrases offer a stark contrast: they offer no consolation, and instead express only pain and isolation.

This bleakness derives from the interpretive environment of these Biblical translations in the 1540s. In the first place, Biblical interpretation had been nationalized and rested, in both statutory practice and Biblical theory, in the person of the King, now Surrey's enemy. Second, evangelical hermeneutics prohibited any but the literal sense. These psalms express paranoia and, by the "lively faith" adopted by Surrey, refuse to do anything *but* express paranoia, held as they are within the literal sense. The hermeneutic environment of these paraphrases serves, that is, merely to replicate the paranoia of the psalms themselves. If paranoia provokes painful and fruitless self-reflection in the mirror, these psalm translations produce, finally, nothing but a mirror image of lonely torment.

The evangelical martyr becomes, in these texts, the truest witness by becoming the textual witness itself, dying not merely *for* the Gospel, but dying in some profound sense *as* the Gospel. Thus in this case the textual witness turns out to be self-consuming. By becoming the textual witness (or *martur* in its literal, Greek meaning), the evangelical courtier becomes a martyr in the modern sense. So the very texts that Surrey chose to express his fury and penitence themselves offer no escape from strict judgment. If these paraphrases attempt to express Surrey's deeply painful and dangerous situation, they do so by *adding to* the pain and danger, and by refusing to console. The textual witness of the dying author, surrounded by false human witnesses, produces the martyr.

🌺 Surrey's paraphrases appear to express protest and outrage against Henry VIII, and against the false witness of Surrey's many friends and family who had betrayed him at the end. The Ecclesiastes paraphrases are spoken in the voice of the king, and in this way they express the sheer grief of power from the inside. Solomon, the royal speaker, is appointed by God to lead his people in the laws of God; at the same time he feels a sense of disgust both for himself and for his people. His efforts to discover truth turn out to be nothing but

> . . . an endless work of pain and loss of time,
> For he, to wisdom's school, that doth apply his mind,
> The further that he wades there in, the greater doubts shall find.[25]
> (Ecclesiastes 1; 48.40–42)

Some of the postures adopted by the Ecclesiastes chapters evoke Surrey's own position: Solomon, like Surrey in disgrace, "like to the steerless boat that swerves with every winde, / The slipper top of worldly wealth by cruel proof I find" (Ecclesiastes 3; 50.1–2). Like Surrey, who died with his new and ambitious palace of Surrey House unfinished,[26] Solomon bewails failed architectural ambition:

> Ancient walls to race is our unstable guise,   [demolish; practice]
> And of their weather beaten stones to build some new devise.
> (Ecclesiastes 3; 50.11–12)

The greater burden of these royal monologues is not, however, to speak for Surrey as Surrey. It is, rather, a fascinating attempt to appropriate the king's voice and to imagine the position from which that royal voice expresses nothing but its own grief and the near-despair of power. Solomon witnesses himself as a deformed and monstrous version of royal justice:

> . . . a royal throne whereas that Justice should have sitt;
> Instead of whom I saw, with fierce and cruel mode,　　[expression]
> Where Wrong was set, that bloody beast, that drunk the guiltless blood.
> (Ecclesiastes 3; 50.44–46)

Surrey forces, or at least wishes into being, a royal self-recognition here, which clearly perceives the futility and injustice of its own exercise of power. He speaks with the voice of an aged king in order to rebuke "aged kings wedded to will, that work without advice" (Ecclesiastes 4; 51.36).

The strategy of these paraphrases is identical to that attributed by Surrey to Wyatt's paraphrases of the penitential psalms. These presented a mirror, so Surrey says, wherein rulers might see "the bytter frute of false concupicence" (38.11). The imagined effect of these psalms is a royal shock of self-recognition and reform:

> In princes hearts God's scourge yprinted deep
> Might them awake out of their sinfull sleep.
> (38.13–14)

That these paraphrases seek to find a position from which to critique the king is corroborated by the fact that Anne Askew, held in the Tower before being burned in July 1546, seems certainly to be echoing Surrey's Ecclesiastes paraphrase, and appears equally certainly to be referring to the king:

> I saw a royal throne
> Where Justice should have sytt

> But in her stead was one
> Of modye cruel wit.   [fierce]
> Absorbed was righteousness
> As of the raging flood.
> Sathan in his excess
> Sucked up the guiltless blood.[27]

Surrey's Ecclesiastes paraphrases, then, would seem to have been welcomed in an evangelical environment, presumably because they offered a space for attacking the king even from within a discursive space that ostensibly belongs to the king himself.[28] It is the king's voice that attacks the king.

If the Ecclesiastes paraphrases exploit a Biblical position from which to criticize Henry VIII, what of the psalm translations, written almost certainly from the Tower as Surrey awaited trial and possible execution? Here Surrey abandons the voice of world-weary Solomon for that of his passionate and penitent father, David. On the face of it, the stated posture of these paraphrases is one of penitence and self-accusation. Two of them are addressed to "friends," Anthony Denny and George Blage, both of them well placed in late 1546 in the new alignment of evangelical and political forces set to assume authority after the death of Henry VIII.[29] The prologues of these works assume a posture of humble supplication, relying on the solidity of both friendship and royal support. After justice had been wrought, Surrey says, by "pryncelye equitie,"

> My Deny, then mine error deep impressed,
> Began to work despair of liberty,
> Had not David, the perfect warrior, taught
> That of my fault thus pardon should be sought.
> (35.5–8)

The actual content of these searing texts is, however, anything but penitent or humble; nor do they have any confidence whatsoever in either friendship or royal protection. On the contrary, their most consistent theme is the perfidy of friends and, only slightly more veiled, the disgusting grossness of unjust kings. The main thrust of the paraphrases is to call down upon these very figures, the ostensible addressees of these psalm translations, the most terrible divine vengeance. Thus Psalm 54 begins by expressing the fundamental position of the psalmist, surrounded by enemies and melting for fear were it not for his single, divine source of succor:

Give ear to my suit, Lord! fromward hide not thy face. [away from me]
Behold, harking in grief, lamenting how I pray.
My foos they bray so loud, and eke threpe on so fast, [also; press]
Buckled to do me scathe, so is their malice bent. [harm]
Care pierceth my entrails, and travaileth my spirit;
The grisly fear of death environeth my breast.
(Psalm 54; 54.1–6)[30]

The opening words imply the legal environment of psalmic address, appealing to God as the judge who alone can see the justice of Surrey's suit, given the collapse of earthly judicial forms. It is precisely to this collapse that the psalm now turns: Surrey (to whom I shall attribute the voice of this psalm for convenience) has, he says, "deciphred" the malgovernance of "our town" in which Guile and Wrong guard the walls, while Mischief governs the market place; Wickedness with Craft "swarme through the strete" (Psalm 54; 54.15–17). Surrey inhabits an irredeemably duplicitous civic world, but what especially provokes his fear and fury is the false witness of intimate, evangelical friends. Known enemies have, he says, less power to wound, but this situation is especially unnerving because it was

Myne old fere and dear friend, my guide that trapped me;
 [companion]
Where I was wont to fetch the cure of all my care,

And in his bosom hide my secret zeal to God.
(Psalm 54; 54.24–26)

A "secret zeal to God" can only be an evangelical zeal, and the repeated accents of these psalm translations, like Wyatt's paraphrases
before them, leave no doubt of Surrey's evangelical credentials. Just
as Surrey had said that Wyatt's paraphrases painted "the lively faith
and pure" and offered a model for the "sweet return to grace" (38.7–
8), so too, unmistakably, do Surrey's texts strategically deploy evangelical vocabulary. He appeals to God "with words of hot effect"
(Psalm 54; 54.30), and with a "lively voice" (Psalm 87; 88.29). God
does not show his tokens, "Whereby each feeble hart with faith
might so be fed / That in the mouth of thy elect thy mercies might
be spread" (Psalm 87; 88.21–2). The impious "suck the flesh of thy
elect and bathe them in their blood" (Psalm 72; 73.24). The "temple
of the Lord" is set within the humble spirit of "simple faith," wherein
"for aye in his word doth rest," and "in boast of outward works he taketh no delight" (Ecclesiastes 4.51–58). Surrey, like many Henrician
courtiers, seems clearly to have adopted the new faith.[31]

The unmistakable evangelical tone of these translations gains all
the more force by contrast with the social world they depict. Spiritual relations are characterized by simplicity; the confirmation of
election by sudden onrushes of grace, and, above all, by the "lively
voice" and unchanging Word in which the elect maintain their "simple faith." By stark contrast, the depicted social world is thoroughly
duplicitous, where the words of false witnesses are crafty and malicious: "Rein those unbridled tongues! Break that conjured league!"
(Psalm 54; 54.13), Surrey implores God. His enemy's tongue is presented by "the wicked sort / Of those false wolves" who swear falsely
(Psalm 54; 54.42–3); his enemies "pierce the simple with their tongues
that can make no defense" (Psalm 72; 56.20).

The spiritual and civic worlds of these texts make opposite hermeneutic demands: while the spiritual Word is simple, unchanging, and
perceptible by trusting faith, the very slippery civic relations are
opaque and wholly unstable; they resolutely refuse to offer up their
meaning. Surrey says that he has "deciphered" the wickedness of "our
town," but decryption is all the harder given that the false witnesses
aligned against him are precisely those who had seemed to share Surrey's "simple" faith. It was "a friendly foe, by shadow of good will,"
the one with whom Surrey had shared his "secret zeal to God," who
had betrayed him.

The contrast between spiritual and social relations has an obvious logic of compensation: an irredeemably duplicitous social world
powerfully recommends a spirituality of faith and simplicity. Similarly, a social experience of total disillusion with the stabilities of human works recommends a spirituality in which works count for nothing. This is especially true of a social world in which those who
profess the "secreat zeale to God" are the very ones who are most duplicitous. The wholly alienating social experience of court life is
likely to produce a spirituality of martyrdom—a spirituality, that is,
that prizes persecution of the single isolated figure as the surest guar-
antor of divine favor.

What is certain is that Surrey was indeed the victim of former
friends and family having turned witness, often demonstrably false
witness, against him. What is equally certain is that other courtiers in
Surrey's situation also saw particular attractions in the posture of the
isolated, betrayed psalmic voice, one true against all false. In the
present context, the most pertinent of these texts is by George Blage,
one of Surrey's former friends who bore witness against him in December 1546, and to whom Surrey's translation of Psalm 72 is dedicated.[32] In July of that same year Blage had himself been in the
Tower, having been condemned to burn for heresy.[33] He presents

himself in precisely the way Surrey does, as the evangelical courtier caught in the treacherous lubricities of courtly conspiracy, imagining his own martyrdom. The parallels with Surrey's psalm translations are striking, although Blage's affinities are more explicitly evangelical. The bishops have painted the Roman Church "with rose color of persecuted blood," "burning incense of a sweet savory wood" (p. 274).[34] Like Surrey, Blage too imagines himself trapped by the very people who should have protected him:

> Our guides have erred and walked out of the way
> And we by them full craftily are trapped
> Whom they should lead they drive out of aray.   [proper bounds]
> (p. 273)

As a victim of those who have "conspired . . . against the living Lord," and of "false conspiracy," Blage depicts himself as the lonely and faithful hero prepared to "abide by thy true word," even unto martyrdom:

> And I O Lord into thy hands do yield
> My faithful soul appointed now of thee
> This life to leave through fire in Smithfield.
> (p. 276)

For Blage (who was in fact finally released), as for Surrey, the promised simplicities and stabilities of the new evangelical religion offer the one point of repair from, and contrast to, an otherwise wholly untrustworthy and mutable civic experience.

※   Thus in obvious ways the psalmic voice is expressive of the Tudor courtier caught in a moment of treacherous transition. Surrounded by the false witness of former friends, the evangelical courtier abandons hope in works and human words, which have proved so untrustworthy, and falls back instead on faith in the simple, abiding Word of God. Endemic distrust might explain why the psalms in particular were so attractive to courtiers like Wyatt, Surrey, Blage and, a few years later, Thomas Smith and John Dudley.[35] As Brad Gregory has said of the psalms and sixteenth-century martyrs' frequent use of them, "For persecuted Christians, these were indeed ancient songs for modern times."[36] Tudor courtiers had especial reason to feel persecuted.[37]

For all their obvious attractions, evangelically inflected psalms offered no deliverance from the frightening social world of the Tudor court. Translated in the political conditions of late Henrician England, and under the conditions of evangelical hermeneutics more generally, the psalms turn out to replicate the experience of paranoia. They lead inexorably to the stake or, in Surrey's case, the block. The Protestant God, like the Tudor king, turns out to operate in wholly unpredictable and opaque ways, and never answers the suppliant, who is himself restricted to the literal sense alone of the Biblical address. That narrow textual space turns out to guarantee his utter powerlessness. The evangelical Tudor courtier, that is, adopts the very theology whose power relations bear the most striking similarities to the practice of Henrician politics. Both the Protestant God and the Tudor king distribute, or refuse to distribute, their grace in ways wholly unconstrained by the effort or estimated self-worth of their suppliants. That, after all, is the very nature of grace in the first place. Furthermore, when the courtier speaks against the king to God, God's word has already been claimed by the king. Both the theology and the politics produce martyrs.

The first-person voice of the psalms, and the intensity of their appeal to God, invite deeply personal appropriation by the persecuted. Twenty years after Surrey's death, Matthew Parker's translation of Athanasius makes this point: "Whosoever take this book [the Psalms] in his hand, he reputeth and thinketh all the words he readeth (except the words of prophecy) to be his very own words spoken in his own person."[38] I turn now to Surrey's paraphrases, and examine how his words, on reflection, are not wholly "spoken in his own person," no matter how much they might try to do just that.

A paraphrase is an extremely exacting form of textual reproduction. By Roger Ascham's account of 1570, only "a perfect Master" should practice it.[39] *Paraphrasis* is challenging because it must work within a very tight demand for change within very narrow possibilities. It is, Ascham says, *audax contentio,* an audacious effort to "think to say better, than is the best" (p. 246). It should use only "other fit words," but not alter the "composition, form, and order" of the original text (p. 248).

Surrey's immediate model for scriptural paraphrase was the paraphrase of the Psalms by John Campensis (published in Paris by the commission of Thomas Berthelet in 1534, and available in an English translation of 1534).[40] For his own paraphrases, Surrey relied on Campensis along with the Vulgate and the Coverdale 1535 translation. He also had a model for such treatment of the Biblical text in Erasmus's paraphrase of the New Testament, a translation of which, by Nicholas Udall and others, was published in 1548–1549. In the preface to his translation of Erasmus's text, Udall defines paraphrase as "a plain setting forth of a text or sentence more at large, with such circumstance of more and other words, as may make the sentence open, clear, plain and familiar" (image 14).[41] His translation of Erasmus's preface to the Gospel of Matthew, addressed to Charles V originally in 1522, is more precise about the tight constraints within which paraphrase must operate. About paraphrase Erasmus says this:

> It cometh to pass that the writers pen is kept shut within the enclosure of an exceeding strait grate, because it is debarred from that liberty,

which all other sorts of commentaries doe suffer and receive (for a paraphrase also is to be reputed as a kind of commentary). (image 18)

The Gospel is so plain, he goes on, that whoever shall make a paraphrase of it "shall seem nothing else to do, but at noontide to light a candle" (image 18). Paraphrase, that is, simultaneously demands lexical variation and exact semantic replication.

Some of Surrey's paraphrases have been described as exceptionally "free."[42] On the whole, however, they hold remarkably close to the paraphrase of Campensis. It is true that Surrey sharpens the evangelical edge of his work with the addition of specifically Protestant vocabulary, but many passages that seem to be personal or political references turn out to have their source in Campensis.[43] Surrey's additions, as we shall see, go beyond merely "lighting a candle at noon," but he does stick remarkably close to his sources, remaining for the most part "shut within the enclosure of an exceeding strait grate."[44]

Is this purely a literary decision, Surrey's way of producing Scripture as his "very own words spoken in his own person," or are his words already spoken for in significant ways? Does the rhetorical restriction of paraphrase have parallels in evangelical and political hostility to additions of any kind being made to Scripture? Do Surrey's translational practices mirror his own circumstance, shut as he is within "an exceeding strait grate"? I propose that Surrey's words are already in important ways claimed by others. There are two, finally convergent, aspects to this question. The first concerns the surprising relation between Henrician and evangelical hermeneutics; the second derives from the evangelical notion of the Biblical text as embodied in the suffering martyr.

In 1542–43 a statute was passed entitled "An Act for the Advancement of True Religion." The situation the act addresses is the seditious and disruptive translation of Scripture. Many "seditious" and "arrogant" people have translated and interpreted the Bible, creating schism as a result of "their perverse forward and malicious minds wills and intents intending to subvert the very true and perfect exposition . . . of the said Scripture, after their perverse fantasies."[45]

The legislative response to this hermeneutic anarchy is to delimit carefully the spaces in which and the social classes by which vernacular Bible reading is permitted, and to disallow Biblical interpretation. Tyndale's translation is proscribed. All "annotations and preambles" to other translated Bibles must be cut out. Moral songs and plays are permitted, as long as they avoid interpretations of Scripture. No women of a class below noblewomen and gentlewomen may read the Bible, and they may only read it to themselves, alone. No other women, and no men below the class of merchant, may read it. Noblemen may read the Bible or have it read by their families and servants in their houses or gardens. Merchants may read it privately. An exception is made for Psalters, primers, the Pater Noster, the Ave, and the Creed: these may be read by anyone "in their houses." This suggests that the Psalter is entirely personal, and without any political or prophetic danger. The last clause of the Act takes care, however, to close off that possibility, declaring that, even within the licit spaces and classes of Biblical reader, no one shall "take upon him openly to dispute or argue, to debate or discuss or expound Holy Scripture or any part thereof . . . upon the pains of one month's imprisonment" (3: 896).[46]

The king's power and responsibility to govern the dissemination and interpretation of Scripture had, by the time of this statute, already been theorized in the vernacular. Very soon after the Act of Supremacy, Christopher St. German had argued in his *Answer to a Letter* (1535) that the King had not assumed any new powers that he did not already possess by the Act of 1534.[47] Those already-possessed powers include control of Scripture. St. German contends that many passages of Scripture are in any case plain, but that where expert opinion is required, this should be the preserve of the king. Discrimination in such matters cannot be the preserve of the clergy, since many of these passages concern the clergy, and so their judgment would be prejudicial. The king has care not only for the material, but also for the spiritual well-being of his subjects, and this includes governance of Scripture. If, St. German argues, any instability should arise from "any exposition of Scripture be it by doctors, preachers or any other, then kings have power to stable them."[48] Kings and their counselors may "make exposition of such Scripture as is doubtful so as they shall think to be the true understanding of it and none but they." Subjects are "bounden even by the law of God to follow their exposition."[49] A theoretical defense of royal hermeneutic supremacy of this kind underlies the strictures in the Act of 1542–43.

Surrey's Biblical translation potentially incurs, then, the penalties of the Law. Translation by a nobleman is permitted (whether in the Tower or not), but what is not permitted is any interpretation of the Biblical text. Surrey's paraphrases actually work within that stricture; indeed, his choice of paraphrase, and a mode of paraphrase much more tightly bound to the scriptural text than, for example, Wyatt's *Penitential Psalms*, may itself be prompted by that stricture. Certainly evangelical commentary on psalm material, even if it stayed close to the literal sense, was proscribed in precisely the period of Surrey's own paraphrases. Thomas Becon's *David's Harp*, published in 1542, is a commentary on Psalm 115.[50] It shares common traits with Surrey's psalm translations: Becon chose, for example, the opening of Psalm (Vulgate) 72 (also paraphrased by Surrey) to express the condition of the persecuted saint.[51] Becon's work was banned in July 1546, along with much other evangelical material, including many psalm translations, in "A Proclamation for the Abolishing of English Books."[52]

Political control of scriptural reading was not the only constraint on Surrey. More profoundly, he was subject to an evangelical, theological constraint, working as he did within a Tyndalian concept of the Biblical text. Tyndale's prologues manifest deep and unresolved tensions between the textual ideals of philological accuracy, on the one hand, and relevance to contemporary readers, on the other. In the preface to his Pentateuch translation of 1530, Tyndale encourages his reader to think "that every syllable pertaineth to thine own self."[53] At the same time, he is committed to philological accuracy, declaring, for example, that he never altered "one syllable of God's word against my conscience" (p. 8). The point where these two often-irreconcilable desiderata meet is in high praise for the literal sense. Scripture is "a comfort in adversity that we despair not," and "this comfort shalt thou evermore find in the plain text and literal sense" (p. 8). To the arrogant learned person who says that scriptural understanding is impossible without the application of allegory, the simple reader of the literal sense should reply thus: "That they were written for our consolation and comfort; that we despair not, if such should happen unto us" (p. 8).

Relevance, then, is found in what medieval exegetes would have called the tropological or moral sense; this, however, is visible at the literal level, without recourse to historical allegory, and without reference either to past or future. For Tyndale, Biblical allegory does not replicate the dynamic of salvation history;[54] on the contrary, allegory is a pedagogical tool, useful only in making an instructional point more forcefully. Biblical interpretation, therefore, should ideally restrict itself to the literal level, and especially to God's promises. At most, it may extend to the moral level. It must not, however, read future promises allegorically encoded in the Biblical text.

Protestant historiography tends to champion the recovery of the literal sense from the deceptions of allegory as a moment of liberation. Given that Henrician legislation often targeted evangelical Biblical material, it looks on the face of it as if Henrician policy, in its conservative phases at any rate, was the enemy of evangelical Biblical translation. Viewed from a larger perspective, however, the clash between Henrician policy and evangelical Bible production may be superficial. Tyndalian hermeneutics look rather less liberating when one realizes that they are in many ways convergent with royal hermeneutic interests: both Tyndale and the official hermeneutics prohibit anything but (in Tyndale's words) the "plain text and literal sense," or they demand (in the words of the 1542–43 statute) "annotations" to be excised. The suggestion that Tyndalian hermeneutics converge with royal interests is implicitly confirmed by Tyndale's discussion of hermeneutics in *The Obedience of a Christian Man*, the work that most explicitly defends obedience to monarchs, even obedience to tyrants.[55] For both the legislation and for Tyndale, the Bible must be read within the strict temporal limits of the literal sense. Of course, Tyndale's Lutheran hermeneutics do see a promise embedded within the literal level, but that promise is, in Tyndale's view, contained only in the explicit covenants made in the scriptural text. Where Scripture does not contain those future promises, the Biblical text might mirror the pain of its reader, but it cannot transform that pain through a promise of future deliverance.

Both evangelical and Henrician hermeneutics, then, leave the Biblical reader suffering within the exiguous confines of the literal sense. In the psalms that Surrey chose to paraphrase, that textual space is the space of unending pain. How do an evangelical theology and hermeneutics accommodate that undeniable suffering?

All of the psalm material that Surrey chose to paraphrase expresses the isolation of an individual totally and terrifyingly betrayed by intimate friends, and calling on a silent God for violent retribution. Until the happy day when his enemies will be ruthlessly exposed and punished, the psalmist must remain suspended in pain: "My eyes yield tears, my years consume between hope and despair" (Psalm 72; 56.45–50). In this social world, suspended between "hope and despair," the psalmist appeals to God as the one source of his comfort. To the "lively name" of God he appeals with a "lively voice," as one of the "elect." This very appeal is made, however, only by way of signaling its uncertainty. Why, the psalmist begs, does God *refuse* to appear in defense of his own,

> To show such tokens of thy power, in sight of Adams line,
>   Whereby each feeble hart with faith might so be fed
> That in the mouth of thy elect thy mercies might be spread?
>   The flesh that feedeth worms can not thy love declare,
> Nor such set forth thy faith as dwell in the land of despair.
>   In blind endured hearts, light of thy lively name
> Can not appear, as can not judge the brightness of the same.
> (Psalm 87; 55.20–26)

The very formulation of the appeal to this God threatens, then, to expose its groundlessness, since God does not respond. God's redeeming action is perceptible only through an unequivocal series of negatives. The more silent God is, the greater the intensity of appeal, but this in turn merely underlines the undeniable possibility that God is silent because the speaker is *not* one of the "elect." This psalmic praise of God moves toward declaring its own impotence, as a voice "in the land of despair," unable to declare God's mercies. A song of praise threatens to die in its very utterance.

Having deciphered the malicious craft of his social world, Surrey is left facing an even more impenetrable God. The hermeneutic challenge posed by this God is that the psalmist should continue to interpret God's apparent punishment and apparent rejection of the sinner as the surest sign of his ultimate favor: the psalmist voices his woe from a bottomless pit, where "O Lord, thou hast cast me headling [head first] to please my foe" (Psalm 87; 55.9). From within the strict limits of unrelieved pain, not only are social relations wholly vitiated by mistrust, but the spiritual relations between the solitary complainant and his inscrutable God offer only present pain and suffering on which to meditate. If the psalmist is to draw consolation from this situation, he can do so only by interpreting pain as a kind of pleasure. The experience of painful persecution must turn out to be a consolation, since it is a very sign of election.

This transformation of pain into consolation is theorized in much evangelical reflection on the experience of persecution. Evangelical writers did not flinch from the necessity of embracing the martyr's death when the occasion presented itself, and to do so they needed to present the horror of pain, and especially of death by fire, as an immolation devoutly to be wished. An example from the same textual environment as Surrey's own psalm paraphrases, Thomas Becon's psalm commentary of 1542, takes especial care to praise persecution as a necessary sign of God's favor. Becon generates his account of the martyr's suffering by reference to the psalmic situation. He translates, indeed, the very psalm (Vulgate 73) that Surrey paraphrases. The psalmist contemplates his own terrible suffering while the corrupt prosper: "My feet were almost gone, sayth David, my treadings had nigh slipped, for I was sore grieved at the wicked to see the ungodly in such prosperity."[56]

Consolation derives from two sources: in the first place, the powerful enemies will certainly be crushed. Second, and more profound, is the belief that persecution is itself a sure sign of God's favor. Martyrdom is, says the psalmist, precious in the sight of the Lord ("Pretiosa in conspectu Domini / Mors sanctorum eius" [Psalm 115.15]).[57] Drawing especially on Paul,[58] Becon theorizes the connection between persecution and favor as follows:

Of all these scriptures it is evident, that it is no sorrowful, but joyful thing to suffer persecution for righteousness sake, for the glory of God, and the promotion of his most blessed Word. Neither is it a token of God's wrath, but rather of his singular benevolence and high good will toward them, which are troubled for his sake.[59]

Persecution is to be welcomed, precisely as the surest sign of God's favor to his chosen saints. The martyred saints are punished in few things, but will deserve reward in many:

God proveth them, and findeth them mete [fit] for himself, yea as gold in the furnace doth he try them, and receiveth them as a burnt offering . . . The righteous shall shine as the sparks, that run through the red bush.[60]

Becon's strategy here is clearly to transform the hard realities of the burned martyr's suffering (furnaces, sparks, and burning bushes) into their opposites—the sure signs of a very bright and hot election.

That encouragement to martyrdom is a fairly predictable rhetorical strategy for a group facing persecution. It also allows for the unsettling possibility, of course, that the group facing persecution must actively *seek* persecution. Not to experience persecution would, after all, be to lack the assurance of God's favor. Such a perception would make sense of the peculiar mixture of doubt and trust in Surrey's paraphrases written in the Tower. In Surrey's situation the Word of God remains locked and hidden, inaccessible to interpretive scrutiny, *even as* Surrey paraphrases the Biblical text. Given the sinner's uncertainty as to his own salvation, he must implicitly distrust the sincerity of his own voice. Confidently declaring "thy worde," even in the very act of Biblical paraphrase, must remain only a future possibility:

And my unworthye lips, inspired with thy grace,
Shall thus forspeke thy secret works, in sight of Adams race.
(Psalm 73; 56.65–66; my emphasis)

If consolation is to be found in the Biblical text, it is not *within* the dynamics of the text itself, as would be the case with a typological reading. Consolation, such as it is, is to be found only in the text's demand that the sinner continue to recognize present suffering as the sign of election.

Thus, both the evangelical martyr and the evangelical Biblical translator (occasionally the same person) are in some ways self-propelled to the stake. The surest way of confirming the authenticity of the Biblical text is to suffer for it. The surest way of confirming the witness of the Gospel is to become a bodily textual witness by being a suffering martyr, or "witness."

The intimate connection between the Biblical text and martyrdom is everywhere apparent in evangelical writing of this period of persecution. To go no further than Becon again, for example, we read that

> the blood of the holy martyrs is the water, wherewith the gospel of Christ is watered and made to grow. So that persecution hindereth not the glory of the gospel . . . but furthereth it greatly. And where most persecution is, there doth God's word most of all flourish.[61]

Metaphorical connections between bodily pain and Biblical growth are frequent: Foxe, for example, reports Tyndale's encouragement to Frith in the Tower awaiting martyrdom. "Your cause," says Tyndale, "is Christ's gospel, a light that must be fed with the blood of faith . . . That oil [must be] poured in every evening and morning, that the light go not out."[62] Thomas Bilney tests his "feeling faith" the night before his burning by holding the forefinger of his right hand steady in the candle's flame, while his left-hand index finger marks the place of Scripture, "When you walk through the fire you shall not be burned, / And the flame shall not consume you" (Isaiah 43:2; see Figure 1).[63] Evangelical martyrs did often die at the stake with this Biblical text attached to their bodies.[64] These connections are underwrit-

1. Thomas Bilney in prison, testing his faith by holding his finger in the fire.
From John Foxe, *Actes and Monuments*, first edition (London, 1563).

ten, in my view, by a deeper connection: the body as authenticating
witness to the witness of the Gospel.

Standard accounts of evangelical hermeneutics maintain that evangelical theorists refused any but written verities, which amounts to
Biblical verities.[65] If it's not written in the Bible, it's not authentic. Sixteenth-century evangelical writers themselves repeat this with great
frequency. For more subtle theorists, however, this is not quite the
full position: they understand that no text can authenticate itself,
since texts need to be established as authentic in the first place. The
late medieval Catholic theorist has no difficulty with this concept:
the Church guarantees the truth of Scripture.[66] Christians receive

that truth through what Thomas More calls a "historical faith," a faith grounded in the ongoing tradition of the Church and its councils.[67] In his dispute with More, Tyndale clearly recognizes that the Biblical text needs a prior, unwritten witness, and that witness is the individual reader's emotional response. What guarantees the authenticity of the text for Tyndale is, as with More, faith. Whereas More's is a historical faith, however, Tyndale's is what he calls a "feeling faith."

Tyndale's metaphors for this faith are metaphors of bodily pain. A man might believe in the capture of a city by historical faith if he trusted in the messengers who had witnessed the battle, since historical faith "hangeth in the truth and honesty of the teller, or of the common fame and consent of many." "Feeling faith" is more a matter of witness and experience:

> As if a man were there present when it was won, and there were wounded and had there lost all that he had, and were taken prisoner there also. That man should so believe that all the world could not turn him from his faith.[68]

The second example, revealingly, concerns burning. When a child's mother tells him that the fire will burn a finger, the child believes this with a "historical faith":

> Even likewise, if my mother had blown on her finger, and told me that the fire would burn me, I should have believed her with an historical faith . . . but as soon as I had put my finger in the fire, I should have believed, not by the reason of her, but with a feeling faith, so that she could not have persuaded me afterward to the contrary.[69]

The ultimate guarantee of Scripture, then, is a "feeling faith," a bodily witness that Scripture is true. Prior to the literal sense of the text is an anterior text, written in the heart itself. "God," says Tyndale of the elect's possession of Scripture, "shall write it in their hearts with his Holy Spirit."[70] Just as we believe, he says, that the fire is hot through experience, so too do the elect have the Law of God written in their hearts.

My argument here goes one step further than Tyndale. I suggest that, for the evangelical reader, the surest way of manifesting that interior textual witness is to suffer for it physically. Betrayed by false human witnesses, that reader must become him- or herself the truest textual witness, which means becoming the martyr. The literal text of the psalms provides nothing but evidence of unrelieved pain for Surrey. The only way he can guarantee his faith that the psalms offer some future consolation is to advertise his preparedness to suffer physically for them. Taken literally, the paranoid, isolated voice of the psalms replicates Surrey's own condition; that voice is a mirror reflecting pain, as "when my glasse presented unto me / The cureless wound that bledeth day and night" (37.12–13). Within the evangelical hermeneutic that Surrey has adopted, the only way of imagining consolation from these texts is to embrace yet further, bodily, pain. Only a hot "feeling faith," against all evidence to the contrary, can bear true witness to the text inscribed on the heart, a text that is rendered legible through the publication of punishment.

🎋 Henrician evangelical courtiers were not the only converts to the new religion who felt betrayed by their most intimate associates. Evangelical translators also fell out appallingly with each other. Thus George Joye, for example, undertook a revision of Tyndale's 1534 New Testament. Joye disagreed with Tyndale's understanding of the Greek word for "resurrection," and translated it as "the life after this life."[71] Tyndale was incensed, and added a second prologue to his New Testament in which he attacked Joye: let anyone translate Scripture for themselves, he says, or

(If they will needs) as the fox when he hath pissed in the gray's hole challengeth it for his own, so let them take my translations and labors, and change later, and correct and corrupt at their pleasures, and call it their own translations, and put to their own names, and not to play boo peep after George Joye's manner.[72]

Tyndale likewise repudiated his former assistant, William Roy, who had helped him with the first edition of the New Testament. Roy's "tongue," Tyndale wrote, "is able not only to make fools stark mad, but also deceive the wisest."[73] The simple Tyndale finds himself surrounded by crafty helpers.

Of course it may be that Tyndale did end up with untrustworthy colleagues. Those who have considered Tyndale's tetchy relations with his helpers have pretty much taken Tyndale's word for the matter, and dismissed Joye as having "personal faults" and Roy as "devious."[74] Although this may indeed have been the case, if we leave the matter there we fail to see how a particular kind of scholarly dispute, and a specific scholarly profile (fragile, distrustful, and philologically aggressive) emerges from these translations.

In his Prologue to the 1525 New Testament, Tyndale encourages correction from those who are "better seen [have more expertise] in tongues." If any such person spots an error, they should "put their hands to amend it, remembering that it is their duty to do so."[75] In the Prologue to *The Parable of the Wicked Mammon*, he says that he offered his New Testament "to all men, to correct it, whosoever could."[76] By 1530, however, the invitation to correct has been deleted from the *Pathway into Holy Scripture* (the 1530 revision of the 1525 Prologue). By the time of the 1534 New Testament Prologue, things are a little more complicated, and a little less welcoming still: in the very first paragraph Tyndale explains what the reader should do if differences are found between the Greek and this text: "Let the finder of the fault consider the Hebrew phrase or manner of speech left in the Greek words. Whose preterperfect tense and present tense is oft both one, and the future tense the optative mode also."[77] Why should Tyndale make this prickly flourish of grammatical terms in his very first paragraph, and why should he write as if each of his readers were now in a position to check the traces of Hebrew remaining in the Greek phrasing? This isn't anyone's idea of the opening paragraph of an open Bible.

Since writing the first New Testament, Tyndale had been translating in large quantity directly from the Hebrew, which is one reason he may be more sensitive to the presence of Hebrew in New Testament Greek.[78] More to the point, I think, is that Tyndale had, between the 1525 and 1534 New Testaments, been subject to a philological battering, by Thomas More in particular, regarding the translation of certain words. As he says in his Prologue to the Pentateuch of 1530, his enemies have "so narrowly looked on my translation, that there is not so much as one *i* therein if it lack a tittle over his head, but they have noted it, and number it unto the ignorant people for an heresy."[79] Tyndale's formulation here is exceptionally revealing: the badly formed letter becomes itself a heresy; this is a treacherous and unforgiving scholarly world, in which bad philology leads directly to humiliation and possibly to the stake. Thus by the time he wrote the 1534 Prologue, Tyndale was ready to defend every tittle, and warned critical readers that they'd better know Hebrew and Greek before making a move.

One can certainly understand why Tyndale should be so defensive in the 1534 Prologue. The defensiveness exposes, however, the evangelical claims about Scripture interpreting itself. Far from that being the case, Scripture requires translation, and translation requires philological skill. If, in an evangelical view, the Church no longer has power over Scripture, interpretive power does not simply vanish from the system. On the contrary, it resurfaces elsewhere, in this case in the philologist's expertise. The text is now the property not of its readers and interpreters, but rather of its translator. Authorial propriety of the text and linguistic expertise rise dramatically in significance, producing new frontiers for confrontation.

It's significant that neither Tyndale nor More attack each other primarily on philological grounds. As we have seen throughout this book, both primarily appeal to prior, ideational texts, the text written on the heart, to authenticate their scripture; that is, they appeal mainly to theological rather than philological arguments. It's true that Tyndale responded on philological grounds to the collection of translations that especially offended More ("congregation" instead of "church," "elder" instead of "priest," "love" instead of "charity," and "repentance" instead of "penance").[80] For the most part, however, these philological disputes arose on the edge of the larger battleground, exposing issues of expertise or authority that both sides, for different reasons, may have preferred to avoid explicitly. Catholics might prefer not to talk about the pluperfect tense in Hebrew, while evangelicals might prefer not to draw attention to the fact that the text has a very precise source of human authority in the person of its translator. It might be the Word of God, but it's the work of a philologist.

The philological issues were for the most part, then, kept well in control in the confrontation between evangelicals and their Catholic opponents. When, however, dissension broke out among evangelicals, those issues were raised very directly. In one such struggle (between Joye and Tyndale), I observe the following: that the voices present themselves as fragile scholarly personae, feeling alone and threatened on the philological battlefield; that many of the insults deployed against Catholics are now used by one evangelical against another; and, above all, that distrust is a constituent part of philological debate about the literal meaning of words, conducted in print, and stripped of conversation.

The title of George Joye's response to Tyndale's attack on him says it all: *An apologye made by George Ioye to satisfye (if it maye be) with Tindale to pourge & defende himself ageinst many sclaunderouse lyes fayned vpon him in Tindals vncharitable and vnsober pystle.*[81] Joye feels seriously aggrieved and betrayed. His text begins and ends with psalm texts: he opens with "Lord, deliver me from lying lips and from a deceitful tongue" (Psalm 119:2). And he ends with the verse from Psalm 54:13–15 that Surrey would use to such effect, even if Joye does not explicitly cite it as a scriptural text, and adapts it to his situation:

> But had it been my enemy that thus had unjustly reviled and vexed me, I could have borne him. And if my hater had thus oppressed me, I could have had avoided him. But it was thou my own fellow, my companion in like peril and persecution, my familiar, so well known unto whom I committed so lovingly my secrets, with whom gladly I went into the house of God. (image 52)[82]

It's unsurprising that Joye should feel threatened and betrayed. For he is faced with an unusual situation in the *Apologye*: Tyndale has accused him of a "crime" for his translation of the word in question (image 2). Evangelicals expected to be accused of heresy by their Catholic opponents, but the Tyndale/Joye exchange of 1534–1535 marks the first splintering of the English evangelical camp, a splintering with a long subsequent history. The accusation of heresy (or "crime" for an imputed belief) inevitably produces its mirror image (that is, the accused accuses), and this is effectively what Joye does in the *Apologye*: he attacks Tyndale's translation of *anastasis* as incorrect (Tyndale translated the Greek with "resurrection").

Joye opens with a "take-no-philological-prisoners" line of attack:

> Here is it manifest that T. understandeth not this place of scripture, neither knoweth whither Christ's argument tendeth . . . and there-

fore no marvel though he giveth not this word "Resurrectio" there his proper signification, of which ignorance this his error springeth, God so suffering us to fall standing too much in our own conceits, thinking our self so highly learned, and to translate and write all things so exquisitely and perfectly that no man is able either to do it better or to correct our works. (image 5)

Joye's critique of Tyndale borrows its ammunition from evangelical critique of Catholic interpreters: Tyndale errs because he doesn't read properly; Tyndale doesn't respect the "proper" signification of a key word; Tyndale thinks he owns Scripture.

There are more such moves: there are many "plain scriptures" on Joye's side (image 7); Tyndale changes the present tense into a future and a passive into a neuter to suit his own position (images 8–9); Tyndale "wrested and wrieth" (twists) texts "contrary to his own doctrine out of their proper and pure sense with feigned glosses to shift and seek holes, he, after his . . . disdainful manner against me filliped [tossed] them forth between his finger and his thumb" (image 17); Tyndale will suffer the "terrible sentence of God threatening all evil speakers" (image 31); in his subsequent protestations about the issue, Tyndale merely "painteth . . . to color his hypocrisy and deadly hatred" (image 32); Tyndale seems to think that the Holy Ghost has breathed on him alone (image 52).

The manner of this exceptionally vituperative attack exposes the authority that now inheres in the philologist: questions of heresy will arise from the translation of single words. The vituperation also reveals that the evangelical position will inevitably produce schism from within itself. This is partly because there are so many key words in Scripture, and each one is a time bomb (Tyndale could not have predicted that "resurrection"—hardly central to the evangelical/ Catholic debate—was going to detonate). Another factor, however, is the nature of written, printed, and public debate. Joye says that he and Tyndale have had four meetings, in each of which Tyndale has failed to deliver a letter agreeing to withdraw the attack on Joye. Tyndale, by Joye's account, keeps failing to deliver the withdrawal, and instead demands, on the fourth visit, a written account of what Joye did, which will be submitted to a third party. So Joye is compelled to write the *Apology* (images 3–4), just as he was, as he later says, compelled by conscience to correct Tyndale's New Testament (image 23).

Evangelicals held that matters of belief depend entirely on written documents. Given that unshakeable commitment, the philological correction of sacred documents will inevitably become a matter of conscience-driven compulsion. When debates are written, printed, and widely available, reputations, along with charges of heresy, stand or fall by the conduct of those published debates. It's revealing that conversation should be swallowed by writing here, and that writing should produce such vituperation: writing demands to be recognized as the only authority, but writing without trust leads directly to more vituperation. Written communication that is not underwritten by trust inevitably produces, after recourse to all other forms of arbitration have failed (as they inevitably do), charges of hypocrisy. It's also revealing that the Tyndale/Joye dispute is not restricted to the two main protagonists: in his 1534 Prologue devoted to an attack on Joye, Tyndale says that Joye's reading of the word "resurrection" has "caused great division among the brethren." "No small number" of them, Tyndale continues, "utterly deny the resurrection of the flesh and body." Talking with them is, says Tyndale, a waste of time, since they are "so doted in their folly, that it were as good persuade a post, as to pluck that madness out of their brains" (p. 71). Every word can be a source of dispute in which the charge of heresy will never be far away, and every dispute will gain adherents.

We can see this failure of conversational trust again in a later dispute that also involved George Joye (clearly a disputatious character). In 1546 Stephen Gardiner, Bishop of Winchester, published *A declaration of such true articles as George Ioye hath gone about to confute as false.*[83] Gardiner first provides the prelude to his dispute with Joye, which involves a series of friendly acts by Gardiner toward Robert Barnes that have been repeatedly repudiated by Barnes. Gardiner feels that his good faith has been betrayed, and now broaches Joye's own malicious accusations. His argument is subtle: he produces a powerful defense of trust in the institutions that envelop Scripture as the necessary condition of productive reading of Scripture (images 83–85).[84] Gardiner accuses Joye of twisting his words, and tumbling them all together in a sack (image 174). The key point is trust: just as Gardiner feels betrayed by Barnes and Joye, so too will all written debate about Scripture end in dispute where trust is absent. Readers of the dispute between Gardiner and Joye will end up divided into opposed camps: "I believe Joye, and I believe Winchester" (image 84); likewise they will believe what they decide to believe in Scripture: "I know what edifieth me, thanks be to the Lord of his gift; my conscience telleth me what is good, and no man shall bring me from that [what] God teacheth me by his Holy Spirit" (image 84). This approach might sound attractive, Gardiner concedes, but without trust, words alone produce endless schism. By Gardiner's estimation, every man would be his own church under the evangelical reading regime, and "each one man to . . . be alone, alone, alone, mine own self all alone, and then to be devoured of the devil alone, without comfort in the wilderness alone" (image 86).

CHAPTER SIX

History as Error

ALL IN ALL, as we have seen, evangelical reading involved a good deal of painful rejection. The following stood threatened with repudiation: the material Church; most of its members; sometimes one's closest allies; and sometimes one's body. What, though, of history? Did the past survive the series of violent repudiations necessitated by evangelical reading?

Evangelical culture will always have a problem with the boundary line between present and past, new and old. Like many other revolutionary cultures, it demanded a clean break with the obscurantist past, and correlatively praised novelty. Its personal model was one of rebirth and conversion, which also produced a historical model of the sudden, absolute turn. Whereas the Catholic sacrament of penance required accretive sequences of effort across time, the evangelical spiritual model demanded of individual lives a turn, sloughing off "the old man with his works" (Colossians 3:10) and putting on the new man. One's own past then becomes valuable as a history of error: one is driven forward into the converted life by energetic and absolute repudiation of one's old self. The writer who made this motif celebrated was, after all, Paul. Paul was the apostle favored by evangelicals, after whose own conversion experience on the road to Damascus, from persecutor to apostle, they modeled theirs.

If the personal schema is one of the sudden turn, so too is the historical model one of sudden, chiaroscuro conversions, where the "scuro" is the benighted past and the "chiaro" the illuminated present: evangelicals played endlessly on the themes of light and darkness, without any shading in between. They acted in order that "the light shall be seen . . . by the space of a whole thousand years stopped up."[1] The particular form of this historical light was institutional: evangelicals reinstituted the True Church by repudiating the Church of the Anti-Christ, and they did so on the basis of their reading: the historical Church could be rejected as a hypocritical Church of the Devil precisely because it had developed nonscriptural traditions. The True Church, by contrast, was designed in exact measure of the text of Scripture, not a word less or more.

This revolutionary accent on novelty, however, created a problem: what to do with, how to narrate, history itself? That problem is at once theological, polemical, and institutional. Theologically, the evangelical God has deterministically decided everything in advance, so history is over before it has happened. Evangelical history does not develop, so much as manifest the entire historical drama of Law and Gospel in each single moment. In each moment, that is, God's interventionist action in the world is immanent and legible. That produces not an account of historical unfolding and progressive revelation but a sequence of moments, each of which replays the same intense drama.

Polemically, the question of history is especially urgent: if the true (evangelical) church is indeed the True Church, then where was it for so long? Was the past *wholly* error (an unlikely scenario), or does the evangelical Church actually have a historical reality? Evangelicals needed rapidly to develop a historiography that could justify the apparent absence of their Church, since it was historically improbable that God would have allowed the Church to err for quite so long. Evangelical historiography also needed to account for very large stretches of history, when the True Church was submerged, as a history of *nearly* pure error; and evangelical thinking managed this need principally by identifying Hebraic error with Catholic error. Once the triple identification of Hebrew culture, Catholic culture, and Error had been made, the way was prepared for three massive repudiations.

Finally, the evangelical promotion of novelty and historical turning created an institutional problem for its own future. If apparent history *is* just error, then that error was likely to survive the moment of clean break as a kind of virus, as it were. The virus of the benighted past is a threat that accompanies all revolutionary moments, not least because the past is, in practice, never extinguishable.

In the revolutionary project of the evangelical Church, however, the virus of the past is likely to attack with especial force. The virulence of further "past attack" was predictable, because the evangelical revolutionary project was hostile not only to its own particular past, but also to the very idea of historical tradition. The word "tradition," indeed, is very frequent in evangelical writing and is always pejorative, used in phrases such as "the stinking puddles of men's traditions."[2] "Tradition" always signals human invention. It signals the accretions of history on the purity and integrity of the Gospel, to which not a word must be added, nor from which a word subtracted. Trying to ensure the immunity of a text, and the immunity of an institution from the virus of history, turns out to be an exacting project.

So the spiritual movement that began with Luther not only tried to delete a particular history, but came very close to wanting to abolish history itself. That abolition powerfully energized the revolutionary moment, since identity remains forever untouched by the passage of time: the Elect remain elect regardless of their conduct in the world.

The abolition of history might energize, but it also proved to be a very unstable ground for any future material institution. For once historical tradition had been rendered so thoroughly suspicious, that suspicion shadowed all further history. It then became very difficult to establish further historical continuities and traditions, since the supercessory moment was founded on total repudiation of the very concept of tradition itself.

The development of a tradition, that is, became a sure sign that the virus of the past had been transmitted. Given the human propensity to develop traditions, any movement founded on the repudiation of tradition will inevitably be unstable. It will be subject to permanent revolution and schism, since the very establishment of tradition will itself be a call to new vigilance, and a new supercession. The evangelical must be ever ready to reject the past and any institution or person that looks like the immediate past.[3] Thus revolutionary societies whose revolution repudiated not only the past but the Past will always be shadowed by permanent revolution.

These intense difficulties with the relation of old and new are in many ways the product of evangelical reading practice. The very distinction between the Old Testament and the New, after all, makes an evident invitation to separate old from new. How do evangelicals respond to that invitation? How do they read the Old Testament past? Is it threatened with irrelevance and violent repudiation because its literal sense applies only to the past? Is it just error? How do they read the Catholic past? Is it, too, just plain error?

Alexander Alesius, a Scot who had studied in Wittenberg, relates that he bumped into the king's Vicar-General, Thomas Cromwell, in a London street one morning in 1537. Cromwell was on his way to Parliament, where the true definition of "sacrament" (no small matter) was being debated by a committee of bishops. Alesius describes the topic of the debate differently (though, in the end, accurately): "Whether all things necessary unto our salvation be contained in the Scripture, or but a part only, and the residue to be taken out of the glosses of the doctors, out of the acts of old councils and out of popes lousy decrees."[4] Alesius happily accompanied Cromwell, without suspecting that he would soon find himself speaking.

Once they arrived in the committee room, Cromwell took his seat, with the bishops seated facing him, "at a table covered with a carpet with certain priests standing about them." Cromwell's opening statement is quoted in direct speech, and it's clear that Cromwell, evidently an expert committee chair, is giving a steer to the bishops. The king, he says, does not want to act without consulting them. In his wisdom, the king desires that the bishops "friendly and lovingly dispute among your selves of the controversies moved in the church, and that ye will conclude all things by the word of God with out all brawling or scolding." Before the bishops can speak, however, Cromwell makes it abundantly clear what they should say, with this unambiguous order: "Neither," he adds, "will his majesty suffer the Scripture to be wrested and defaced by any glosses, any papistical laws or by any authority of doctors or councils." That is clear enough, but Cromwell adds this for good measure: "Much less will he [the king] admit any articles or doctrine not contained in the scripture, but approved only by continuance of time and old custom and by unwritten verities as ye were wont to do" (images 6–7).

The phrase "unwritten verities" is a buzz word of sixteenth-century evangelical polemic; in evangelical usage it signals the soufflé of unscriptural Catholic doctrine, which can be effortlessly deflated with the sure pin of Scripture.[5] The intended topic of debate into which

Alesius stumbled should be less about Scripture than the sacraments, but the bishops fell into immediate dissension over unwritten verities. An argument about the status of Scripture and the unwritten constantly derails the sacramental argument. Cranmer (onside with Cromwell in the carefully defined factions) intervenes among the dissenting voices to insist that these are weighty matters; the issue ostensibly being debated is "whether the outward work . . . doth justify man or whether we receive our justification through faith" (image 8). In fact, however, the debate quickly turns on the authority of Scripture: Cranmer says that they should put all dissension aside and draw their authority about the number of sacraments from Scripture alone.

Suddenly, without warning, Cromwell bids Alesius to speak. Alesius, unprepared but undaunted, himself appeals to scriptural authority to argue that there are only two sacraments (baptism and the Eucharist). At this the Bishop of London, John Stokesley, erupts in disagreement, only to be silenced himself by the Bishop of Hereford, also fresh from Germany. Hereford intervenes to remind the bishops that all this argument will get nowhere, and that, above all, they should be arguing only from Scripture, on orders from the king; there's no way of escaping the force of Scripture, now that it's available in the vernacular: "Think ye not, said he, that we can by any sophistical subtleties steal out of the world again the light which every man doth see" (image 12). Encouraged by this intervention, Alesius continues his impromptu speech in favor of only written verities being adduced to decide issues concerning the sacraments.

It's interesting that this debate about the sacraments has turned into a debate about where authority is located. The undertow of the argument pulls all the interlocutors back to the fundamental ground of authority: Scripture or the Church? written or unwritten authority? Stokesley intervenes a second time, once again making the real argument explicit. Even if baptism and the Eucharist are authorized by Scripture,

> you [are] far deceived if ye think that there is no other Word of God but that which every souter [shoemaker] and cobbler do read in their mother tongue. And if ye think that nothing pertaineth unto the Christen faith but that only that is written in the Bible, then err ye plainly with the Lutherans. (images 14–15)

What's also interesting is that the very form of this text is announcing its uselessness. The text is highly dramatic, vividly reporting the dialogue of a council session in direct speech. Direct speech, however, gets nowhere, since everyone ends up only in dissension. At a certain point, just as Cromwell is about to wind up the session for that day, he signals the uselessness of discussion with the benighted Bishop of London, who has been resisting the evangelical case for written verities only. That futility is signaled at the moment when Cromwell, Cranmer, and their fellow evangelicals hear Stokesley again: "They smiled a little one upon another for as much as they saw him flee even in the very beginning of the disputation unto his old rusty sophistry and unwritten verities" (image 15).

Here the knowing, unspoken signal expresses the uselessness of ecumenical councils (a frequently made evangelical point), including this very council;[6] it also signals the moment in which written documents replace verbal persuasion: Alesius is persuaded not to return the following day, out of concern for his safety. Instead, he writes a document defending only written, scriptural verities. The rest of the text consists of citation of the written document sent by Alesius to the bishops. Thus the written word has swallowed the spoken word in this text itself. That formal move in Alesius's text (from dialogue to text) is, after all, the essential point of the text's own argument: only written, scriptural texts have authority, not "any glosses, any papistical laws or . . . any authority of doctors or councils." The existence of the plain text makes any further talk futile; indeed, it renders any further texts useless except those that insist, as this one does, that all nonscriptural forms of authority are invalid. The past swallows the present; text swallows voice.

That absolute primacy of the scriptural text, which we have seen in previous chapters, might look like a purely interpretive point. It is equally, however, a historical point: interpretation amounts, after all, to the reception of texts across time. Prohibition of any commentary on the texts is, by definition, a prohibition of historical tradition. In Alesius's written document which he now cites, Alesius argues the case for only written verities, authority derived solely from the written text of Scripture. This definition of authority is also, immediately, a case for total historical arrest at the moment of scriptural inscription: with that moment of inscription, history is effectively over. From that moment on, history should, by rights, amount only to exact repetition.

Alesius's first textual exhibit in support of this case is Deuteronomy 4:2: "You shall put nothing unto the word which I command you, neither do ought therefrom, that ye may keep the commandments of the Lord your God which I command you."[7] This insistence on textual arrest is repeated in Deuteronomy 12:32: "But whatsoever I command you, that take heed ye do: and put naught thereto, nor take ought therefrom."

In Deuteronomy more widely, this call for textual fixity is associated with cultural fixity and exclusivity: Deuteronomy 4:2 enjoins textual fixity precisely by way of guaranteeing conquest of the Promised Land. Deuteronomy 12:2 extends that cultural fixity to the destruction of other religious cultures in the land of Canaan: "See that ye destroy all places where the nations which ye conquer serve their gods . . . Overthrow their altars and break their pillars and burn their groves with fire and hew down the images of their gods." In Deuteronomy 20:16 the injunction to religious fixity is extended to the annihilation of the peoples who inhabit the land of Canaan: "In the cities of these nations which the Lord thy God giveth thee to inherit, thou shalt save alive nothing that breatheth. But thou shalt destroy them without redemption, the Hethites, the Amorites, the Cananites, the Pherezites, the Hevites and the Jebusites, as the Lord thy God hath commanded thee."

The reception of treasured canonical books into a new culture is always a challenge for cultural history. Those books will inevitably be at variance with the demands of the new order, sometimes brutally so. These texts from Deuteronomy, for example, unequivocally demand the death of all prior inhabitants of the land destined for the followers of Moses. The New Testament contains many passages that will strike many modern ears as equally repellent: Paul, for example, recommends that those practicing homosexual sex, who are guilty of "fornication, wickedness, covetousness, maliciousness, full of envy, murder, debate, deceit," are, by God's decree, "worthy of death" (Romans 1:24–32). Paul also directs slaves to obey their masters (1 Timothy 6:1–2). Such cultural variance between canonical texts on the one hand, and the present into which they are received on the other, is inevitable, especially when the texts derive from cultural formations very distant in time or place from the present. The texts of Deuteronomy were, for example, written in perhaps the seventh century BCE, and their subject is the time of Moses (around the fifteenth century BCE). The authentic texts of Paul were written before Paul's death in about 67 CE. Perfect cultural fit between the societies of such texts and those of sixteenth-century Europe won't be likely.

On the face of it, the Lutheran and Tyndalian response to that lack of fit is to accept the text exactly as it is, and to apply it to the pres-

ent. One must neither add nor subtract, regardless of the pain this in-
flicts. Luther and Tyndale, that is, apply a "rationalizing" principle
that new forms of literacy always import: that the written text applies
everywhere, to all people, in all times, without distinction.[8] Luther,
for example, in his *Bondage of the Will* (1525), mocks Erasmus's argument that it is not expedient to speak the truth to "everybody at every time in every way."[9] On the contrary, Luther exclaims, the Word
must be proclaimed whole and without respect to persons, regardless
of the tumult it causes. In fact the tumult is a sign that the Word is
being truly preached: even pagan writers recognize, he says, that
change requires "tumult . . . and bloodshed"; "for myself, if I did not
see these tumults I should say that the Word of God was not in the
world; but now, when I do see them, I heartily rejoice."[10] Tumult is
necessary, he goes on, because history is necessarily a soporific to the
real vitality of the scriptural text: "The Word of God and the traditions of men are irreconcilably opposed to one another, precisely as
God and Satan are mutually opposed, each destroying the works and
subverting the dogmas of the other."[11]

Tyndale also frequently makes the point that Scripture is to be
taken whole, regardless of the consequences. In *The Obedience of a
Christian Man*, for example, he enjoins (unsurprisingly) obedience;
however, obedience must be to the very letter of God's Law: "Without God's law do nothing. And to his word add nothing, neither pull
anything therefrom, as Moses everywhere teacheth thee." Tyndale
stresses the point by targeting any good intention not grounded in
the written Law: "Serve God as he hath appointed thee and not with
thy good intent and good zeal . . . God requireth obedience unto his
word and abhoreth all good intents and good zeals which are without God's word. For they are nothing else than plain idolatry and
worshiping of false gods."[12]

So any well-intentioned effort to please God that is without scriptural warrant is itself a foreign, idolatrous practice. It marks divergence from the Law and historical accretion—the very thing that Deuteronomy targets for destruction.[13] A good but scripturally unfounded intention represents an addition to the Law; it must therefore be subject to the Mosaic injunction against idolatry, whereby Moses enjoins "that ye destroy all places where the nations which ye conquer serve their gods."

God's Law, that is, constitutes an unbreakable whole; it must be preserved entire, exactly as it is, free from all interpretation. To do otherwise is to add, and to add is to create tradition: "It is a manifest blasphemy to say that we may be saved or damned by any traditions of man," as Alesius says in the text cited earlier. We are not to "imagine god to be like some ignorant poet which hath given us a patched and an imperfect work" (image 21).

Evangelicals, then, chose the option of accepting the text, in all its angularities, and applying it to, even inflicting it on, the present. What about their Catholic predecessors? The full answer to that question would require many books; happily those books have been written, and the position may therefore be stated with brevity.[14] There are, in the broader history of hermeneutics or textual interpretation, two remaining solutions to the problem of how old canonical texts apply to the present: one either rejects the past text, or one invents ways of reading that render manageable the dangerous potential of the past text. The position of the pre-Reformation Church clearly did not reject the Hebrew scriptures. It did, however, invent ways of reading that were able to manage the astonishing but frequently violent force of those scriptures.

The pre-Reformation Church's essential strategy of managing the past was to allegorize it. The Hebrew scriptures were characterized, as we saw in Chapter 4, by one principal division, between the literal sense and the mystical senses. The literal sense designated the historical actuality of an event; the mystical senses designated what the historical event meant for the present. This primary division is of cardinal importance in recognizing the historical truth of a past event: allegory of this kind does not merely see through a past event to its true meaning and then discard the event. On the contrary, it preserves the historical substance of the event related by the text. That said, it then makes that historical event relevant to the present, in three ways: in the first instance, the past event points forward to its historical fulfillment in Christ (the figural, or allegorical sense). Next, the past historical event provides imitable ethical models (the tropological sense). Finally, the past event points forward to a future, eschatological fulfillment at the end of time (the anagogical sense).

This scheme had its roots in comments made by Paul about the relation of the Hebrew scriptures to the Christian dispensation.[15] The full scheme may seem rather unwieldy, but the fact that it survived for so long as the prime interpretive model of sacred Christian texts for western Europe (more than a thousand years, from the third to the sixteenth century) suggests that it answered to profound needs. Evangelical polemicists found it easy to mock the analytical distinctions as academic jargon ("chopological" senses),[16] but the scheme was, in practice, more like a flexible frame within which interpreters could develop one interest or another. Rarely, in fact, did interpreters feel compelled to account laboriously for each level of meaning.[17]

Brief reflection on the scheme reveals how it responded so fully to need. Any interpretive school wants its canonical texts to remain historically pertinent to the present; often interpreters want canonical texts to have ethical application; and some interpreters also want their texts to retain a hold on the future. Figural allegory provides a schema within which these different temporal needs can be satisfied. Allegory recognized the past without being a prisoner to it;

tropology underlined the ethical force of the text for the present; and anagogy clarified the way in which the text points to the future and to the end of time.

Figural allegory is, in short, fundamentally a way of managing history. It preserves the precious historical document without becoming its prisoner. It creates dynamic relations between past, present, and future, and also between history and ethics. It recognizes historical rupture and change, since it takes account of the reality and difference of the past; but it also countenances an ongoing historical tradition of reception.[18] It is also fundamentally a poetic system, insofar as the allegorical connections between past and present are likenesses: Abraham's readiness to sacrifice Isaac is simultaneously real *and* metaphorically resonant with a later event, God's preparedness to sacrifice Christ. If evangelical reading seeks out God's explicit, covenantal dicta as the core of Scripture,[19] figural allegory seeks out images. If evangelical reading satisfies a need to have the Law explicated, figural allegory satisfies a pleasure for poetic, imagistic code-breaking whose solution reveals the sense of salvation history.

In addition to the historical grid through which the unruly Biblical text was to be managed, patristic expositors also added a further controlling grid, that the literal sense must not be taken to affirm anything impossible, absurd, or unworthy of God. Thus Augustine determined that every reading of Scripture should end up in the same place: charity. In characteristically brilliant paradoxes, Augustine puts the matter in this political way:

> With the tyranny of cupidity thus overturned, charity reigns with most just laws of love of God for God. Let this rule apply therefore in figurative [biblical] statements, that a reading be diligently considered until the interpretation should be led to the realm of charity. If the statement leads to charity through its literal sense, then it is not to be considered a figurative statement.[20]

This passage places an extraordinary power in the hands of the reader, and removes that power from the literal level of the text itself, since it directs the reader to keep reading a given scriptural text until it should offer up a charitable sense. Whatever the ostensible *literal* force of the scriptural text, the reader should read with a charitable "prejudice." That prejudice should be so strong, indeed, that it becomes the very measure of what is to be taken as figural: if a text does not lead into the "realm" of charity, then it is, *by definition*, to be understood figuratively. This readerly power is promoted not as a way of ignoring authorial intention; rather, it reveals God's charitable intention as author. We are to assume charity to be God's intention, whatever the ostensible literal force of the text.

Augustine's rule of reading for charity, and the system of figural allegory of which it was a part, was fully alive in later medieval and sixteenth-century England. The translators of the late fourteenth-century Wycliffite Bible, for example, had no hesitation in adducing figural allegory, as well as Augustine's rule about charity, as the ground rules for interpreting their own Bible.[21] Even later, humanist scholars on the cutting edge of Biblical philology recognized the power of mystical readings. Thus Erasmus in chapter 2 of his *Enchiridion Militis Christiani* (written around 1503; translated into English by 1534) describes the literal sense of Scripture as "hard" and "unsavory," but, he says, "get out the spiritual sense and nothing is more sweeter nor more full of pleasure and sweet juice."[22] This text was admittedly early in Erasmus's career; it was possibly translated by Tyndale himself. In it Tyndale found praise for allegory: among scriptural exegetes, for example, Erasmus encourages his readers to choose those who "go *farthest* from the letter . . . for I see the divines of later time stick very much in the letter and with good will give more study to subtle and deceitful arguments than to search out the mysteries" (my emphasis).[23]

The allegorical scheme was also alive in art forms, even as Tyndale was about to attack it. Precisely because it was dependent on metaphoric similarities, it lent itself with especial ease to visual representation. The magnificent set of windows in the chapel of King's College Cambridge reveals the system's grandeur of conception in action. This scheme, commissioned by Henry VIII, and preserved, presumably, from the iconoclast's hammer because of that royal commission, relates the Gospel story in a vast horizontal narrative; each Gospel scene is also related vertically to its Old Testament figure, or shadow. Thus Moses crossing the Red Sea is set above Christ opening the way for the souls imprisoned in Hell; the resurrected Christ issuing forth from the tomb in the adjacent window is answered by Jonah being vomited forth by the whale.

The figural system, then, is designed, at least in theory, both to recognize and to redirect history. History exists, but it's changed; in the words of John Fisher in his 1521 sermon against Luther, "The law of Moses and the governance of the synagogue of the Jews was but a shadow of the governance of the universal church of Christ."[24]

In the sixteenth century, however, this reading system suddenly looked fragile. Both humanist philology and evangelical culture expressed a new confidence in the literal sense, which made the figural scheme look suddenly rheumatic, laborious, and implausible. Faced with an evangelical interpretive program that was designed to promote the literal sense alone, to replicate history in all its destructive power, and to explicate doctrine explicitly, this system looked very vulnerable. The evangelical program described figural allegory as, precisely, tradition; as human invention laid upon and disfiguring the pure text of Scripture; as the work of those who have "nailed a veil of false glosses on Moses's face, to corrupt the true understanding of his law."[25] Allegory is "the trash and baggage stuff that through papistical traditions had found a way to creep in."[26]

The assault on allegory has remained dominant in Western culture, partly because the Protestant Reformation established the literal sense as the default position; partly because humanist philology also sought to elucidate the literal sense above all; and partly because Enlightenment textuality promoted written, contractual, and literal statements in, for example, the constitutions of France and the United States.

❊ Evangelical readers, then, must take the text of Scripture whole. They must repudiate allegory, "traditions of their [Catholic interpreters'] own making, founded without ground of scripture, and partly in juggling with the text." Such allegories are produced without due attention to the whole text and its order, to what Tyndale calls "the process, order and meaning of the text."[27]

A moment's reflection will reveal this rejection of allegory to be a tall order. If the reader is not to allegorize, but to take the Law as it is offered, without adding or subtracting, then the reader is also, on the face of it, submitting herself to an exacting and imprisoning textual master from the foreign country of the past. How, one might ask, could a sixteenth-century reader possibly obey the commandment of Deuteronomy 20:16: of the peoples living in the land to be inherited by the followers of Moses, "thou shalt save alive nothing that breatheth. But thou shalt destroy them without redemption, both the Hethites, the Amorites, the Cananites, the Pherezites, the Hevites and the Jebusites, as the Lord thy God hath commanded thee." The sixteenth-century English reader had no Hethites handy to "destroy without redemption."

That last comment may sound facetious, but it reminds us that no ancient text can be taken literally and remain pertinent to contemporary readers. Tyndale frequently insists that readers make the text of Scripture intimately pertinent to their own lives: "As thou readest therefore think that every syllable pertaineth to thine own self, and suck the pith out of scripture."[28] On the one hand, readers must understand the whole of Scripture, without changing anything; on the other, they must make it intimately relevant to their own lives. These two choices were available to sixteenth-century textual consciousness, but they were seen as *exclusive* choices: some humanist philologists argued that philological recovery was designed to reproduce the exact shape of history (regardless of pertinence to the modern reader); other scholars promoted the idea that the purpose of recovering ancient texts was to provide models for contemporary readers, regardless of historical integrity. One version of textual recovery was stringently historical, while the other was unashamedly presentist.[29]

Evangelical theorists wanted to have it both ways. They wanted, that is, to preserve both the exact integrity of the text, and its pertinence to modern readers.[30] How could they manage that? The rest of this chapter reveals the impossibility of this reading challenge. It also elucidates the strategies adopted by evangelical theorists to disguise that impossibility. In order to sustain their approach, evangelicals had effectively to reject any sense of historical tradition within Scripture itself. Everything is always as it was. They also had to invent ways of reintroducing allegory in thin disguise. Evangelical allegory was, however, an interpretive machine for repudiation: most of history was error, both Hebraic and Catholic. That shared error between Hebraic and Catholic observance produced allegory (Hebrew error equals Catholic error), though this allegory was designed to reject rather than incorporate.

The position argued here is parallel to the argument in Chapter 4 about the literal sense: both the wholeness of the text and the literal sense are not so much descriptions of evangelical reading practice as ideological weapons in the evangelical armory. Both are in fact unsustainable positions that placed terrible pressure on evangelical readers. I use Tyndale's prologues, to both Old and New Testament, as my main sources.

✖✖✖ The main evangelical challenge in dealing with the Hebrew and Christian scriptures was to flatten any sense of historical development. For Luther and Tyndale, "Old Testament" and "New Testament" do not designate two material corpora distinct in time. On the contrary, Old and New Testament are primarily concepts, equally available throughout all Scripture. In the Preface to the 1525 New Testament Tyndale begins by saying something apparently straightforward: that the "Old Testament is a book wherein is written the law of God," while the "New Testament is a book, wherein are contained the promises of God." That suggestion of historical difference is immediately blurred, however, by reference to the meaning of "evangelion (that we call gospel)": this means "good, merry, glad and joyful tidings," but it can apply to the Hebrew scriptures, "as when David had killed Goliath the giant."[31] The potential application to the Hebrew scriptures is then extended: "evangelion or gospel . . . is called the New Testament," and it was available as well to Old Testament figures: "To strength such faith withal, God promised this his Evangelion in the Old Testament by the prophets."

Tyndale is here recapitulating the basic terms of Luther's theology: Law and Gospel. These terms are not specific to a period of history, nor do they designate any historical unfolding.[32] Instead they designate the Law by which Christians are damned and the promises by which they are saved; Law and Gospel are both dispersed across the Hebrew and Christian scriptures. Tyndale is more explicit about this in the Prologue to Exodus:

> The new testament is those everlasting promises which are made us in Christ the Lord throughout all scripture. And that testament is built on

faith, not works . . . The new testament was ever, even from the beginning of the world. For there were always promises of Christ to come
by faith, in which promises the elect were then justified inwardly before God.[33]

The distinction, then, between Old and New is not a historical one;
it is instead a distinction that applies to the spiritual life of every
evangelical believer, before and after Christ. It designates the Lutheran dialectic of abjection and gratitude, through whose painful
passage the evangelical reader must pass.

This redistribution of the New Testament equally across all Scripture serves two ends, one theological and the other polemical. Theologically, it serves the Lutheran investiture of God with his proper
omniscience and omnipotence. God's decisions cannot be subject to
the vagaries of human volition and human history. Given the absolute need to preserve that divine prerogative, all God's decisions need
to be wholly available across time. Lutheran ontology effectively
does away with historical sequence, since the spiritual life will swing
between two poles that are always available, without respect to period. All has always been as it already is. Because Christ is always already there, the historical tension goes out of reading; it is replaced
by a spiritual and psychological tension for each reader, that of the
explosive paradox of the Gospel buried within the Law.

Luther's distinction between Gospel and Law is effectively a demolition of history: just as the history of the individual is demol-
ished through predestination, so too is historical progress flattened
through the eternal immanence and legibility of the Word. Progressive revelation is, as a result, massively reduced. This is why Luther
and Tyndale privilege statements of covenant over narrative:[34] covenant produces meanings that are wholly independent of the unfolding of narrative. The entire drama of salvation is enacted in the read-

ing of any given covenantal statement. Things just become clearer after Christ; it's a cognitive rather than a historical change.

The point of reading the Hebrew scriptures under this regime is not to intuit historical foreshadowings; it is rather to undergo the dialectic of despair and hope that each of the heroic figures of the Hebrew scriptures themselves underwent. As Tyndale says in his Prologue to Exodus, with regard to the events of that book: "Note thereto how God is found true at last, and how when all is past remedy and brought into desperation, he then fulfilleth his promises, and that by [i.e., for] an abject and a castaway, a despised and refused person: yea, and by a way impossible to believe."[35]

In short, the historical relation between Old and New Testament is subsumed by the problematic facing each reader. Historical relations are replaced by an emotional dialectic of fear and gratitude for individual readers. The reader now occupies the central position in the drama of history, since that drama has been subsumed into the psychological drama of works and faith, Law and Gospel, despair and hope.

The bearing down of history upon the reader is apparent in a painting entitled *The Law and the Gospel* (1529) by Luther's friend Lucas Cranach (Figure 2).[36] The image is obviously divided by a binary division of Law to the left and Gospel to the right. Images of the Law dominate the left-hand panel, arranged in a semicircle: the withered tree, the Mosaic reception of the Law, the scene of original sin, the corpse, and finally Moses bearing menacingly down on the naked central figure.

Each of these images is mirrored by its Gospel counterpart: flourishing tree, Virgin, crucified Christ and sacrificial lamb, risen Christ and John the Baptist. Although this disposition appears to represent a historical distinction (Old on the left and New on the right), the posture of the figures suggests otherwise. Moses the lawgiver might

2. Lucas Cranach the Elder, *The Law and the Gospel* (1529).

glower threateningly, but his left hand points across to the crucified Christ; above all, the central figure is effectively the reader of Law and Gospel, caught between the two. His naked body is turned toward the Law, while his head is turned toward the promises of the Gospel. The division, that is, is not historical so much as psychic, and it is expressed in the divided posture of the reader, torn between fear and gratitude. The naked reader is not faced with a choice, since the choice has been made by God's election; the reader is instead faced by the challenging psychic test of persuading himself that he has been chosen to arrive on the right-hand side. Salvation history and individual choice have both been subsumed by psychic drama.

The absence of historical tension and unfolding is underlined in an alternative version of the same image, made by Cranach in 1528: here the scene of the Law is overseen by Christ at the end of time: everything is already as it will always be.[37]

Typology is not altogether absent from this scene: an Old Testament scene from Numbers 21:8 is bounded by the semicircle of images of Law and death. That passage from Numbers relates how the Israelite followers of Moses are bitten by poisonous snakes sent by God to punish them for their grumbling recalcitrance to Moses' command. Moses is ordered to set up a fabricated serpent on a pole; everyone who looks upon it will be cured. In the Cranach painting we see not cure but death; the promise of cure is embedded in the image, but not activated.

The image of the brazen serpent was traditionally taken to be a figure for Christ, based on poetic correspondences between Old and New dispensations. In Cranach's image that poetic correspondence is evoked but neutralized, since the formal placing of the brazen serpent scene in the background implies a different status for typology. The center of this image is no longer the passage of history itself, but the reader's problematic in a world in which history has been replaced by psychic stress.

The flattening of history, or rather the subsuming of the drama of history into the psychic drama of the reader, is produced by theological persuasions: God's omnipotence must not be compromised in any way by the unfolding of human history; history must not challenge God in any way, or leave him in the dark. It's over before it has begun, both in individual lives and in salvation history.

❊   The flattening of history provides a massive polemical advantage for a revolutionary church. One of the most frequent objections to the evangelical church was that it had been absent for so much of history. If evangelicals did constitute the True Church, then where was it for so long? In his *Dialogue Concerning Heresies* (1529), for example, Thomas More capitalizes on the historical priority and continuity of the Roman Church in an attempt to render the evangelical church illegitimate. The question of priority is obvious for More: "The church of Christ is before [that is, prior to] all the churches of heretics, and . . . all congregations of heretics have come out of the church of Christ." So too is the question of continuity. More cites Christ's words from Matthew 28:20: "And lo I am with you always, even until the end of the world." Now if Christ is always with us, he is with the Church, not sometimes with it and sometimes not. Christ's Church is, therefore, "and ever shall be continual without any times between." For More, that is, there can be no "middle age," or time "in between" when the Church was absent, after the coming of Christ.[38] More was no medievalist.

The evangelical church seems, by contrast, to have been absent; the only existence it has is ideational. Heretics are, says More, "driven to deny for the church the people that be known for the church."[39] As a result, by logical necessity, they "go seek another [church] they neither know what nor where." The ghost of More's own *Utopia* (1516) returns to haunt him here, since now it's his enemies who are inventing powerful but wholly ideational institutions: they "build up in the air a church all so spiritual."[40]

How might the flattening of history help evangelical polemicists faced with powerful arguments of the kind produced by More?[41] They capitalized on the Lutheran theological understanding of history to say that the evangelical church actually pre-existed the Roman Church. In fact, they maintained, the true, evangelical church pre-existed Hebraic religion too. Evangelical theorists adopted, that is, the very position that More mocks, of building a wholly ideational church that trumps human history. Once again, everything has been

decided in advance; everything is as it always was. Identity is untouched by the passage of time and by engagement in history.

This was clearly an implausible position to defend, but evangelicals did nevertheless make such a defense. Miles Coverdale offers a
bold example. In 1541 he translated a text by Heinrich Bullinger,
with this title in English: *The olde fayth, an euydent probation out of the holy
scripture, that the christen fayth (which is the right, true, old & undoubted faith),
hath endured sens the beginnyng of the worlde.*[42] Coverdale's essential strategy is to argue that the Roman Church is the new one, whereas the
evangelical church is the True Church. As will be clear from the title,
Coverdale doesn't go for half measures here: the true form of the
church has existed since the beginning of the world. To adopt the
evangelical church is not, then, to adopt a novelty; on the contrary, it
is a conservative choice that repudiates the false, posterior, accreted
novelty of tradition represented by both Hebraic religion and the
Roman Church.

How does Coverdale mount this improbable argument? The essence of the true believer is faith. Anyone who had faith in Christ, either before or after Christ, signals the existence of the True Church.
With that premise in place, Coverdale moves through Biblical history, proving that history does not progressively unfold; history is a
series of moments in which an identical drama of faith is played out.
He says this about Adam, for example: "It is easy to understand what
faith and knowledge Adam had of our lord Christ. Namely, that he
knew in him very godhood and manhood, and that he saw in faith
his passion and cross afar off" (image 21). This is not typology, but a
replay of the single act of faith through which the fullness of the
Christian dispensation is already available. Once Coverdale has established that "the holy Patriarchs also were Christen and saved by
Christ," he establishes a broader division from which to read Hebraic
narrative and, indeed, from which to read the entire narrative of sal-

vation history. Abel was the "first martyr and instrument of God and of Christ in the holy Church, whereas Cain is the head of the citizens of the serpent. The free men of the city of God and of Christ, do cleave only unto God . . . [and] build only upon Christ" (image 23).

As will already be evident, futurity is almost entirely banished from this startling historical vision: everything is known already by a small and covert band of the faithful who represent the true, *Christian* Church. Christianity is older than paganism and older than the Jewish faith. Abraham was "God's friend and justified or made righteous, or [before] ever he was circumcised" (image 23). Even if many Israelites practiced idolatry learned from the Egyptians, many nevertheless kept the "old" faith (that is, the Christian faith) (image 29). The delivery of the Law in the Mosaic tables changed nothing: "The Lord began no new thing with his people when he delivered them the tables of the law" (image 32).

Coverdale acknowledges that his position will seem "new and strange in many hearts," but trusts that those who have understanding will recognize that this is "the true, old, right and godly Divinity and Theology" (image 39). However strange and forced his position may seem, one can readily see why it was so attractive (and, not least, necessary) to him. For a start, Coverdale adopts a position from which he can gain leverage on all observances and customs as posterior, accreted tradition. This will serve him when he comes (as he does) to attack the Roman Church as a form of Hebraic idolatry: both Catholics and Jews are belated, fallen additions to a pure religion of the Christian Gospel that was written on the hearts of the faithful since the beginning of the world.

Above all, the position serves Coverdale's essential historical need: the evangelical, True Church has always existed; *it* is the old Church; the Roman Church and the panoply of Hebraic custom are Johnny-come-lately *arrivistes.* We must remain fixed on the originary moment:

"God's testament or bequest" must "remain still," with "nothing . . . added to it or taken from it" (image 33).[43]

Coverdale produces a new form of vernacular exegesis here, reading the Old Testament retrospectively as an exact confirmation of all that became clearly known after Christ. The spiritual athletes of the time before Christ were Christians, full members of the True Church. The positive version of Old Testament history survives only in the persons of these single survivors, solitary figures who perceive and experience the dialectic of Law and Gospel, and whose authenticity can be guaranteed, for the most part, only through persecution.

All history aside from these spiritual athletes (that is, most of history) is a history of belatedness, textual divergence, human tradition, and error. All that anyone alleges against this true faith is "nothing worth," says Tyndale: "whether it be concerning holy men, old age, multitudes, learned men, general councils, convocations or parliaments, fathers, acts, statutes, tokens and wonders" (image 55). Coverdale thus establishes the attack position of a new historiography, in which the function of the historian will be to hollow history out, as error is exposed. The job of the historian is to scrape away, to get back to the True Church below. Most history was a mistake; that is, most history was just human tradition.

The title page illustration of Foxe's *Acts and Monuments* of 1563 (Figure 3) exemplifies the polemical advantage of flattening historical sequence. Its lower divisions represent a historical battle: on the middle left the persecuted evangelical saints burn, with trumpets raised to hail the elect on Christ's right. On the bottom left the Word is preached, without a word added to or subtracted from the Tetragrammaton in Hebrew letters, which illuminates the sermon. On the bottom right, by contrast, a Corpus Christi procession leads toward the celebration of the Eucharist in the middle right panel, in which the Host is offered up, as if to the devils, on Christ's left.

The contrast between the right and left sides of this illustration is

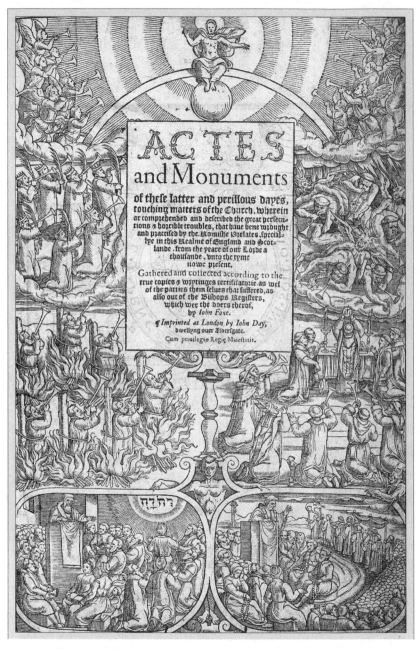

3. Title page, John Foxe, *Actes and Monuments*, first edition (London, 1563).

polemical and historically specific. Nonetheless, it borrows iconography from another, ahistorical scheme. The image of Christ seated on the rainbow at the top, drawn ultimately from Revelation 4:3, also derives from standard iconography of the Last Judgment. Very often this scheme was painted over the chancel arch of churches. In Foxe's image Christ is not, however, judging the sinners and the saved at the end of time; instead, he already judges the faithless and faithful in this life. Eschatology, or the end of time, is thus transferred to what looks like the flow of time and historical conflict. It is also transferred from Church to book. The absolute judgment is made in this life, and it's made by virtue of reading, or hearing, the Law in its original form. Election is coterminous with lection. Because the True Church is truly known across time, indifferent to historical sequence, nonscriptural practice can be damned with the confidence of divine approval. Evangelical satire is not reformist so much as damnatory; it can damn because it works in confident possession of God's absolute decision.

If figural allegory registers the unfolding of time, evangelicals have no need of it, since time, for them, does not unfold. For both theological and polemical reasons, the True Church was always fully formed. Once that point has been made, however, evangelicals reintroduce allegory with a vengeance.[44] But while allegory in the figural scheme was a means of historical recuperation, evangelical allegorizing becomes a waste-disposal machine. Allegory is a way of disposing simultaneously with Hebraic custom and Catholic observance.[45]

Tyndale returns to the question of allegory frequently; he is especially preoccupied with it in discussion of Old Testament books that promote works and observances, since these threaten to capsize his program of scriptural reading altogether. Leviticus, for example, is a book of very specific laws and observances, such as dietary and medical injunctions (including, for example, some probably ineffective measures for the treatment of leprosy). Reading this book under a regime that forbids addition to or subtraction from the Law is an exacting challenge. It is revealing that Tyndale should repudiate allegory so forcefully here, since allegory is the very thing he most needs, and the very thing he promptly reintroduces.

In his Prologue to Leviticus, Tyndale holds that allegorical interpretation is a kind of interpretive anarchy. He is especially aware of this danger with regard to Old Testament ceremonies, since these come perilously close to works. Thus he forcefully repudiates allegorical interpretation, in which readers "feign every man after his own brain at all wild adventure without any certain rule."[46] In fact this anarchy suggests diabolic deception, since, Tyndale goes on,

> we had need to take heed every where that we be not beguiled with false allegories, whether they be drawn out of the new testament or the old . . . but namely [especially] in this book [i.e. Leviticus]. Here a man had need to put on all his spectacles and to arm himself against invisible spirits. (p. 148)

Once the "invisible spirits" of allegory have been frightened off with eyes empowered by spectacles, however, Tyndale welcomes allegory back: "But the very use of allegories is to declare and open a text that it may be the better perceived and understood" (p. 148). How can Tyndale make this startling move, and why should he make it?

He can make it because for Tyndale allegory is retrospective. Once we have the clarity of the knowledge of Christ, we can retrospectively "borrow figures, that is to say allegories, similitudes or examples to open Christ" (pp. 145–146). So allegory is demoted from a principle of salvation history and reinstituted as a pedagogic princi-

ple, since allegories "lead a man's wits further into the pith and marrow and spiritual understanding of a thing."

Why should Tyndale reintroduce the feared category of allegory?
Why especially in the Prologue to Leviticus? Leviticus is a legal text,
constituted wholly by statements of Law. For Tyndale the Law serves
not to persuade us that we can fulfill it, but rather as a corrosive to an
old sore, designed to inflame the sore of the "abject and castaway" in
order to provoke a radical capitulation to divine grace. Belief that we
could fulfill the demands of the Law, and the observances demanded
of God, is a form of idolatry and obeisance to foreign gods. At the
same time, the reader must absolutely not add anything to or subtract anything from the Law. These understandings of the Law are
evidently difficult to sustain; in the case of a text like Leviticus, they
become pretty well impossible. Tyndale is therefore required to miti-
gate them in this case.

He meets this challenge from the very beginning of the Leviticus
Prologue. The observances demanded in this book were ordained by
God "to occupy the minds of that people the Israelites, and to keep
them from serving of God after [that is, according to] the imagination of their blind zeal and good intent" (p. 145). So "ceremonies" (a
dangerously Catholic practice for Tyndale) are not necessary, but are
rather a kind of playpen, designed to keep the children from harm.
They were a kind of primary literacy, an

> A. B. C. to learn to spell and read, and as a nurse to feed them with
> milk and pap, and to speak to them after [according to] their own ca-
> pacity and to lisp the words unto them according as the babes and
> children of that age might sound them again. (p. 145)

So Tyndale does depend here on a notion of history as develop-
mental: ceremonies are "fantasies" designed to "satisfy the children's
lusts"; they are useful until things of "greater earnest" should arrive

(p. 145). They are, in fact, reading lessons. Although they provide no ground to build on, in retrospect we can see that they have some similarity to the Christian dispensation, as circumcision bears some relation to baptism. Once these possible but retrospective similitudes are conceded, Tyndale slips into something much more prospective:

> And though also that all the ceremonies and sacrifices have as it were a starlight of Christ, yet some there be that have as it were the light of the broad day a little before the sun rising, and express him, and the circumstances and virtue of his death so plainly as if we should play his passion on a scaffold or in a stage play openly before the eyes of the people. As the scapegoat, the brazen serpent . . . the Passover lamb . . . (p. 146)

Tyndale moves within a whisker of becoming an admiring spectator of a mystery cycle here, even down to the moment of sunrise that initiates a day's cycle. At this point he seems on the very verge of conceding a prospective, figural understanding of allegory. At this surprising moment, however, he retreats to the Coverdale position outlined above: that "a few familiar friends" of God in Old Testament times knew Christ completely. So the appearance of startling, figural similarities is a mirage: the similarities derive from the fact that the gifted figures of the Old Testament knew wholly about Christ. In their case, there was no historical development. From there Tyndale goes on to pull the sting of ceremonies even more: ceremonies worked not because they were of any value in themselves, but rather for the faith with which they were performed.

This discussion is, in short, balanced on a knife-edge, just as the entire book of ceremonies is balanced on a knife-edge. Allegory proves nothing, and yet allegory is the only possible way of saving this book. That irreducible doubleness is registered at the end of the Prologue, when allegory is praised and blamed in rhetorically balanced clauses: there is not "a more subtle and pestilent thing in the world to persuade a false matter than an allegory"; but "there is not a better, vehementer or mightier thing to make a man understand withal than an allegory" (p. 150).

This rather tortured retrieval and simultaneous denial of allegory is exemplified in no less spectacular form in Tyndale's *Obedience of a Christian Man* (1528). Here, though, allegory becomes a fully operational waste-disposal machine for Old Testament ceremonies.

As we have seen, evangelical writers treat the heroes of the Old Testament very much as theorists in any revolutionary period treat figures from the past. These revolutionary theorists wish to define the past in clearly segmented periods, and to demonize those segments that obscure the revolutionary truth. The past, however, can never be wholly repudiated, so figures from the past who foresaw the enlightened present are consistently isolated from the benighted past by which they are surrounded. They are isolated in order to be praised as prophets, as figures wholly in possession of the enlightened truth. Once that move has been made, then the way is clear for a much larger and more aggressive repudiation of the benighted, superstitious past. The isolated figures prove the rule of obscurantism by exception. Sixteenth-century evangelical writers recuperated figures from the late medieval Catholic past,[47] as well as from the Hebraic past. Adam, Abel, Noah, Abraham, Jacob, Moses, David, Hezekiah, Josiah, and so on—these figures knew of Christ, but they were surrounded by idolaters who worshipped foreign gods. They were surrounded by idolaters, that is, who bore striking resemblances to the Catholic Church.

That move produces vibrant and abundant allegorization. It is, however, an allegorization designed to generate waste rather than to recuperate. It's an allegory that gives free reign to detestation of both Hebraic observance and Catholic ceremony. In the *Obedience* Tyndale begins, as he does in the Prologue to Numbers, by violent repudiation of allegory. The cause of the Church's current captivity "sprang first of allegories"; the reader must understand the sophistry and blindness of allegories, in order that "thou mayest abhor them and spew them out of thy stomach forever."[48] That point made, he encourages, as he does elsewhere, ethical readings of the Old Testament.[49] The story of David and Bathsheba, for example, is designed to strengthen us: "For if we saw not such infirmities in God's elect, we which are so weak and fall so often should utterly despair and think that God had clean forsaken us" (p. 163). So too with the "homely gest [story]" of Noah's drunkenness: Tyndale's reader will remember what happened to the "cursed children of wicked Ham which saw his father's privy members and jested thereof to his brethren" (p. 163). Readings of this kind are very close to the so-called tropological or moral sense of the four-fold scheme, even if Tyndale subtly shifts such readings from being strictly ethical to being replays of the drama of salvation: "Thou seest what infirmity accompanieth God's elect be they never so holy, which is yet not imputed to them" (p. 164).

That Tyndale should make tropological readings is entirely unsurprising. What is surprising is that he should then go on to make spectacular allegorical readings. He proceeds in this case to read the story of Ham mocking his father's nakedness in the most startling series of allegorical connections. The narrative provides "an apt and handsome allegory . . . to describe our wicked Ham, Antichrist the Pope." For just as Ham mocked his father's nakedness, so too for hundreds of years has the Pope as Anti-Christ "done all the shame that heart can think unto the privy member of God, which is the word of promise or the word of faith . . . and the gospel and testament of Christ wherewith we are begotten" (p. 164). The identification of Noah's penis and the Gospel is startling enough, but Tyndale goes on from here to develop the connection between Ham and the Pope in a dazzling series of Old Testament "similitudes": just as the descendants of Ham grew into giants, so too have the Pope and his minions become "mighty giants above all power and authority." One of the descendants of Ham was Nimrod; Tyndale expects his readers to know this, since he goes on thus: "They [the Pope and his minions] heap mountain upon mountain, and will to heaven by their own strength." Just as God destroyed these giants, so too will he destroy the Pope.

After this bravura display of Old Testament references woven into an allegorical narrative, Tyndale settles once again into sober, anti-allegorical mode: "The similitudes prove nothing, but are made to express more plainly that which is contained in the scripture and to lead thee in the spiritual understanding of the text."[50] This move looks rather like special pleading: allegory proves nothing except the true meaning of the text. Insofar as Tyndale is effectively saying that, he is borrowing the interpretive and poetic ingenuity of his opponents. We should note, however, that Tyndale uses allegory only to repudiate. The Old Testament is famously full of recalcitrant figures, full of those who complain against the strictures of Moses, or who insist on practicing the idolatrous worship of surrounding peoples. These figures provide ample grist for the interpretive mill of identifying recalcitrant, idolatrous Israelites with recalcitrant, idolatrous Catholics:

> As it went with their kings and rulers, so shall it go with ours. As it was with their common people, so shall it be with ours. As it was with their spiritual officers, so shall it be with ours. As it was with their true prophets, so shall it be with ours until the world's end . . . As there was among them but a few true hearted to God, so shall it be among us: and as their idolatry was, so shall ours be until the end of the world.[51]

Tyndale offers a template here for a new allegorization: there will always be a few elect; they will be persecuted by the powerful and the idolatrous. So a few Old Testament figures survive, but the rest of the history of Israel is a history of error that points directly forward to Catholic error. The divine violence visited on Old Testament idolatry thereby legitimates, if not demands, a violence against the idolatry of the Catholic Church. Allegory has become a machine for isolating and disposing of error.

In short, Tyndale wants to read history as both whole and almost empty. He wants to take the entire text whole, without addition or subtraction of any kind. He simultaneously needs a way to reject most of the text's narrative as a narrative of error, by way of rejecting both Hebraic and Catholic confidence in the observances of the Law. The Book of Numbers provides revealing examples of both these positions, since the narrative of Numbers contains the promulgation of laws, recalcitrant Israelites, and idolatrous foreign religious practices that need to be driven from the land of Canaan by the invading Israelite army. The Israelites who died before reaching the Promised Land may have observed the Law, but they did so without faith. Tyndale draws two historical parallels with these faithless observers of the Law: the Pharisees and the Roman Church. The Israelites wished to please God with their "holy faithless works," and this prompts comparison with the Pharisees at the time of Christ, who laid the "foundation of free will" on this example. Because they "built holy works after [according to] their own imagination without faith of the word," they "fervently . . . slew the king of all holy works."

This anti-pharisaic outburst leads directly into its parallel in post-Christian, Catholic history, itself idolatrous with its "setting up" of the altars of free will:

> Then look again on our hypocrites which in like manner, following the doctrine of Aristotle and other heathen pagans, have against all scripture set up free will again, unto whose power they ascribe the keeping of the commandments of God.[52]

Most of the rest of the Prologue to Numbers is taken up with the question of vows, where Tyndale develops his theme of the continual resurfacing of historical error. Not so subtly, he insinuates direct parallelisms between pharisaic and Catholic practice: Christ rebuked the Pharisees for "long prayers, for fasting, for tithing so diligently that they left not so much as their herbs untithed, for their cleanness in washing before meat and for washing of cups, dishes, and all manner of vessels . . . and for giving of alms." The Book of Numbers itself goes into great detail about the precise utensils to be used within the Ark of the Covenant (Numbers 4:5–15); Tyndale is clearly distancing himself from those Hebraic observances prescribed by God himself.

So some things do need to be added to or subtracted from the Law. Tyndale's reading of the Old Testament is poised on a knife-edge of commitment to the integrity of the Law on the one hand, and visceral distaste of the precise, material injunctions concerning observances, on the other. That distaste is most obvious and mild when he is describing plainly idolatrous practice, but the distaste spills over into all but anti-Semitic repudiation of Hebraic observance prescribed by the Law itself. Like Luther, who encourages his readers to love Moses for the Law and to stone Moses for hatred of the Law,[53] Tyndale both loves and distrusts the Old Testament. He distrusts not only idolaters, both Israelite and Canaanite, but also prescribed Hebraic observance. In his *Brief Declaration of the Sacraments*, for example, he begins by noting the remarkable similarities between Hebraic and Christian events and "sacraments." Passover was

a very prophecy of the passion of Christ, describing the very manner and fashion of his death, and the effect and virtue [strength] thereof also. In whose stead is the sacrament of the body and blood of Christ come as baptism in the room or stead of the circumcision.[54]

Once Christ came, however, Passover ended, since "in the room [function] thereof (concernyng that spiritual signification) came the sign of the sacrament of the body and blood of our Saviour Christ. As baptism came in stead of circumcision" (image 12). After that decisive break, persistence in the Old Law (not adding to or subtracting from it) amounts to hatred of Christ: these observances are "clean unprofitable." "And as the circumcision in the flesh, their hearts still uncircumcised. But hating the Law of God and believing in their own imaginations, were circumcised unto their great damnation" (image 14). Once that negative account of Hebraic observance has been underlined, the next move is predictable: Catholics, too, persist in idolatrous practice: "The same I say came thereto to their greater damnation: I pass over with silence the wicked and damnable doctrine of these servants of Mammon [that is, the Roman Church], which for lucre, pervert the true use of the sacrament [of penance] and hide it from the people" (images 14–15).

The pattern of Tyndale's use of the Old Testament is now clear. Like other evangelicals, he has a tortured relation with the Old Testament: on the one hand, it's Scripture and the Law, to which nothing must be added, and from which nothing must be subtracted. On the other, it brims with very specific prescriptions concerning observances that suggest confidence in works, from which a great deal must be subtracted. Tyndale in fact adopts a variety of shifting positions regarding Old Testament observances: either they must be taken whole, or else they are foreshadowings; or else they are foreshadowings that must now be repudiated; or else they are idolatrous accretions on an earlier, truer Christian dispensation.

This shifting attitude to the past is equally a shifting reading practice: sometimes the Law is literal, at others it must be allegorized. The common strand in these shifting positions is, however, a hollowing out of history: almost all history is bunk; only an elect few were ever in possession of the truth (then as now), which existed from the beginning of the world. That persuasion allows the evangelical church to present itself as the true, original Church; it also allows simultaneous condemnation of Hebraic and Catholic practices as equally idolatrous. Hebraic ritualism is an allegory of its Catholic counterpart. As with the literal sense, commitment to the integrity of the Law is purely ideological, a neat way of preserving polemical superiority in any situation.[55] The identity of the Elect, like the identity of many revolutionaries, remains untouched by the experience of history. No matter how much they err, they are always, and they always have been, saved.

CHAPTER SEVEN

Thomas More and Textual Trust

EVANGELICAL reading practice looks, in short, pretty bad. Even after we set aside the obvious ways in which it looks bad to nonevangelical readers whose church will be rejected by it (not a negligible exception), evangelical reading still looks unattractive. It can commit evangelical readers to a good measure of self-loathing and unending anxiety; it can produce moral authoritarianism; it can isolate its readers; and it can recast history as almost entirely errone-ous. The future, it might be added, becomes a story of schism fore-told.

To declare that practices from the past look bad can be otiose. Per-haps the historical practice has no bearing on the present, or perhaps those practices had no alternative from within their own historical moment. In either case, disapproval is little more than idle presentism. In the case of sixteenth-century reading, however, the charge is not idle, since sixteenth-century evangelical reading does have powerful consequences that extend into twenty-first-century Western moder-nity. And the tradition of liberalism, which traces its genealogy from sixteenth-century Protestantism, is the very tradition that is most threatened by the real child of sixteenth-century evangelical culture (that is, Biblical fundamentalism). If liberalism wants a future, it had best be clear about its past.

There is, however, another reason why it's worth saying that sixteenth-century evangelical reading looks bad: powerfully argued alternatives to it *did* exist within its own historical moment. Not only that, but those alternatives have themselves been consistently made to "look bad" in dominant historiographical traditions. In this chapter I'll look at the ways in which an exceptionally prescient Thomas More foresaw the outcome I have been describing in the previous four chapters.

More's positions, usually dismissed by historians as the manic reflex of a persecutory temper, turn out to be deeply meditated, brilliantly argued, and, up to a very precise point, extremely plausible. The essence of his argument is that texts are trustingly made and remade in human history and by human institutions. The literal sense is only ever a fragile thread whose sense can be constructed within trustworthy communal understandings and traditions, some of them necessarily unwritten. The society of pure contract, along with the clarity and fullness of the literal sense, is always only a fiction.

After the resurgence of this textual tradition (now called "pragmatism") in the twentieth-century liberal academy, we are, possibly, in a position to regard its sixteenth-century ancestor with a little more understanding and tolerance.[1] Of course we must also admit into an account of More's "plausibility" the fact that he actively promoted the burning of heretics. We must not hide that, and I will confront it directly in the following chapter. Neither should we allow it, however, to swamp More's whole position immediately.

✦ According to the plausible terms of William Roper's biography of his father-in-law, *The Life of Sir Thomas More* (written around 1557, published in 1626),[2] Thomas More often found himself on precarious ground from the moment he entered the service of King Henry VIII in 1518. Congratulated by Roper sometime around 1525 for his familiarity with the king, More acknowledged the king's singular favor but also marked its distinct limits: "For if my head could win him a castle in France . . . it should not fail to go."[3] From at least 1530, of course, Henry VIII was rather less well disposed toward More, given More's opposition to the royal divorce and remarriage, and given the king's stated intention (in early 1531) to establish himself as the Supreme Head of the Church in England.

The fragility of More's position, especially after his resignation as Lord Chancellor on 16 May 1532, necessitated an adroit response to texts. In February 1534 he was implicated in the campaign against Elizabeth Barton, whose published visionary revelations had been critical of the king's divorce. The authorities managed to destroy all copies (seven hundred, by one contemporary estimate) of the book of Barton's revelations.[4] More escaped that charge, despite the king's desire to incriminate him, but there was no escaping the Oath of Supremacy.

In April 1534 More still saw some legal resources by which he might evade imprisonment, since, in his estimation, the oath was "not agreeable with the statute"; his enemies were not "by their own law able to justify my imprisonment" (p. 240). This avenue of escape proved illusory, however, as Thomas Audley (More's successor as Lord Chancellor) and Thomas Cromwell introduced a new statute "for the confirmation of the oath so amplified with their additions" (p. 241).

As More's enemies moved ever closer, the poignant relation between death and texts becomes ever sharper. A civil servant, one "Master Rich," sent to pack More's books in prison, engaged More in conversation about the jurisdiction of Parliament. Parliament had the power, More conceded in a set of hypothetical arguments, to make Rich the king; he denied, however, that Parliament had the power to make Rich a pope, or that "the Parliament [could] make the King supreme head of the Church" (p. 245). Once in possession of this incriminating evidence of a statement attributed to More, More's enemies felt able to strike: "Upon whose only report was Sir Thomas More indicted of treason upon the statute whereby it was made treason to deny the King to be supreme head of the Church" (p. 245). The indictment adds these words about the *manner* in which More had made the alleged denial: "maliciously, traitorously, and diabolically" (p. 245).

Faced with the charges, More first scrutinizes the adverbs just listed. If they were removed from the indictment, he would see (adding his own adverb) "nothing justly to charge him." From here More goes on, as we might expect from a lawyer, to discredit the source of the allegation and to question its likelihood: Rich (whom More has known since Rich was a youth in the same parish) had an ill reputation; was it likely, More appeals to his judges, that he (More) would "utter the secrets of my conscience touching the King's Supremacy" to such a person? "Can this," he asks, "seem likely to be true?" (p. 246).

Even if what Rich alleges to have been spoken had been spoken, the charge does not stand, More maintains: it was spoken in "familiar secret talk, nothing affirming, and only in putting of cases without other displeasant circumstances." If it had been merely hypothetical, then it had nothing of malice, if we take *malitia* to mean "malevolence." If we take *malitia* to mean "sin," then we are all guilty. So either no one is guilty (by the law of the land) or everyone is guilty (by God's law) (pp. 246–247).

Despite these arguments (and many more), the jury found More guilty. Once convicted, More changes his discourse: he no longer appeals to secular law, but to ecclesiology, in denying the right of Parliament to make laws appointing the King to be Supreme Head of the Church. Once actually judged guilty, More abandons argument of any kind, and instead expresses a wish. He imagines a future reconciliation between himself and his judges: even though Paul was present at the stoning of Stephen as one of his persecutors, now Paul and Stephen are saints together in heaven; so too, More says to his judges, he hopes that "we may yet hereafter in heaven merrily all meet together" (p. 250). More was executed at the Tower of London, by beheading, on 6 July 1535.

In Roper's representation at any rate, More displays many virtues under fire: he's well-informed, cool-headed in his own defense on a capital charge, and magnanimous in defeat. Not least, he is skillful in his treatment of texts. The text of the conversation reported in the indictment is unlikely to be true: Rich is not a credible witness. But even if the literal sense of the text of the indictment is accurate, it is not the full story. Genre constitutes meaning (so hypothetical arguments do not affirm anything); and *manner* also contributes to meaning (these hypothetical arguments were not made with malicious or traitorous intent). That is, the real sense of the text is not contained in the literal force of its words. More's argument moves from what the words mean (always various) to what his judges should take the words to mean. He reveals that interpretation that is both just and accurate is not a matter of the literal sense alone. Even if More did utter these words, his intention was not to contravene maliciously the terms of the statute. Once we take intention and circumstance into account, the written words mean something different. The sense of written verity is profoundly modified by unwritten, circumstantial verities.

More was by no means the only courtier in the reign of Henry VIII to face capital charges on the basis of a few words. Thomas Wyatt

was twice imprisoned in the years 1536 to 1541, and he escaped
death by an apparently very narrow margin in 1536. In 1541 he was
accused of "falsely, maliciously and traitorously" slandering the king.[5]
Wyatt asked his judges to consider the intention of the words he was
alleged to have uttered: their manner did not correspond to these adverbs. Besides, Wyatt goes on,

> it is a small thing in altering of one syllable either with pen or word
> that may make in the conceiving of the truth much matter or error.
> For in this thing "I fear," or "I trust," seemeth but one small syllable
> changed, and yet it maketh a great difference, and may be of an hearer
> wrong conceived and worse reported.[6]

This careful defense may never have been delivered, since Wyatt
was excused without trial, "yielding himself only to His Majesties
mercy."[7]

Wyatt's own poetry expresses the predicament of the Henrician
courtier, caught in a world of pretty much ubiquitous verbal mistrust.
His *Paraphrase of the Penitential Psalms*,[8] for example, recounts the fearful
isolation of the sinner, surrounded by enemies and abandoned not
only by "friends most sure wherein I set my trust"; the sinner is also,
disturbingly, abandoned by "mine own virtues": "reason and wit unjust / As kin unkind, were farthest gone at need." In place of any
source of succor, enemies surround the sinner, and the malice of
those enemies is, above all, verbal: "So had they place their venom
out to thrust / That sought my death by naughty word and deed. /
Their tongues reproach, their wits did fraud apply." Faced with this
ubiquitous verbal menace, the sinner is "deaf and dumb," "Like one
that hears not nor hath to reply / One word again."[9]

Henrician courtiers were not the only subjects of Henry VIII to
suffer intense and interrogatory scrutiny of their careless utterances.
The radical new jurisdictions required by Henry VIII's divorce de-

manded a strict program of surveillance. In 1534 the definition of high treason was for the first time explicitly extended to verbal utterance: it became an act of high treason to pronounce the king a heretic, schismatic, tyrant, infidel, or usurper of the crown "by express writing or words."[10] In April 1535 Henry's chief minister, Thomas Cromwell, gave some teeth to the legislation. He sent a letter to lay and ecclesiastical authorities throughout the kingdom, instructing them to arrest anyone promoting the jurisdiction of the Bishop of Rome.[11] Geoffrey Elton's book *Policy and the Police* amply documents, yet appears to admire, the effectiveness of this surveillance campaign; Elton reports that by June 1535 "the first task was now completed and the net strung over the realm: bishops active in proving themselves and moving their clergy, justices of the peace everywhere keeping an eye on the bishops" (p. 241).

Elton tells of the "readiness of all sorts of people to speak up and give evidence." One reason for the willingness of informers to volunteer incriminating information was, Elton feels confident, love of the king: "Far too many people spoke against their neighbors without the stimulus of either private malice or public fear to allow one to overlook the very real devotion to King and realm and authority which manifestly existed" (p. 371). There was also, of course, plenty of evidence of "the stimulus of . . . private malice," of private feuds gathering "fresh strength from the government's revolutionary policy" (p. 371). Whatever their motive (private malice or "devotion to the King"), informers responded vigorously to the call for information.

According to Elton, this was no "universal pall of terror," and besides, he says, "what seemingly shocked people was not the pillorying or executing of little men for talking too freely without meaning much by it, but the attacks on the great" (p. 371). Despite Elton's own plentiful evidence of damaging information ending up on Cromwell's desk, Elton does not imagine how "little men" may have felt about other "little men" being executed for "talking too freely without meaning much by it." Elton's sympathy instead goes to the bureaucrat Cromwell, with such an overflowing in-tray.[12] "If there was terror," Elton declares, "it existed in the mind only" (p. 374).[13]

In short, there is plentiful evidence that the environment in which Henrician writers, readers, listeners, and speakers wrote, read, listened, and spoke was pervasively menacing.[14] Words with either political or religious import were easily vulnerable to malicious readings that stripped them of their personal circumstance. Such words could be manipulated as impersonal weapons against those who uttered them. With their mitigating circumstance removed, the literal sense of words exposed speakers and writers to the whim of predators, both local and distant. This system, no less than the invasive and much more efficient surveillance systems of the modern era, actively *desires* discourse to be stripped of its circumstance. For, thus stripped, the literal sense (or what the words might mean) can be wielded to power's desire—can be wielded to, in the words of Cromwell in his letter demanding that seditious speakers be arrested, "our further pleasure."[15] Stripping words of their unwritten circumstance is to effect a redistribution of interpretive power: no longer does the aura of the utterer inform interpretation of the utterance, in an environment of trust. Instead informers and judges govern utterances at will, in an exercise of interest and power. All that is needed by the predatory powerful is the simple, literal sense.

Beyond the specific dangers of political and religious utterance, early Tudor England was also, of course, grappling with the challenges of other forms of powerful textual impersonality. The relatively new textuality of print was at the same time commanding and thoroughly impersonal. It was commanding not least because its power of reproduction was so immeasurably greater than that of manuscript reproduction; it was impersonal because it was so much more uniform than the system of manuscript transmission. Texts that were reproduced in vastly greater numbers, with much higher levels of identity one to the other (and therefore much higher levels of impersonality), claimed new forms of recognition and respect. Those new levels of uniformity and impersonality contributed powerfully to the simplification of jurisdictions in England and Wales, in, for example, both law and liturgy.[16] Modernity is nothing if not the "rationalization" of complex, smaller, and disjunctive jurisdictions into simpler, larger, and unified jurisdictions. The impersonal technology of print makes that process of rationalization practicable; and the process of rationalization itself heightens the sometimes fearful impersonality of its textual instruments.

The effect of that new technology is easy to imagine but difficult to calibrate. The effect of the censorship is much more specific; its force can be calibrated in any number of early Tudor documents where the force of incriminating words is being underlined. Stripping words of circumstance amounts, in effect, to stripping them of adverbial force, or manner. A statement spoken hypothetically, jokingly, ironically, allegorically—all such statements are now up for grabs. Stripping words of their adverbial force is to strip the discursive realm of a kind of faith.[17] It neutralizes, that is, a civilized readiness to entertain the ever-present possibility of *difference* in meaning between what was uttered and what was meant. In an interpretive environment deprived of circumstance, what is uttered is what is meant; the literal sense is the only sense. Any faith that the speaker or writer may have meant something different is banished.

When the grounds of verbal faith have collapsed, the protocols of interpretation loom menacingly. Questions regarding interpretation themselves become urgent, in all contentious fields of discourse. In the early sixteenth century this was no less true for evangelicals than it was for those defending the established Church.

In this predicament of semiotic fragility, one powerful response was that of evangelicals. As we have seen, instead of questioning the cruel impersonality of the literal sense, they passionately embraced that impersonality. They appealed to the absolute solidity and incontrovertible clarity of one locus of the literal sense, the text of Scripture, because that was written by God. They also appealed to a God who alone could verify meaning by access to an interiority now wholly impenetrable by human intelligence. In the same passage of the *Penitential Psalms* discussed earlier, Wyatt describes the appalling situation of David, surrounded by pitiless and ferocious courtly tongues and abandoned by his own reason. David articulates the one source of understanding left: "O Lord, thou know'st the inward contemplation / Of my desire. Thou knowest my sighs and plaints. / Thou know'st the tears of my lamentation / Cannot express my heart's inward restraints."[18] All exterior signs are now susceptible of suspicious readings, and only God can be relied upon to read the inner text of the heart.

A world in which the counters of secular faith, such as words and gestures, have been entirely devalued is equally a world in which faith rises to the position of prime spiritual category. This is as true of sixteenth-century England as it was of late fourth-century Rome,[19] or as it is of twenty-first-century America. High levels of faith are constant in all societies (the conduct of everyday life is impossible without it). The collapse of faith in the secular realm produces extreme commitments to religious faith. It is precisely when faith in the conduct of political life has collapsed that revolutionary spiritualities of "faith alone" rise rapidly and aggressively to prominence.

Of course those movements also tend to preserve traces of the profound *collapse* of faith from which they have arisen: after all, evangelical readers insisted on the explicit, written covenants in Scripture as the sure rock of their faith. Contracts are the product of a lack of faith, of a need to have everything written. The "faith alone" culture is, as we saw in Chapter 3, symptomatic of the "no faith" culture.

In this environment of urgent discursive danger and interpretive fragility, were there alternatives to evangelical reformulations of faith? There were, and these alternatives established the grounds of meaning in legal as much as religious discourse. I began this chapter with reference to More's legal trial with the aim of stressing three things. First, disputes over meaning in the sixteenth century (as in fact in any literate society) are no "academic" matter; or rather the academic matter of interpretation was often, in legal as much as scriptural fields, a matter of life and death. Second, disputes over sixteenth-century Biblical reading were inflected by a larger interpretive environment in which the production of meaning was under pressure in many fields.[20] Finally, More approached Biblical meaning not as a theologian, but as a lawyer extremely well informed in current theological disputes. More's legal approach allows him to see with much more rapidity than the theologians the primacy of reading and interpretation in any debate with Lutherans. And his experience as a lawyer leads him directly to much deeper social, historical, and institutional implications of reading practice than his ecclesiastical peers were capable of proposing.

It's true that More's understandings of textuality and of reading were produced within specific, scriptural debates. At their broadest reach, however, More's arguments offer an alternative to a variety of textual impositions and receptions characteristic of early modernity. That said, it's also true that he was unlikely to win this debate: for More's profound position demands that we take verbal, pre-textual circumstance into account. But in the new environment of polemics conducted in print, with print's new and demanding impersonality, debate had itself become a written phenomenon. As More fought in print, and as he fought by extensive, precise quotation of the printed works of his enemies, he was fighting in a mode that ran counter to his persuasion that intuitive and/or oral pre-texts are the real determiners of meaning.[21] More's polemical works were fighting, that is, under a debilitating handicap: the formal *manner* of encounter into which he was drawn ran directly counter to the *content* of the position to which he was most deeply committed. Although he fought in printed texts, he believed that only oral or unwritten context made sense of written texts.[22]

Unlike their continental contemporaries who took up the fight against Lutheranism, Fisher and More quickly understood that the central issue between Lutherans and their enemies was reading. As More says in the *Confutation of Tyndale's Answer* (1532–33), "All the question for the more part riseth . . . not upon the scripture self, but upon the construction thereof." No one is arguing about what's scriptural or not, but only about "the true sense and right understanding" of Scripture.[23] Whatever the theological issue raised by Lutherans, the attempted resolution quickly became a matter of scriptural reading, precisely because Lutherans claimed authority only from Scripture. Unless the opponents of Luther and his followers could develop an account of the place of Scripture within Catholic practice, they were doomed to lose.

The so-called "controversialists" (Romanist defenders of the papal Church against Luther) were slow to realize the significance of the status of Scripture, as was the official Church itself. Certainly some early opponents of Luther expressed their bewilderment as they attempted to pin him down with written authority. Already in 1519 Jerome Emser complained that, while Luther set himself up as a judge, he refused to be judged by any known authority: if an opponent cites canon law and the decretals, he (Luther) calls them "cold," and even the Fathers of the Church are dismissed as "mere men." If, on the contrary, "I defeat him with the gospels, he will simply say I haven't understood him properly."[24]

Despite these exasperated expressions of impatience with Luther's textual tactics, the major early attacks on Luther do not broach either his soteriology or his scripturalism. The papal bull excommunicating Luther, *Exsurge Domine* (15 June 1520), for example, has nothing to say about either of these topics. It has a good deal to say, as is characteristic of this early stage of the encounter with Lutheranism, about indulgences, the sacraments, and papal authority.[25] David Bagchi, the most recent commentator on the early opponents of Luther, concludes that overall, "the hierarchically ordered cosmos of the Pseudo-Aeropagite was a central feature of the controversialists' approach to Luther."[26] Most of them were theologians, wrote in Latin, and wrote only one treatise (precisely because it was dangerous to attack Luther under a papal curia that did not support and, astonishingly, was ready to distrust those who engaged in the dispute).[27]

By 1545, however, the place of Scripture in the debate with Luther had changed. Scripture was very high on the agenda of the Council of Trent. The fourth session of the first meeting declares that, while Scripture is the source of all salutary truth, the true path to salvation is contained both in sacred Scripture and in the "non-written traditions that, received by the apostles from the mouth of Christ himself, and transmitted as if by hand to hand by the apostles, under the dictation of the Holy Spirit, have come down to us."[28] The same decree declares that the Latin Vulgate is the authentic version of Scripture.[29]

In each respect, Thomas More differs from the other controversialists. He was not a theologian, nor even a priest; he wrote the majority of his works against Lutheran doctrine in English; he wrote many more than one anti-Lutheran tract; he did not make any sustained reference to the divine right of the Pope;[30] he did not defend (or attack) figural allegory; he defended the existence of vernacular scripture;[31] and, above all, he was a long way ahead of the lumbering official Church's recognition of the primary importance of reading in the entire debate. More recognized the significance of the issue of scriptural reading and authority from the very beginning.

Already in the first version of the *Responsio ad Lutherum* (1523),[32] More engages the question of Scripture more thoroughly than his brief required. What was his brief? In 1522 Henry VIII had published his own response to Lutheranism, the *Assertio Septem Sacramentorum*,[33] a treatise that may have been ghost-written by More himself.[34] Though a professional piece of theological work, the *Assertio* does not get to grips with the full measure of Lutheranism. Instead it makes defenses, again characteristic of this first phase of the confrontation, of indulgences, of Purgatory, of papal authority, and, above all, of the sacraments. Only in passing does it make reference to the status of Scripture, with undeveloped arguments in favor of unwritten verities.[35]

Luther replied, abusively, to Henry also in 1522.[36] As it was beneath a monarch's dignity to become engaged in dispute, and especially abusive dispute, it seems likely that More was commissioned to respond, abusively, to Luther's response (even if More himself assumes masks for both versions of the *Responsio*).[37] More completed one version in February 1523, which was not published until December of that year.[38] The second, enlarged version was probably written before the end of September 1523.

Good lawyer that he was, More observed both his brief and the appropriate rhetorical level. In the first version of the *Responsio*, he restricts himself to rebuttal of Luther's *Contra Henricum*, but even there he expands on the question of unwritten verities, while following Henry on the sacraments.[39] Having cited Luther's words to the effect that only Scripture and no human inventions can be authoritative,[40] More (after some strikingly vituperative and brilliantly imagined preliminaries) mounts a rapid and full-scale attack on Luther's understanding of Scripture's authority. He cites the passages from the *Assertio* itself that defend unwritten verities, and concludes that the king

> points out that many things were said and done and taught by Christ which are not recorded by any of the evangelists, which are not contained in any writings of the apostles, not repeated in any scriptural text. Since his associates held these details fresh in their memory, however, they have been passed on successively, as though from hand to hand, since the time of the apostles and have come all the way down to us. He also shows that the catholic church . . . is taught and governed by the Holy Spirit.[41]

These formulations may have been the very ones that ended up in the Tridentine decree cited above,[42] but the concepts defending unwritten verities would soon become routine in anti-Lutheran polemic.[43]

Despite using the king's words, which may in fact have been his own, as his cover, More now moves out from behind the king's voice. He expands the argument for unwritten verities by enlisting key scriptural texts that would soon become crucial weapons in the debate. More cites Christ's parting words to the disciples, as recorded in John 16:13: "When the Spirit, the Paraclete, comes He will lead you into all truth."[44] More insists on the unwritten quality of the promised guidance by the Holy Spirit: Christ did not promise that the Holy Spirit would write, or even that he would speak; rather, Christ promised that the Spirit "will incline you inwardly and by His inspiration direct your hearts into all truth." That text is sustained by citation of Christ's last words as cited in Matthew 28:20: "I am with you even unto the consummation of the world."[45]

Having adduced his key textual exhibits for unwritten verities, More develops the argument by casting doubt on the alternative, that of textual truth and only textual truth. In part he insists on the partiality and fragility of the textual tradition of Scripture: the fact that Paul wrote was an accident of history; he would not have written his epistles had he been able to speak to his addressees personally; many of his epistles are lost; of those that are extant, some are incorrectly or ambiguously translated. More also points out that there is disagreement about the literal sense of Paul's texts: there is "incessant controversy about their meaning" (*de sensu certatur incessanter*).[46] Arguments based solely on the literal sense will never end: "The man who admits nothing but the evident scriptures will never lack pretext for denying what he wishes and for asserting what he pleases."[47]

If truth is partly unwritten, and if there is in any case dispute about the literal sense, More, like all the other controversialists, must adduce some locus for that truth.[48] At this point More introduces what is already a familiar *topos* and text used by evangelicals themselves, the concept of the Law being written on the heart.[49] As we saw in Chapter 4, evangelicals repeatedly evoke the words and text of Hebrews 8:10 and 10:16: "I will put my laws upon their hearts and upon their minds I will write them." Just as God wrote the first law in stone and eternally, so too, according to More, will he "write the new law inwardly by the finger of God on the book of the heart."

Both evangelicals and anti-Lutheran controversialists, that is, drew on exactly the same support text to locate the scriptural text of highest authority. This was an immaterial text, written not on "harder material" but, as More says, on the "most pliant" (*materia . . . mollissima*) of the heart itself.[50] Each side clearly needed this anterior text, precisely because each side disagreed with the other about the meaning of the material text. For More, however, there is no contradiction in laying claim to this interior and prior text. Evangelicals, as we have seen, claimed stridently that all scriptural truth was wholly available in the accessible and incontrovertible literal text. Only under pressure did they retreat to the anterior text written on the heart. More, by contrast, is in no way embarrassed to lay claim to this "unwritten" text. After all, he posits from the beginning that texts, however important, are but fragile bearers of truth; they exist in tandem with other, often unwritten carriers of meaning and trust, the sum of which can be expressed by the metaphor of a scriptible and legible heart.

More does not leave the question of Scripture in the *Responsio* there, but enough has been said to show that he recognized the significance of the issue of Scripture from his first public encounter with Luther. His defense of unwritten verities is, however, more developed and subtle in the *Dialogue Concerning Heresies* (published in 1529, followed by the second edition in 1531).[51] In the *Dialogue* More penetrates the activity of how we make sense of any texts as we read. From our engagement as readers of sacred texts, More develops an understanding of both institutions and history.

As was probably the case with the *Responsio*, the *Dialogue* was commissioned as well. In 1528 Cuthbert Tunstal, the Bishop of London, promulgated a license for More to read books adjudged heretical, imported from Germany but translated into English, in order that he, More, should compose a reply for the "simple and unlearned" ("simplicibus et idiotis hominibus").[52] More's *Dialogue* was the result. The *Dialogue* promises to offer more illumination than the *Responsio*, not least because its very form is more promising than that of the *Responsio*, which was directly aimed at Luther in vituperative mode. The *Dialogue*, by contrast, is an extended conversation between "More" and a young man of Lutheran tendency. The young man is profoundly stimulated by, but as yet undecided about, the "new learning." Contrary to More's commission to write for the simple and unlettered, however, the young man as depicted is not at all simple or unlearned.

As we saw in Chapter 2, John Fisher made a conciliatory offer to any Lutheran disciple in his sermon of 1526. He promised a dialogue and space for free discussion: if the disciple should wish to come to him in confidence, then Fisher promises to spare him the time "to hear the bottom of his mind." The disciple will hear Fisher's thoughts in return. The playing field will be even: "And I trust in our Lord that finally we shall so agree that either he shall make me a Lutheran, or else I shall induce him to be a Catholic and to follow the doctrine of Christ's church."[53] In the *Dialogue*, More creates the fictional scene for precisely this dialogic model.

The *Dialogue* consists of the written record of four conversations between Chancellor More and a young scholar, sent to More by one of his friends in the provinces. More's friend clearly admires the young man; he has employed him as a tutor to his sons, and regards him as a friend. He also tells More that the young man is very bright: he's possessed of a superb memory, has a "merry wit," and is not at all tongue-tied (1:25/24–31).

The text opens with three preliminaries: an address to More's readers, explaining why he has written and published a record of his conversation; full citation of the letter of introduction regarding More's young interlocutor, sent by More's friend; and full citation of a letter from More back to the friend, written after the dialogue. Then begins the *Dialogue* proper, which is divided into four books. The books measure conversation sessions, and the first and last two books are each punctuated by the sharing of meals. Between the conversations recorded in the first two and the last two books, a fortnight's break intervenes, during which time the young scholar returns to visit old friends at his former university.

Exactly why the young man has been sent to see More is not made entirely explicit at first: there are some people in the locality of More's older friend who talk very strangely of letters sent from London by a priest or two. It is soon abundantly clear, however, that the young man is exactly the well-educated and intelligent kind of person who might be inspired by the evangelical program. After their initial meeting, More confesses in his letter to the friend, he had initially suspected that the young man was, "as young scholars be sometime prone to new fantasies, fallen into Luther's sect" (1:34/29–30). But it's also as if the older friend wants to hear what More has to say about the new religion: he has sent the young man because he can't come himself; he knows the young man's memory is prodigious; and he trusts the young man to report accurately.

Despite some doubts, trust surrounds and undergirds the text of the dialogue at almost every point. The older friend has "confidence and trust" in both More and the young man (1:25/20); that trust is reciprocated. The dialogue is a true dialogue: the older friend tells More that the young man is to speak frankly, saying "what him list" (what he desired), and not retreating before More's authority or his arguments "but if [unless] he be borne back with [by] reason" (1: 26/1–2). More should speak to the young man as he would to his older friend. Writing to his friend after the dialogue, More expresses his confidence that the young man will have "faithfully" made a "plain and full report" of the conversation (1:26/19). The conversation is represented as taking place not in official sites, but rather in More's domestic environment at Chelsea, in his study or garden. It's true that, as Chancellor, More did detain and interrogate suspected "heretics" on his own property,[54] but the conversations of the *Dialogue* are no interrogation; this is a friendly, frank dialogue interspersed with hospitality, conducted in an environment of trust.

That trust surrounds the text of the *Dialogue*. Texts are insufficient records of the real event, which here is conversation, but we rely on the texts as second best in a structure of trusting acts. The letter the older friend sends to More is a "letter of credence," a standard term for a letter of recommendation, but one whose formal title has resonance in this context of texts deriving from and reproducing trust. The very text of the *Dialogue* generates trust in a prior event, and itself demands a certain trust. More clearly emphasizes that direct conversation is preferable to texts, but he signals equally that texts confirm and give credence to conversations. The older friend would certainly have preferred to be present at the dialogue rather than to read it; and the young man will certainly have given a true report. More, in consultation with friends, has nevertheless decided to write it up all the same: "and surely, sir, in this point ye may make yourself sure that I shall never willingly deceive your trust" (1:27/1–2).

So the text is both a useful and a trustworthy record of a conversation. But it is also a bulwark against other, distrustful conversations: in his opening address to his readers, More tells us why he wrote the conversation. Some parts of the matter are intricate, and need to be attentively read and considered. Moreover, it's not impossible that the young man's report of these treacherous matters should get into the wrong hands, and it's not absolutely inconceivable that the young man might be improperly suborned. Although More trusts the good will of the young man, it's not impossible that he might purposely "mangle the matter" for some "sinister favor" (1:21/30–22/10), in which case the young man's master (More's friend) would be unable to judge the truth of the matter. But a handwritten record of the conversation is also insufficient: what if outright heretics got hold of this manuscript and printed it maliciously? So More now decides, after consultation with friends who have read the book (always following the majority view), to publish the dialogue as a printed book in order to provide a secure record.

This rather elaborate series of screens and preliminaries to More's

Dialogue, as with the elaborate preliminaries to other works by More, repays close attention. In this case More is making a profound point about the form of the *Dialogue*, a point that we have already seen him make in his treason trial: that texts are insufficient. They are a record to which one can appeal, and they might stabilize the evidence from which meaning will derive. But they only work productively between trusting partners. The full meaning of texts is not available in their literal sense, or on the page; that meaning is dependent instead on layers of necessarily unwritten trust. It wouldn't be trust if it were written.

This formal point about the *Dialogue* as a text is in my view at the core of More's argument in the *Dialogue* about the text of Scripture. And the reading of Scripture is at the heart of the *Dialogue*. By the time we read More's prefatory letter to his friend, we understand that the young man is unquestionably drawn to evangelical religion; he is also properly exercised about persecution of both evangelicals and their books. He's especially concerned about the recent burning of Tyndale's New Testament. All this persecution is for no other purpose, the young man is reported as saying to the Chancellor, than "to keep out of the people's hands all knowledge of Christ's gospel, and of God's law except only as the clergy themselves list [desire] now and then to tell us" (1:29/1–4). Convinced that the clergy are determined to pull Scripture out of the people's hands only to prevent perception of the truth, the young man wonders if what Luther wrote was so bad after all. The young scholar cites precedents against violent Christian persecution of heresy. He clearly thinks this persecution is offensive for its violence, and also corrupt because it's self-interested.

Above all, though, the young intellectual cares for Scripture: he's swept away by a new experience of reading. He no longer cares for the other liberal arts, for "man, he said, hath no light but of holy scripture" (1:33/33–34). He learns many scriptural passages by heart, and is exhilarated by new, active possibilities of interpretation: he has no patience for the glosses of interpreters, who distract him from the "great sweetness in the text itself"; instead he sets himself to search out "the sentence [meaning] and understanding" of Scripture "as far as he might perceive by himself" (1:33/33–34). Later in Book One the young man again reveals himself as a passionate reader: will Chancellor More prohibit the reading in which "a man has so great affection to the study of scripture alone that he for the delight thereof feeleth little savor in anything else"?

Again in Book Three, on return from "the university" (presumably Cambridge, much more influenced than Oxford by Lutheranism), the young man reports his conversations with fellow students. The question of Scripture will not go away. Though almost all of the fellow students were persuaded by More's arguments for the orthodox position, one student took exception with regard to one single, important point: "For ought [anything] I could bend upon him he could never agree that the faith of the Church out of scripture should be as sure and bind us to the belief thereof as the words of scripture" (1:248/24–27).

The question of Scripture is, in short, not a theoretical matter in the *Dialogue*; it's informed by passionate reading experience and conviction. But neither is More's treatment of the matter simply a repetition of standard arguments about unwritten verities. More gets in very close to the actual processes of reading and interpreting, and he moves out from there to larger questions of trust, institutions, and history. *The Dialogue Concerning Heresies* is in good part a dialogue about the licit function, and limitations, of sacred texts.

The actual discussion of Book One of the *Dialogue* begins with a nexus of orthodox practices to which evangelicals objected: pilgrimages, images, and belief in miracles (1:12–19).[55] It then moves on to

Scripture (1:20–31),[56] a discussion that tips increasingly into a discussion of the Church. In Book Two the young man acknowledges everything that has been argued about the interdependence of Scripture and Church in Book One, but then he immediately fires a torpedo at More's ecclesiological assumptions: what if More is right about the fact that the Church cannot err, and cannot mistake Scripture, but wrong about which Church he is talking about? What, that is, if More is in fact talking about a hypocritical, fake Church, and not the True Church? In the rest of Book Two More defends the proposition that the Church he has in mind is plausibly the True Church; he recurs to questions of saints, pilgrimage, images, relics, and miracles in the course of that defense.

Book Three takes place after the young man has returned from a fortnight spent with his university friends. The discussion again begins from the ever-resurgent question of Scripture and writing, but quickly moves to the more contemporary issues that were raised by the young man in the Prologue: the abjuration of Thomas Bilney (who was not burned until August 1531), including the role of witness in heresy trials (3:2–7); the burning of Tyndale's New Testament (3:8–10); the Wycliffite Bible, which includes discussion of both Arundel's Constitutions (1409) and the controversial case of Richard Hunne (3:14–15); and More's strong though guarded defense of translating Scripture into English (3:14–16). Book Four broadens the horizon to continental Europe, as More prepares to defend the persecution of heretics. More discusses Luther's opinions, including predestination (4:1–6; 10–12); the 1524 Peasants' War in Germany and the sack of Rome in 1527 (4:7); and, finally, the persecution of heretics past and present, even at the stake (4:13–18).

This structure has some obvious sense, and some initial puzzles. The most obvious factor is the need to create a certain distance: More clearly begins with more theoretical issues, and moves only in the last two books to contemporary, applied cases. Thus the structure and the form of the *Dialogue* are both designed to create space, moving only in the final pages to the cruel exigencies of the present and future. More also creates wider horizons in the relation of the last two books to each other: he begins with English cases and then broadens the purview in the final book to the larger European scene, before returning to his final and grievous defense of persecution. Those structuring principles are clear; but why should More begin the *Dialogue* with pilgrimages, images, and miracles? And if Scripture is the central question here, why should discussion of Scripture be sandwiched between discussion of popular practice and ecclesiology?

In my view the answers to these questions are as follows: More prepares the ground for his cardinal argument that reading is dependent on faith by leading the reader through faith-dependent practices (especially miracles); and for More there can be no independent discussion of Scripture precisely because Scripture is not, for More, an independent entity. Scripture is only ever a partial and subsidiary resource of the Church. Outside that set of resources, an independent Scripture would collapse. Both these answers will gain in substance if we turn now to the *Dialogue*'s arguments concerning reading.

By More's account, texts do not generate faith, but are dependent on a prior faith. He tackles these issues in Book 1:24. There More poses the hypothetical case of a child's scriptural education; the young man (himself a tutor, after all) affirms that the hypothetical child should be put to the study of Scripture very early on. But should the child not first learn his Creed in his mother tongue, More asks. The young man agrees that the child should learn the Creed first, but immediately denies that the Creed should be used by the child to "judge and examine holy scripture thereby" (1:133/31).

Let us then, suggests More in quietly forensic mode, leave aside "this Christian child of ours," and consider instead the case of a "good old idolater" who had never heard of any god but the man in the moon whom he (the idolater) worshipped "every frosty night." What if this fellow were presented with a Bible translated into the vernacular: would he learn the articles of the faith from it? The young man replies that this would not be impossible, but More presses him. What if the whole thing struck him as lies? Response: plain reading of the book would teach him otherwise. This would be true, More agrees, "were it all one to read a thing and learn a thing" (1:134/14–15). What if another book, of likely truth but in fact untrue, were presented to the old infidel: how should he believe that the Bible, with all its miracles, is true? "Nay," replies the young man, "that must he needs believe or else he can perceive nothing" (1:134/19–20).

More now moves in to capture his territory: "Well . . . then is there one point of faith, one great lesson to be learned, without the book, that must be learned somewhere either by God or man, or else the whole book will do us little service?" (1:134/21–23). But even if the idolater did believe that it was all true, would he discover for himself the articles of our faith, and, if so, how long would it take him to do so? While we wait for him to find them out, let's return, says More, to take another look at "our good little godson, the boy that we christened right now." Would he need only his Creed before he started on Scripture? The young man thinks so, whereupon More imagines the little boy coming across this passage (Psalm 81:6, Vulgate): "Gods ye be all, and children of the high God." Will the child be led astray by that text? More gently pushes the young man into recognizing that the child will need the Creed to understand the figural meaning of some texts. He will need to use the marble cutter's leaden ruler, or "Lesbian rule." This celebrated concept is drawn from legal discussions of practical reasoning, according to which the rule of law should be adapted to the specifics of the case in hand. Likewise, in the *Dialogue*, the marble is the Creed and the Scripture the leaden ruler, to be bent according to the shape of belief, rather than vice versa (1:135/33).[57]

More now expands on the scriptural self-education of the little boy, who is already using reason in the application of prior belief in his reading. He is, to say the least, unlikely to avoid any number of errors (More uses the example of the Trinity) in his scriptural reading, if he were to read without the articles of faith (1:137/7–16). We don't read as a *tabula rasa*, in merely passive reception of textual content; instead, we construct meaning at every point by hypothetical suppositions applied to, and not supplied by, the text.

These observations about the priority of faith in reading, observations drawn as much from scriptural as from legal practice, require from More an account of the source of this faith. Faithful, unwritten intuitions about the pre-textual truths that produce meaning as we read are not in the least nonevidential. On the contrary, as a lawyer More understands that *all* knowledge is dependent on faith of one kind or another; deciding where we chose to place our faith depends on choosing the best evidence. And that's a matter of the most credible witnesses. In the case of miracles, for example, More acknowledges that someone who has not witnessed a miracle is not bound to believe it. But such a person might seem negligent "if they nothing inquire" into such a question; or if they

> have diligently made ensearch, then must it needs be that they have heard of [by] so many told, and rehearsed by the mouths and the writing of so good and credible persons, that they seem unreasonably suspicious if they think altogether lies that so many true men or men like [likely] to be true so faithfully do report. (1:63/19–24)

A faithful reading in no way dismisses evidence; on the contrary, one puts one's faith in the most credible witness. Just as More tried to discredit the witness in his trial on a capital offense, so too, as would any lawyer, he asks his interlocutor to think about the credibility of witnesses. In the case of reading Scripture, he tries to persuade the young man that all interpretive acts imply belief, at some point, in credible witnesses.

If pre-textual, faithful commitment to credible witnesses is part of any reading experience, More's pragmatist program must locate those credible witnesses. Like the twentieth-century pragmatist interpreters who located the engine of reading in the "interpretive community," More located it in a community that was both historical and present.

Earlier in Book One the young man affirms that Christ left Scripture to his Church, in which Christians could "sufficiently see both what they should believe and what they should do." Having supplied this sufficient source of truth, God, by the young man's account, "letteth them alone therewith, without any special cure [concern] upon their faith and believe" (1:113/25–30). Reading is a sufficient record of an absent God, and a sufficient guide for wayward Christians. More disagrees. As he does consistently in the *Dialogue*, he defends his position with the weapon of scriptural authority, in order to control that authority.[58]

Why did Christ say "I am with you all the dayes until the end of the world" (Matthew 28:20)? What purpose would Christ's ongoing presence serve unless he "should not keep [preserve] his right faith and believe [belief] in his Church"? (1:114/6–7). The young man confidently replies that Christ's presence is a *textual*, and only a textual, presence. Then why, More asks, did Christ never leave a book of his own making behind, as Moses and the prophets did? (1:114/32–35). Besides, the New Testament was not yet written when Christ uttered these words. When Christ said that his words would not pass away (Matthew 24:35), he was speaking of his "promises made in deed, as his faith and doctrine taught by mouth and inspiration"

(1:115/20–21). He was not referring to written Scripture, of which some parts, More asserts, are already lost, perhaps more than we know. Other books of Scripture are textually corrupt. When Christ promised to inspire the apostles as they stood in judgment before kings (Luke 21:12–15), he was not promising remembrance of written Scripture, but "words new given them by god inspired" (1:116/6).

More then presses home his understanding of the insufficiency of Scripture. If the young man is correct in thinking that Scripture is all we have of Christ's ongoing presence, then did God, More asks, also leave behind the "right understanding of holy scripture"? (1:116/28). If God didn't leave this necessary supplement behind, then Scripture would be about as useful as "a pair of spectacles" to "a blind friar." Happily God did leave this understanding, the young man confidently states, in Scripture itself; we arrive at the true understanding by collation of one scriptural text with another. He proposes, that is, the *scriptura sui ipsius interpres* concept. More has him readily acknowledge, nevertheless, the attestable existence of many readers for whom Scripture has somehow not managed to interpret itself correctly, and who have, as a result, fallen into heretical error.

In the wider dispute, either side must recognize the possibility of heretical reading, since each side considers the other heretical. This irreducible and mutually acknowledged fact of disagreement over scriptural interpretation drives both positions. As we saw in Chapter 4, evangelicals, under pressure from the fact that the open text of Scripture was not open to all, redefined the group who were capable of understanding the self-sufficiency of Scripture. The elect, that is, had the text already written on their hearts. Thus evangelicals were appealing to an exclusivist notion of textual authorization. More, by contrast, appeals to an inclusivist notion. For him, the meaning of Scripture is authorized within the historically continuous and inclusive institution of the Church. Scripture may be the letter, but the historically continuous institution of the Church is, as it were, the envelope in which the letter arrives, and which makes sense of the letter. The fullest "Scripture" is not the canon of written texts; it is, instead, the "substance of our faith itself, which our Lord said he would write in men's hearts" (1:143/5–7).

How can we have confidence in the Church as the source of our pre-textual faith? More replies thus: Christ clearly wanted his Church to be continually in the world (Matthew 28:20), not sometimes there and sometimes not, "without any times between"; he also wanted his Church to be in possession of faith. If the Church had a continual existence and a continual possession of faith, then the Church also had continual possession of the "right understanding of scripture." This continuity is achieved by the influence of the Holy Spirit, informing readers across time: when reason fails to discriminate between competing texts, then the Holy Ghost, through grace, "should lead them into all truth" (John 16:13). Christ did not say that the Holy Ghost would write them the truth, nor tell them the whole truth by mouth, but that "he should, by secret inspiration, lead them into all truth." So, in addition to Scripture, "there is another present assistance" to ensure that the Church does not err in the understanding of Scripture.

"We are arrived back," More remarks to his young interlocutor, "to the same point again that ye would so fain flit from" (that is, the historical existence of an institution with continuous presence and an ever-fresh, inspired understanding of Scripture) (pp. 117–119). More and his young partner in dialogue have arrived back, that is, at a prior set of unwritten persuasions that make sense of the written. In particular, they have arrived back at the Church, without which we would not, More says elsewhere in the *Dialogue,* know the canon of Scripture in the first place. There were many gospels, but who could be sure which were the true ones? The Church, "by secret instinct of God [has] rejected the remnant and chosen out these four" gospels. "And therefore," he cites Augustine as saying, "I should not believe the gospel but if [unless] it were for the Church" (1:181/14–17 and 10–12).

Later in Book One the young man recurs to his opinion that Scripture can be interpreted from within Scripture: "Me thinketh [it seems to me] . . . the text is good enough and plain enough needing no gloss but if it be well considered and every part compared with other" (1:168/16–18). In this later instance, More proves that everything needs a gloss: "Hard it were," he says, "to find any thing so plain that it should need no gloss at all" (pp. 168/19–20). Everything needs a gloss, even two times two makes four. For two times two geese doesn't make four ganders—so even talk about geese needs a gloss, More says playfully, before moving to his serious point: that collation of scriptural texts is *itself* a gloss, whose principles of collation are not provided from within Scripture itself (pp. 168–169).

In short, More's position derives from the nature of reading itself. He makes no defense whatsoever of figural allegory, but rather goes deeper to reveal that all texts are in a sense allegorical: all texts "say one thing and mean another."[59] Texts do not and cannot sufficiently teach us how to read them. If they came with written instructions, then those instructions would themselves need written instructions. Pure textual transparency is impossible: no text can simply deliver its meaning of its own accord; all texts must find their voice within interpretive environments that draw on a range of unwritten, faithful intuitions. Those intuitions are based on decisions about credible witnesses and likelihood of evidence. In the case of Scripture, Scripture itself tells us that the Holy Spirit will continue to inspire our perception of Scripture, and the likeliest tradition for that ongoing inspiration is the institution of the Church, instituted by Christ and in possession of a continuous and long tradition.

※   In Chapters 3 through 6 of this book I explored the dark, energizing paradoxes of one extremely influential current of early modern reading. I now revisit each of those chapters on evangelical reading, armed with a More visiting card. In each case, More provides a less energizing but also a saner and profoundly historical view of scriptural meaning.

Chapter 3 examined the Lutheran doctrine of salvation and its immediate effect on reading. Lutheran reading promises the truth about one's salvation, but that promise can only be arrived at through detestation of oneself and the text, since the injunctions of the text can't be fulfilled. The point of injunctions, we remember, is not to encourage humans to fulfill them; on the contrary, injunctions are there to rub in the sheer depth of human incapacity. When they seem to mean "do this," they really mean "face it: you can't do this."

What does More make of this soteriology and its implications for reading? The *Dialogue* is primarily focused on Scripture and on the Church as Scripture's faithful pre-text. More does broach questions of predestination, however, in Book Four. He finds Luther's predestinarian position deeply shocking: that God, from the beginning of time, should have chosen or damned people; that works should be judged only in the light of God's acceptance and not at all by their worth—by this view God is, according to More, nothing short of vicious. It makes of God "the cause of all evil and such cruel appetite as never tyrant and tormentor had."[60] Nor is More slow to see the implications of predestination for reading Scripture:

> Now turn they the triacle [balm] of holy scripture quite into poison. For this false error once taken for truth, whereof should all scripture

serve? Whereof should serve the exhortations to good works if men neither any do, nor any can do, neither of themselves nor with the help of grace? . . . Whereof shall serve all the dehortations [dissuasive exhortations] and comminations and threats in scripture by which God calleth men from sin and evil works? (1:403/10–23)

Predestination makes a cruel and sadistic tyrant of God, and produces a Kafkaesque world of tormented uncertainty for readers. It is as if (to draw on a passage from the *Confutation*) God had made a written proclamation in such a way that only those to whom God had given "a secret privy knowledge" could read. All the others will want to read the proclamation, but are unable to discover its meaning for want of "that token which he kept from them." And because they don't have the token, God will "hurl stones at their heads because they fulfill it not."[61]

In Chapter 4 I examined the paradoxes of a literal sense whose claims so stridently excluded opacity or institutional mediation as to produce exactly the opposite of an open literal sense. Evangelical textuality turns out to depend on an invisible, secret text, and that text has an institutional status. By making such non-negotiable and extreme claims for the sufficiency of the literal sense, that is, evangelicals necessarily produced an anterior text, written on the heart, which made sense of the literal. And that anterior text turned out to be exactly coterminous with the institution of the True Church of the Elect.

In the present chapter I have already clarified More's profound opposition to overweening confidence in the literal sense. More is a textual pragmatist, for whom the sense of texts can be constructed only in the context of non-written, faithful (though credible) *préjugés*. Those pre-textual dispositions have an institutional source, in the Church. That said, More's defense of unwritten authority might seem to offer him pretty well unlimited ground for the formulation of that authority: whatever the Church says has to be right, unchecked by textual restraint.

Is More specific about the restraints on unwritten authority? He is, by reference to councils. Whereas Tyndale was profoundly hostile to councils, textual authority in More's Church derives from conciliar decision (not from papal supremacy). These differing estimations about the value of councils derive from different conceptions of the Church. Tyndale's Church is exclusivist and new; More's, by contrast, is inclusivist and old. Thus More quickly recognizes the idealist and exclusivist nature of the Lutheran Church. Lutherans must deny absolutely the material Church, and that total repudiation produces an idealist alternative Church: Lutherans "build up in the air a Church all so spiritual," peopled exclusively by the predestinate. This is a church, in the words of the young man, unknown to the world, but known only among the predestinate (1:198/24–26). This is a church of paradox, since it's made up only of the virtuous, whereas Luther knows that no one is virtuous (1:204/26–28).

More, in turn, repudiates that idealist, secret, and invisible Church, not least because it arrogantly collapses the rhythm of judgment and history into a single, complete moment. In his view, evangelicals move last things forward, creating a church of the elect here on earth, while More's orthodox Catholic position reserves that eschaton for the last days. For More, that is, the ultimate discrimination between the saved and the damned will only take place at the end of time; in the uncertain meanwhile, the Church is made up of all Christians. Absolute judgment is premature and presumptuous:

> The Church therefore must needs be the common, known multitude
> of Christian men good and bad together, while the Church is here in
> earth. For this net of Christ hath for the while good fishes and bad.
> And this field of Christ beareth for the while good corn and cockle, till

it shall at the day of dome be purified and all the bad cast out and only good remain. (1:205/4–10)

More's Church is known, not secret; visible, not invisible; inclusive, not exclusive. It contains "some sick, some hole, and all sickly" (1:205/26). The only people it rejects are heretics, whom it casts out "for fear of infection" (1:205/28).

This Church is not only visible, but it has a demonstrable history. In keeping with his lawyerly emphasis on credible evidence, More frequently recurs to arguments of probability regarding the Church, given its age. Christ's Church must be the oldest, he says (1:195/22–23). He asks his interlocutor how he comes to know that the matter of the Gospel is true. The young man articulates More's very point in his answer, relying on an account of faithful transmission of truth across time. God did not tell him that the Gospel is true directly, "mouth to mouth," but, he says,

. . . he hath told it to other in the beginning . . . and after that it was once known, the knowledge went forth fro man to man. And god hath so wrought with us that we believe it because the whole church hath always done so before our days. (1:180/32–38)

More believes in the judgment of history, partly because his Church has a demonstrable and long history (fifteen hundred years), a durability that God would not have permitted had that Church been erroneous. If, More says in the *Confutation*, the known Church has been so aberrant for eight hundred years, then "where hath been all this while the right congregation of Tyndale's Church?"[62]

Authority in that enduring historical institution is not located in a single person, and certainly not in the person of the Pope. More defended papal supremacy for the last time in his polemical works in the *Responsio* (1523). In that instance he was sustaining Henry VIII's rather premature defense of papal supremacy made in the *Assertio*, a defense from which More, according to Roper, had tried to dissuade the king.[63] The known Church's authority in the *Dialogue* resides, rather, in collective decisions made across time.

By More's accurate account, Tyndale distrusts conciliar decision, both of Parliament and of the Church: Church councils were not, he reports Tyndale saying, inspired by God, but only by "the wit and affections of men."[64] Although in the *Dialogue* there is no sustained discussion of councils, More does stress the centrality of consensual decision making. He does not, he insists to the young man, appeal to the judgment of only one or two learned men, but to "the consent and common agreement of the old holy fathers," and "the common consent of the church" (1:169/32). There is an element of grace in this position, but it is a grace that manifests itself in conciliar rather than personal experience; its authenticity can be proven only by its duration across the history of the Church.

More's sustained and explicit defense of councils grew stronger, indeed, as his distance from Henry VIII grew. By the time of the *Confutation of Tyndale's Answer* (1532–33), More had resigned the Chancellorship and was writing as a private citizen. In this text More defends councils much more forcefully. He cites Robert Barnes's objection to councils, that they err because they are merely representative, and do not constitute the whole Church, which consists of the Church of the Elect.[65] More's imagination immediately takes off, picturing the council hall that will be big enough to accommodate the whole Church, and so satisfy Barnes's call for a council that is not restricted to representatives. Salisbury Plain should serve, as long as it be fitted with a roof in case of rain. Everyone must be welcome, including all those judged heretical by the Roman Church.[66] This inclusive council would, of course, need to be imagined eight hundred years ago, before the Church fell into error, so let it be in the time of Saint Gregory (late sixth century). More presses the absurdity of the nonrepresentative council for a little longer than it deserves, before articulating his serious point about the necessity of representation in councils:

> General councils should be . . . not of the whole number of all Christian people, but of some such convenient number as conveniently might assemble, and the same, though it were not the whole Catholic Church indeed, but . . . only representative, should yet have the same authority and the same full credence given unto it, as though there were at it all the whole Christian people.[67]

In Chapter 5 I focused on the paranoia produced by relentless insistence on the literal sense. Such social distrust is everywhere answered by More's hermeneutics of credible, unwritten sources of confidence. More's hermeneutics is always, that is, underwritten by communal understanding.

Chapter 6 examined another dark paradox, that of a reading culture that prized historical integrity in so relentless a way as to produce a hollowing out and repudiation of history. For evangelicals, history was complete in its every moment; Scripture was complete at its inception; the True Church was always present in all its fullness. For More, by contrast, Scripture was never complete, and history does unfold. In sharp distinction from the evangelical position, writing is for More an essential part of the divine message, but not the whole. All writing has a historical existence, located within specific institutional and rhetorical situations that determine what is and is not written. This applies no less to scriptural writing than to nonscriptural.

More imagines his way rapidly into plausible historical scenarios in which scriptural texts were written in the first place. No evangelist or apostle ever sent the written testimony of faith to any nation unless they were first informed by word that the Church had an

existence in that country (1:144/26–29). And besides, the evange-
lists and apostles wrote in circumstances that were both dangerous
and rhetorically challenging, given the mixed nature of their intended recipients. They did not, accordingly, write everything down
(pp. 144–145). Paul, for example, did not write everything because
his audience was not prepared to tolerate the full truth: "I have given
you hitherto but milk and not strong meat" (1 Corinthians 3:2)
(1:145/30–31). Because Paul's audience was mixed, he wrote with appropriate rhetorical discretion, measuring his statement to the capacities of his readers.

In his *Bondage of the Will* Luther stridently dismisses a rhetorical understanding of Scripture, lambasting Erasmus for wishing to consider
the "times, persons, and ways in which the truth ought to be spoken."[68] More, in keeping with a powerful pre-Reformation tradition[69]
and with his own profoundly rhetorical culture,[70] does propose a rhetorical understanding of Scripture. That tradition applies not only
to the times, places, and persons in which and to whom Scripture
should be read; it also applies to the situations in which and the
audiences for whom the Scriptures were written in the first place.
In More's understanding, the rhetorical shaping that applies to any
other document applies to the writing of the Scriptures themselves;
very little transcends history.

Even God, by More's account, works rhetorically, by making his
revelation known variously, "from time to time" (1:146/19–25).[71] It's
not surprising that More should believe in a progressive revelation,
from an older to a newer dispensation. Nor is it surprising that he
should give credence, as he does, to the testimony of historical duration. What is surprising is his relaxed understanding of continu-
ing, progressive revelation. In the *Confutation*, for example, More argues that Tyndale gains nothing by insisting that the doctors of the
Church disagreed among themselves:

For God doth reveal his truths not always in one manner, but sometime he sheweth out at once . . . Sometime he sheweth it leisurely, suffering his flock to come and dispute thereupon, and in their treating of the matter, suffereth them with good mind and scripture and natural wisdom, with invocation of his spiritual help, to search and seek for the truth, and to vary for the while in their opinions, till that he reward their virtuous diligence with leading them secretly in to the consent and concord and belief of the truth by his Holy Spirit . . . So that in the mean while the variance is without sin.[72]

In short, we have two models of reading on offer. Tyndale proposes a form of fundamentalism, while More proposes a consensual, historically grounded account of reading. This reading practice is premised on the limitations of the literal sense, and is generated by trust. In the view of cultural history, however, More is regarded as the manic persecutor, whereas Tyndale is the forerunner of the Bill of Rights. How do we account for this?

One answer is that More actively promoted and engaged in the persecution of "heretics." In the final chapter I will ask whether or not he could have avoided doing that.

CHAPTER EIGHT

The Tragic Scene of Early Modern Reading

IN CHAPTERS 3 through 6 of this book I argued that evangelical culture of the first half of the sixteenth century produced an exclusivist, intolerant, persecutory, distrustful, and inevitably schismatic culture of reading. In the last chapter I presented Thomas More as contrastive in every way: he promoted a reading culture that recognized the fragilities of the literal sense; trust as the ground of an interpretive community; the inevitable immersion of texts in human history; and the function of capacious, historically durable institutions in managing unruly canonical texts.

More also promoted, however, the violent persecution of readers he defined as heretical. If John Fisher rightly diagnosed the intolerant persecutions that would flow from evangelical Bible culture,[1] More presents the obverse case, with its own ignoble history prior to, and well beyond, More himself: the Catholic persecutor of books and readers.[2]

In this chapter I ask whether or not More's very active embrace of persecution was inevitable. I argue that persecution was not the product of the reading culture that More so ably defined and defended; instead, both More and his evangelical opponents were the victims of a reading culture whose punishing disciplines were well beyond their control—that is, the victims of a textual virus of distrustful literalism. Both sides contracted this virus from a wider textual environment that was simultaneously compelling and imprisoning. Far from fleeing that textual contagion, evangelicals embraced their alien, energizing, and punishing text with a passion. In More's case, he contracted the virus by fleeing it. More turned into an exact replica of his intolerant and literalist opponents even as he fought them. In fact, he did so *by* fighting them. In short, both sides ended up mesmerized and exhausted by punishing versions of early modern reading and writing.

In the opening of the *Dialogue Concerning Heresies*, More has his young interlocutor persuasively attack the physical persecution of heretics. The young man reports that in many men's eyes it's unreasonable that simple and unlearned men, even if they have fallen into error, should, "in stead of teaching, be beaten cruelly with abjurations and open shame, with peril of burning also."³ Such persecution is also both unchristian and unhistorical, since "a good many good and well learned men thought plainly that the clergy . . . do contrary to the mildness and merciful mind of their master, and against the example of all the old holy fathers, in that they cause, for any error or wrong opinion in the faith, any man . . . to be put to death" (p. 31/ 15–20).

At the very end of the *Dialogue* More returns to these cardinal arguments, by far the most serious in the entire work. Initially he confirms them, in his own voice: Christ demanded that we "live after him [according to his example] in sufferance and patience" (p. 406/18); and, despite the frequency of "heresy" in the early centuries of the Church, a long list of Church Fathers is cited accurately to the effect that heretics were not then punished with corporal punishment. (The text makes no reference to later medieval examples of savage persecution for heresy, such as the Albigensian Crusade in the early thirteenth century.) In the early centuries of the Church, More confirms, there was no other punishment for heresy except argument and verbal confutation, either in dialogue or in writing; condemnation of heretical views by synods and councils; or, finally, excommunication (pp. 406–407).[4] The young man agrees, longing for a practice whereby all "violence and compulsion" would be expelled in both Christian and pagan contexts, and where "no man were constrained to believe but as he could be, by grace and wisdom and good words induced" (p. 407/27–28).

More evokes here the humanist vision he had himself expressed earlier in *Utopia*. Soon after his conquest of the island, King Utopus issues a decree "that it should be lawful for every man to favour and follow what religion he would."[5] Europeans bring two things to Utopia, Greek learning and Christianity. Both are readily appreciated, but the second introduces fanaticism: the Utopians quickly exile the Utopian convert to Christianity who becomes a Christian bigot (p. 270). Varieties of religious persuasion are permitted, and even heretics who oppose the broad terms of orthodoxy established by Utopus are allowed to defend their positions, within certain confines (pp. 272–277).

In the *Dialogue*, then, More voices persuasive arguments against the physical persecution of heretics, arguments that are in keeping with More's confidence in the historical tradition of the Church, expressed throughout the *Dialogue*. The last pages of the *Dialogue*, however, defend such persecution. What's different about this heresy that demands violent repression? Even if the Church were to leave heresy unchecked by violent repression, More declares his confidence in the Church's easy survival: just as Christianity grew with God's help in the early centuries of the Church, so too would the majority of Christians hold with the Church now (pp. 407–408).

So why persecute Lutherans? More's first response is the violence of the reformers themselves: if they had used less violence (More is referring to the Peasants' War in Germany of 1524–1525), then perhaps Christians might have used less violence toward them (p. 407/ 8–15). But—and this is his main defense—since the new heretics practice violence themselves, and do not allow Christ's faith to be preached, anyone who permits such a situation would be a "plain enemy to Christ" (p. 408/15).

This is a vulnerable argument in any case, but even more so when applied to More's English situation in 1529, where evangelicals were by no means in the ascendancy. It's true that the Reformation Parliament at the end of 1529 initiated currents that would eventually sweep More and his Church aside, but More was not confronted with anything like full-scale threat when he wrote the *Dialogue*. In our own case, More says, we should nip heresy in the bud, for "by covenant with them Christendom can nothing win" (p. 408/32–33). Contradicting his earlier statements about the lack of capital punishment for heretics in the early Church, More claims Augustine and Jerome as supporters of violent persecution of heretics, failing to point out that they did not recommend the death penalty (p. 409).[6] He then goes on to say that heresy has been punished by fire in every part of Christendom, including England, where heresy "hath long been punished by death in the fire" (p. 409/24). More is on firmer historical ground with regard to continental Western Christendom in the later medieval period, where the burning of heretics had indeed been practiced from the early eleventh century.[7] In England, however, the first statute for burning of heretics was, as More knew, of relatively recent date (1401).[8]

From these arguments More now shifts onto even weaker ground: he makes the case for just war, and then applies it to the defense against heresy, since heretics, if allowed to convert others, will produce "common sedition, insurrection and open war within the bowels of their own land" (p. 416/4–5). If the few trouble-makers are "well repressed," others will be less willing to follow; and talking heretics out of their heresy is doomed to failure (p. 416/9–13) because they are ineradicably devious and proud. More ends by arguing that Luther and Tyndale are worse than previous heretics (and that Tyndale is worse than Luther). He then brings in a pile of marked books for the young man to read, citing one question from Canon Law that justifies the punishment of heretics by death.[9]

This, then, is the best More can do in defense of the burning of heretics. The case is weakly argued in every respect: the only actual authority More cites is the Canon Law question, while all his scriptural and patristic examples get him nowhere with respect to the death penalty, let alone burning, for heretics. More tries to blur the question of heresy with sedition.[10] Moreover, his powerful sense of historical unfolding, developed throughout the *Dialogue,* now abandons him: whereas everything else, including the meaning of Scripture, unfolds across time and depends on historical precedent, Lutheran heresy is not a historical phenomenon; it's just madness, or "frantic." More the defender of a living tradition becomes More the defender of a dead traditionalism, the idea that nothing should change. While his practice throughout the *Dialogue* depends on argument between trusting conversationalists, both argument and Christian trust are abandoned in the face of the diabolically untrustworthy Lutherans.

✳ Why did More defend the burning of heretics when he was demonstrably capable of imagining stronger arguments to the contrary, and when his approach to the persecution of Lutherans is so out of keeping with the entire thrust of the *Dialogue Concerning Heresies?* His fragile arguments in favor of persecution of heretics give us some idea, but the sheer violence of More's linguistic treatment of heretics elsewhere tells us much more. Before he knew about Luther, in his letter to Martin van Dorp (1515), More dismissed argument with heretics, saying that it's a waste of time, and not half as effective as fear anyway: the heretics will be "more intimidated by one little bundle of faggots than daunted by many bundles of syllogisms."[11] Once he is engaging specifically with Lutheranism, in the *Responsio ad Lutherum* (1523), More imagines Luther's burning with relish: charges "of shameless folly and madness" ("impudentis stultitiae ac furoris") will brand Luther's name with ignominy and "cling to the ashes of his body when it has been burned . . . even though these ashes be scattered into a thousand seas."[12]

In the *Confutation of Tyndale's Answer* (1532–1533), More treats the flaming torments of his enemies with heartless mockery: "these arch heretics" are

> very glad, and great glory they take when they may hear that any man is brought to burning through their books. Then they boast that they have done a great maistry [a wonderful work], and say they have made a martyr, when their poisoned books have killed the Christian man both in body and soul.[13]

Later in the *Confutation* More blithely recommends burning both Tyndale's books "and the likers of them with them" (1:221/4). Later still, he narrates the martyrdom of Thomas Bilney (d. 1531) with a frankly vicious self-confidence, saying that, after falling back into heresy, "God caused him to be taken, and Tyndale's books with him too, and both two burned together with more profit unto his soul than had been happily to have lived longer and after died in his bed" (1:359). More's reasoning here is that Bilney rejected Tyndale's books in order to save his soul, even if it was too late to save his body.[14] Perhaps the most vicious image of all in the *Confutation* is that of Tyndale being forever unable to shake off the "faggot that lieth so surely bounden on his shoulder" (1:484/33–35).

This catalogue of More's uncontained, pitiless relish at the prospect of Lutherans and their books in flames could be extended.[15] Leaving aside other such textual references, we should also remember that More, as Lord Chancellor, had been very active in the legal pursuit and punishment of Lutherans. Even if, as Stephen Greenblatt reminds us, we need not believe Foxe's story of More personally whipping James Bainham in More's Chelsea garden,[16] six evangelicals did burn under More's chancellorship (1529–1532).

Despite all his persecution of heretics, we should not take More as exemplary of a century of massive English medieval persecution of heresy, soon to come to an end with the advent of Protestantism in 1558, after which "anything at all can be said—or thought—without a charge of heresy."[17] David Daniell, from whom that last quotation is drawn, makes a sharp contrast between Catholic and Protestant England in the matter of persecution for heresy. He points out that there was no heresy legislation after 1558; in the reign of Elizabeth there was, he avers, only "political" censorship, which has in any case been exaggerated, and which was "different from the repression of all independent thought of any kind" characteristic of the century and more from the anti-Lollard legislation of 1401 and 1409.[18]

Daniell's distinction is mistaken as to fact and ignores one important legal point. It's untrue that there was no heresy legislation after 1558: the 1401 statute for the burning of heretics was not abolished until 1677, and even if that statute suppressed the death penalty, it nevertheless maintained sanctions against heresy.[19] Daniell also ignores the merging of treason and heresy as crimes in English law.[20] From 1534 legislation devoted to heresy was also treated under legislation devoted to treason, since in that year the English monarch also became the Head of the English Church. Once the Pope had declared Elizabeth a heretic in 1570, English Catholics were, for example, subject to "savage" parliamentary legislation ordering "death, banishment, life imprisonment, forfeiture of property or fines."[21] To say that the existence of "political" persecution is preferable to persecution of heretics is to misunderstand the nature of English polity: after 1534 "heresy" could be dealt with under the heading of treason.

Daniell's distinction between Catholic and Protestant England also ignores the numbers of people executed for religious reasons. Here the startling difference in England is not between Catholic and Protestant, but between the pre- and post-Reformation periods. The Constitutions of 1409 were certainly draconian, but the actual number of people burned or executed for heresy between 1414 and 1521, although difficult to calibrate, stands at 33 by one authoritative, if perhaps conservative, estimate.[22] England saw no Lutheran martyrs before 1529. Between 1529 and 1532 (the span of More's chancellorship), 6 people were burned for heresy (including Thomas Hytton, Thomas Bilney, Richard Bayfield, John Tewksbury, and James Bainham).[23] Under the vice-gerency of Thomas Cromwell (1532–1540), 308 people were executed for treason. It is impossible to tell how many of these were executed for what before 1534 would have been regarded as heretical practice. But 178 were executed in the pro-Catholic Northern Rebellions of Lincolnshire and Yorkshire in 1536; 63 people died for words against the supremacy; and 6 people died in the Nun of Kent affair. Thirty-two of the executed were members of the clergy.[24] Between the Six Articles of 1539 and the death of Henry VIII in 1547, 39 evangelicals were executed, and at least 14 people were executed for continued allegiance to the papacy.[25] Once the middle of the sixteenth century is approached and passed, the figures become very high. Approximately 4,000 West Country people died at the hands of the royal army in the Western rebellion of 1547–1549, one important aspect of which was rejection of the Book of Common Prayer.[26] The reign of Queen Mary (1553–1558) witnessed up to 300 evangelicals burned for heresy. Between 1581 and 1590, under Elizabeth (ruled 1558–1603), 78 priests and 25 laypeople were executed for religious reasons, with 53 priests and 35 laypeople executed for the same reason between 1590 and 1603 (a total of 191). Taking into account the executions of Catholics in the reign of Elizabeth and the further executions of 70 Catholic priests between 1601 and 1680, Diarmaid MacCulloch states that "England judicially murdered more Roman Catholics than any other country in Europe, which puts English pride in national tolerance in an interesting perspective."[27]

Daniell also contrasts Oliver Cromwell's "generally benign and very English Protectorate" with the "iron grip" of the Rome-imposed repression after 1409. This statement properly recognizes Cromwell's tolerance toward Jews, but it ignores the massacre of upwards of 3,000 royalist troops and Catholic clergy in Cromwell's earlier invasion of Ireland in 1649.[28]

Thus the actual numbers executed under More's direction don't come close to matching the statistics for later sixteenth- and seventeenth-century English religious persecution. But enough has been said about the ferocity of More's pursuit of heresy to suggest that his confrontation with Lutheranism was deadly serious. Even if, however, More sometimes presents himself as a self-confident hero engaged in an epic struggle, for the most part he knows, from the beginning, that he's going to lose.

Part of the difficulty in fighting heresy is the choice of weapon: even before he had ever heard of Luther, More expresses skepticism about the value of argument with heretics. In his letter to Martin van Dorp of 1515, More had already foreseen the Sisyphean labor of this fight well before it began. Fighting with heretics will be useless, for "the very problems with which they are assaulted afford them no end of material with which to strike back, so that the plight of both parties is very much like that of men fighting naked between heaps of stones: neither one lacks the means to strike out; neither one has the means to defend himself."[29]

The most dangerous aspect of heresy for More is, however, that it's contagious; to touch it is to contract a kind of virus. Confrontations of non-negotiable difference (that is, revolutionary confrontations) necessarily produce fear of contagion, since these are the moments when avoidance of touch is most necessary, yet the likelihood of touch is highest, given the proximity of each side to the dark and filthy opponent. More himself feels threatened by verbal, if not theological, touch with his enemy from the beginning of his confrontation with Lutheranism.

Fresh for the fight ahead in the *Responsio ad Lutherum* (1523), More imagines that he is Hercules dragging the "blind serpent . . . from his disgusting and darksome hiding places into the light" (1:85/32–33). Already in the *Responsio*, however, he expresses disgust as much with his own tactics as with Luther's position. After attacking Luther for what amounts to more than 150 printed pages of the modern edition, More recognizes his own degradation: he now understands, he says, the adage that "'He who touches the pitch will be defiled by it.' For I am shamed even of this necessity, that while I clean out the fellow's shit-filled mouth I see my own fingers covered with shit" (1:311/38–313/1–2). The only way he could have avoided being befouled himself would be not to have touched the scurrilous book in the first place ("scurrilem librum . . . non attingere"; 1:684/11). Lutheran books are pestilential and infectious;[30] they are "full of pestilent poisoned heresies, that have in other realms already killed by schisms and war many thousand bodies, and, by sinful errors and abominable heresies, many more thousand souls."[31]

As More prepares to attack Tyndale in the *Confutation* (1532), he is still summoning up epic images: just as the poets imagine that Hercules drew the mastiff Cerberus up from Hell, so too shall More never leave Tyndale "a dark corner to creep into" (1:34/35–35/4). In the *Confutation* itself there are, however, signs that More is failing in the fight. The most obvious symptom is exhaustion. More says that a terrible weariness has overcome him: "as help me God I find all my labour in the writing not half so grievous and painful to me as the tedious reading of their blasphemous heresies" (1:36/11–13). More speaks from within the heat of the endless labor of combat, as if from a nightmare: he wishes not only that the heretics could just be forgotten, but, even more revealing, that his own books could be burned too. He wishes, in fact, that the whole disgusting and wearisome business could be erased from memory. "After all my labour," he desires nothing more than oblivion: all memory of pestilent Lutheran heresy should be erased from the hearts of the English, and their "abominable books burned up." But that's not the only thing that More wants forgotten: along with the Lutheran books marching to the flame, More desires that "mine own were walked with them, and the name of these matters utterly put in oblivion" (p. 36/13–17).

By the time of the *The Answer to a Poisoned Book* (published in 1534), More is refining the dangers of heresy: the words exchanged in the treatment of heresy are themselves a way of catching the disease. If, More says in the Prologue to that book, the faithful were as loath to hear Lutheran heresy as to speak it, then they would "hate and detest and abhor utterly the pestilent contagion of all such smoky communication."[32] In the *Answer*, the heresy problem has become primarily verbal: it is through the "evil communication" that "the contagion crepeth forth and corrupteth further, in the manner of a corrupt cancer" (p. 4/35–37). We should therefore be very cautious in dealing with heretics, lest we catch the disease, as "the pestilence catcheth sometime the leech [doctor] that fasting cometh very near and long sitteth by the sick man busy about to cure him" (p. 5/5–9).

More had in fact caught a disease from his opponents, but it was not so much a theological as a textual virus. Although More never once acknowledges the theological force of Lutheran doctrine, he does contract a deeper, formal "disease" from his enemies. More contracts, that is, the virus of distrustful literalism, which also attacks his commitment to fiction and the imagination. More is on the textual back foot, defending a trustful, nonliteralist, and conversational pragmatism. But he makes that defense in a textual mode of both print and exact, word-for-word citation. One danger of word-for-word citation is that one voices, and therefore spreads, the precise doctrines of one's opponents. A deeper danger in More's case is that he adopted the textual practice and the exclusivist, distrustful, and utterly self-convinced textual assumptions of those opponents. The deepest danger of all is that no one reads such books: extensive, exact quotation produces dull, ponderous books. The textual mode to which he saw no alternative committed More to nothing but exhaustion and inevitable defeat.[33] It also cornered him into an abandonment of fiction, or what his enemies called "poetry."

🏵 In his *News out of Heaven* (1541), Thomas Becon, a personal chaplain to both Cranmer and Protector Somerset from 1547, offers a novel account of why Christ came to earth. In his view, Christ's coming is primarily a textual event. The world is corrupt with idolatry and poisoned with its own imaginations; those responsible for this are the individuals in charge of texts: the "head priests, bishops, lawyers, and Pharisees," who have corrupted "the holy scriptures . . . with their pestilent glosses." It's therefore necessary that Christ come to mankind as a kind of divine philologist, in order to "redress these great absurdities, reducing and bringing the divine scriptures again to their true sense."[34]

However extreme this subordination of Christ to Scripture might seem, Becon nevertheless reveals the most consistent feature of evangelical culture observed throughout this book: the primacy of place it awards to the text of Scripture. Faced with that claim to a single, textual source of irrefragable authority, intelligent opponents of evangelical culture themselves adapted their rules of engagement. Any serious opponent knows that one must choose avenues of attack that one's enemy cannot afford to ignore. Opponents of evangelical biblicism accordingly adapted their textual weapons in fighting evangelicals: they, too, adopted primarily scriptural sources in their attack. As we saw in the previous chapter, Thomas More consistently cites Scripture as his prime resource in the *Dialogue Concerning Heresies*, even as he attempts to downgrade the absolute authority of Scripture.

This single-eyed focus on Scripture could look like a welcome labor-saving device, even to those wanting to rebut evangelical claims: Erasmus, for example, thanked Luther for having saved him the trouble of needing to cite Church Fathers or scholastic theologians.[35] But the saving on labor was a mirage, since even if there was only one source from which to cite authoritatively, that source needed to be cited in full. As we saw in Chapter 6, evangelicals were insistent that nothing be added to, or subtracted from, Scripture. In practice this amounted to a demand that the whole context be taken into account, or what Tyndale calls "the process, order and meaning of the text."[36] Those who fail to observe this textual injunction, both humanist and evangelical, can be accused of "wresting the scripture unto their own purpose" (p. 4).

Why, then, did More adopt the practice of extensive citation of his enemies' prose? That evangelical demand to respect the whole of

Scripture converged with a humanist, philological practice whereby texts were reconceived as primarily verbal, rather than ideational, artifacts. Late medieval university scholasticism had placed ideas above texts: intellectual direction was generated by extracting and summarizing ideas drawn from authoritative texts, before submitting those ideas to the scrutiny of reason. Humanism, by contrast, placed texts above ideas; or rather, the idea of a text was seen as inseparable from its whole expression. An idea is inseparable from its context and its style.[37] Fifteenth-century humanism's aggressive and largely successful attack on scholasticism amounted to a disciplinary victory of Rhetoric over Logic.[38] The victory of Rhetoric meant that formal instantiation of words was prized above ideas in both the production and the interpretation of texts. Thus humanism's mockery of scholasticism's "barbarous" Latin is really mockery of a culture in which ideas (expressed, in fact, in a conceptually refined if inelegant, wholly readable Latin) count more than the words that express them.

Full citation may also be a matter of new technological possibilities. Reproducing words is cheaper in print than in manuscript: one could reproduce more words for a much lower cost.

Finally, full citation is also the result of new possibilities of verification produced by print culture: if the *ipsissima verba* of a writer are easily available and verifiable, then an opponent must be sure to cite them accurately. More himself tells a revealing story in 1515 about having an argument in a bookshop about what Augustine said about a particular question; More resolved the argument by simply taking the relevant (now printed) work by Augustine from the shelf and citing the very words at issue.[39] The printed word replaces discussed ideas as the primary bearer of meaning; and the book displaces *viva voce* disputation. The need for accurate, demonstrable verification is all the more acutely necessary in a threatening discursive environment, where "it is a small thing in altering of one syllable either with pen or word that may make in the conceiving of the truth much matter or error."[40]

The humanist, philological principle that one should respect "the process, order and meaning of the text" implies, then, that the "meaning" of the text is inextricably embedded in its "process" (that is, narration) and "order." The principle applies not only to the understanding of canonical texts, but also to the understanding and discussion of all texts. Certainly throughout More's polemical career, with the interesting exception of the *Dialogue Concerning Heresies*, he feels compelled to follow the order of the texts he wants to rebut, and to offer ample citation of the exact words of those texts. More uses the method of exact citation in the following works, for example: *Responsio ad Lutherum, Confutation of Tyndale's Answer, The Apology, The Debellation of Salem and Bizance*, and *The Answer to a Poisoned Book*.

More recognizes the cumbrousness of the practice with increasing frankness across his polemical career. In the Preface to the *Dialogue* he says that he has seen examples "of right holy men which in their books answering to the objections of heretics in their time have not letted [failed] to rehearse the very formal words of them whose writings they made answer to."[41] The books to which More refers might indeed be his own, since already in the second version of the *Responsio* he had an imagined interlocutor prompting the imagined, fictional author (one "Ross") to reply to Luther using exactly his words: "You will faithfully quote and compare the words of each writer (*citabisque, et conferes utriusque verba fideliter*); then in your own comments you will render the strengths of Luther conspicuous so that every passage will stand out" in which Luther falls down.[42]

All these vectors—humanist philology, the economics of printing, and verbal danger—influenced More toward exact citation of enemies throughout his polemical career. In the *Confutation*, for example, he takes care to protect himself against the charge of having mangled Tyndale's words by "patches and pieces"; he will instead cite "his [Tyndale's] whole chapter together, without any word of his either omitted or changed."[43] More is here observing an evangelical principle—neither adding to nor subtracting from his text.

The forces pressing More to exact citation are especially pronounced in his *Apology*, a text published at Easter 1533 in response to the anonymously published *Treatise Concerning the Division between the Spirituality and the Temporality*, thought to have been written by the jurist Christopher St. German.[44] The tone and content of the *Treatise* are very measured and Erasmian; it argues for reform of certain jurisdictions of the English clergy, including their right to try cases of heresy. One might expect More to respond to its legal arguments with a measured, legal approach. He does recognize that it's written in a "goodly, mild and gentle fashion" (p. 5/25–26), but More won't have any truck with mild reformism; he treats its author as one of what he now calls "the brotherhood," and strenuously resists all the proposed changes. I am not concerned here with the content of More's reply, but rather with its form. For that form, relentlessly textual and literalist as it is, undoes the force of More's broader position with regard to unwritten verities.

More now writes as an unprotected subject of the King, rather than as Lord Chancellor, as he had been in the *Dialogue*. He is, accordingly, much more defensive and cautious: he opens by saying that no one should look to his works for "such exact circumspection and sure sight" (p. 4/15) as can be found in the words of the prophets, Christ, and the Apostles. At the same time, he is certain that all his works will be scrutinized in minute detail by the "bad brethren": the texts will be "sought out and sifted to the uttermost flake of bran, and largely thereupon controlled and reproved" (p. 3/26–29).

More is especially sensitive to the charge that he has attacked the "bad brethren" with textual partiality, "that I do but pick out pieces at my pleasure, such as I may most easily seem to soyle [deal with, refute], and leave out what me list [it pleases me]" (p. 5/31–33). More returns the charge, but denies it with regard to his own textual practice: when necessary, he cites in full, "as of all their own words I leave not one syllable out" (p. 6/34). Even as he defends this procedure, the rhetorician in More recognizes that it's a loser: almost everyone, including his enemies, complains that his books are too long and tedious. He would have made his book much shorter, but it's easier, he says, to write a short heresy than to refute one briefly. The reader might go astray if at any one point he were not armed with all he needed to know, so "the labour of all that length is mine own, for ease and shortening of the reader's pain" (p. 8/ 33–34).

More sounds remarkably like his evangelical opponents here, as he sinks into a painful, demanding, and endless textual world. Extra-textual talk for More is, now, only dangerous and negative: "bold, erroneous talking is almost in every lewd lad's mouth" (p. 11/9–10); he's surrounded by "some say," hearsay, heresy.[45] Like the psalmic complainant, he's surrounded and threatened by malicious talk: "These heretics be so busily walking, that in every ale house, in every tavern, in every barge, and almost every boat, as few as they be a man shall always find some, and there be they so busy with their talking" (p. 159/36–p. 160/1–3). All that's left for More is to produce texts and to read texts. Some of his readers are entering the same world of endless textual work; they appreciate the length of his works, they have read these long tomes over three times, and they have made tables of indexes for their own reference (p. 8/7–9). Others need only read individual chapters, since each is fitted with all that's necessary.

More is entering the evangelical world of endless, exacting, and exhausting textuality, in which the stakes are very high over every mark of print. Tyndale had been subject to intense textual scrutiny; his enemies had "so narrowly looked on my translation, that there is not so much as one *i* therein if it lack a tittle over his head, but they have noted it, and number it unto the ignorant people for an heresy."[46] More's works have also, he says in his *Apology*, been "sought out and sifted to the uttermost flake of bran" (p. 3/27–28). And just as Tyndale not unreasonably expresses the pain associated with textual labor,[47] so too More now inhabits a world of indigestible textuality. Books have become hard, rebarbative objects. If any evangelical preacher can persuasively rebut More by writing, in many more words than the mountain of words that More has used, then he should keep one copy of the rebuttal for himself, and send the other to More. More promises that he "will be bounden to eat it, though the book be bounden in boards" (p. 14/15–16). The world of the *Dialogue*, and the possibility of dialogue around and about texts, have now vanished; all that's left is the hard graft of producing and reading more texts, all of which expose the author to danger and none of which will persuade their target audience. Both More and his opponents are learning the punishing disciplines of literalism. Tyndale does nothing now, says More, but "mark, mark, mark" as he "sitteth and marketh other men's faults."[48]

　🦋　The abandonment of literary discourse is an intrinsic part of the punishing discipline of literalism. And in abandoning literary in-direction, More becomes uncomfortably similar to his evangelical enemies.

Tyndale delivers a revealing attack on More in *An exposycyon vpon the v.vi.vii. chapters of Mathewe* (1533).[49] He argues that More is really persuaded by evangelical culture, but acts hypocritically through covetousness. Covetousness, says Tyndale, makes many, whom the truth first pleases, go on to persecute the truth. More, "who knew the truth and then forsook it again" (image 95), is a good example. At first he conspired with Wolsey to deceive the king, but

> . . . when the light was sprung upon them, and had driven them clean out of the scripture, and had delivered it out of their tyranny, and had expelled the dark stinking mists of their devilish glosses, and had wiped away the cobwebs which those poisoned spiders had spread upon the face of the clear text, so that the spirituality . . . were ashamed of their part . . . yet for all that, covetousness blinded the eyes of that glaring fox more and more and hardened his heart against the truth, with the confidence of his painted poetry . . . grounded in his unwritten verities, as true and as authentic as his story of Utopia. (image 95)

In this fascinating passage Tyndale uses the tactic, and possibly believes the charge, that one's enemy is actually a closet adherent of one's own position. Deep down, More is one of us, Tyndale is saying; the fact that he pretends otherwise is nothing more than hypocrisy. Hypocrisy, further, has a weapon, which is "poetry"; unwritten verities are no more solid than imaginative, man-made (and therefore idolatrous) constructions like the commonwealth of Utopia. Tyndale is claiming profound identities between himself and More, identities disguised by hypocrisy and "poetry."

As we have seen, More and Tyndale do in fact share one absolutely central conviction, which is that the truest scripture is that written in the heart. More's declaration of that interior text is relaxed, committed as he is to unwritten verities. By contrast, Tyndale's commitment to the cardiac text puts him on the back foot, since his more strident commitment to the plain and incontrovertible literal sense should preclude the need for any other text. For all that, both More and Tyndale use the textual image drawn from Hebrews 10:16: "I will put

my laws upon their hearts and upon their minds I will write them."
Thus, even as More attempts to keep textuality within due bounds,
he uses a textual metaphor. If that represents a concession of sorts to
the evangelicals, so too, though much more powerfully, does More's
abandonment of fiction, conversation, and dialogue in his polemical,
pre-Tower works.

By the end of More's polemical career, Tyndale's description of
More's identity with the evangelicals is true in a profound respect.[50]
By the end of that career, More, like his evangelical enemies, has
no confidence in "painted poetry." Even if he continues to defend
unwritten verities, his own polemical writing expresses nothing so
much as a growing, if punishing, commitment to relentlessly explicit
textuality of a kind favored by the evangelicals.

In keeping with their detestation of "imagination," evangelicals
were certainly opposed to "poetry."[51] In Thomas Elyot's dialogue *Pasquil the Playne* (1533),[52] the two speakers Pasquil and Gnatho represent, respectively, plain speaking and discretion. Pasquil sees Gnatho
and notes that he is holding a New Testament in his hand, for all to
see. Pressing indiscreetly further, he sees that Gnatho is hiding a
book in his coat, which turns out to be Chaucer's *Troilus and Criseyde*:
"Lord," he exclaims, "what discord is between these two books!" (image 4). This in itself is a dangerous comment, but Gnatho promises
not to report it, and to take it in jest. The conditions of literary dialogue are preserved by trusting interlocutors, one of whom trusts,
even if he feels he needs to hide, the literary text.

In the *Obedience of a Christian Man* Tyndale had also specifically
targeted "Troilus" among the books that compete with Scripture:
even as they forbid the reading of Scripture in the vernacular, ecclesiastical authorities permit the reading of "Robin Hood and Bevis of
Hampton, Hercules, Hector and Troilus with a thousand histories
and fables of love and wantonness and of ribaldry as filthy as heart

can think."[53] That opposition between secular writing (especially romances) and the text of Scripture was by 1539 a *topos* of the civil service. A draft Cromwellian policy paper produced in that year declares, for example, that the Reformation is going well in England: "Englishmen have the Bible in hand in place of 'the old fabulous and fantastical books of the Table Round, Lancelot du Lac, Huon de Bordeaux, Bevy of Hampton, Guy of Warwick.'"[54] Even if that policy paper remained a draft, its hostility to literature survived in the official book of evangelical sermons that priests throughout England were required to read from after 1547: the sermon on "The Reading of Holy Scripture" asks what answer shall be proffered at the Last Judgment by those who "delight to read or hear men's fantasies and inventions."[55]

Although negativity toward secular literature has a long tradition in Christian writing, it is, in its evangelical formulation, not merely hostility to certain easily targeted books of romance. Evangelicals entertain a more profound detestation for the unscriptural "poetry" and "imagination" of the entire Catholic Church, for, as Tyndale says in the *Obedience*, nothing "bringeth the wrath of God so soon and so sore on a man, as the idolatry of his own imagination."[56] Like Luther, who dismissed the humanists as "poetae," Tyndale preferred explicit discourse to narrative, assertion to dialogue, and the plain, transparent literal sense to the indirections of literary or religious discourse.[57]

In the *Dialogue Concerning Heresies* More resists the evangelicals' marginalization of all secular disciplines in favor of the study of Scripture. Among the disciplines More defends is "poetry": "and albeit poets been with many men taken [by many men considered] but for painted words, yet do they much help the judgement" and furnish "a good mother wit."[58] More's use of dialogue in that work is, however, the last such use he made of dialogue in polemical works. (He would return to dialogue in the *Dialogue of Comfort*, written in the Tower.) As the *Dialogue* ends with its pile of books endorsing the use of violent persecution of heretics, so too does More's use of dialogue (and, almost, of fiction) come to an end, in his engagement with heresy at any rate.[59] The trusting conditions of dialogue no longer exist, and More becomes helplessly committed, like most writers in treacherous revolutionary moments, to explicit, unironic discourse that eschews the fertile indirections of literature.

More's rejection of "poetry" can be measured not only by the formal quality of his later polemical texts themselves, but also by his repudiation of Erasmus's brilliantly and unstably ironic *Encomium Moriae* (*Praise of Folly* or, with its punning possibility, *Praise of More*), which Erasmus had begun in More's household in 1509. In 1515 More defended Erasmus's delightful satire to Martin van Dorp, who had criticized it. The wicked deserve chastisement, says More, and especially so when the correction is "more decorously and less violently [achieved] by assuming the character of Folly."[60]

By the time of the 1532 *Confutation*, More's understanding of the *Encomium Moriae* has changed utterly. In that text More broaches the contemporary force of Erasmus's text, twenty or so years after its composition. He begins by insisting on its literary quality, saying that "Moria doth indeed but jest upon the abuses" of the Church, "after the manner of a disour's [jester's] part in a play." In any case, the satire is not so critical by far as the satire of the young scholar, he says, "which I have yet suffered to stand in my dialogue."[61] By the 1530s, however, the discursive environment has changed and narrowed: given the infectious poison of heresy, "men cannot almost now speak of such things in so much as a play, but that such evil hearers wax [grow] a great deal worse" (1:178/29–30). As William Barlow says in his own dangerous dialogue of 1531, words about religion are now dangerous, since, by the "deceitful spirits" of Lutherans, "it is come so to pass that a little fault is not only taken to the worst,

but whatsoever is well done, spoken, or written, is oftimes interpreted amiss."[62] So More, ever one to recognize the logical consequences of a given position, now declares himself ready to burn "not
only my darling's books [that is, those of Erasmus], but mine own
also," given the readiness of readers to read them amiss. More would
"help to burn them both with mine own hands" (1:179/15). In a single move, More closes down a literary text and literary textuality.
The environment of texts is now to be wholly distrusted; and as one
distrusts the public, one distrusts the nonliteral texts and carts them
off to the fire. More even goes so far as to return the charge of writing "poetry" to Tyndale: if poetry be nothing but feigning, then Tyndale "useth in his writing much plain poetry" (1:177/5). Tyndale and
More compete with each other to claim maximal clarity and total ex-
posure of the mischievous, poetic indirections of their enemy.

The more energetically More pursues his enemy, in short, the
more he becomes his enemy. I do not mean to lay the blame for the
collapse of More's brilliantly literary mode at the door of evangelical culture. On the contrary, my point is much broader: Tyndale
and More were both the victims of a new, immensely demanding,
and punishing textual culture marked by literalist impersonality. The
conditions of sixteenth-century early textual modernity produced a
monster of sorts, which pushed its victims into rigid, exclusivist,
persecutory, and self-punishing postures.

We are the heirs of that imprisoning moment, whether as liberals
we have partially mastered and understood those punishing textual
demands, or whether as fundamentalists we still render obeisance to
the idol of a text to which nothing must be added, nor from which
anything subtracted. The liberal tradition would understand the punishing demands of literalism better if it stopped tracing its own an-
cestry to the moment that produced its most vigorous opponent.

Abbreviations

Notes

Index

Abbreviations

Concilia	*Concilia Magnae Britanniae et Hiberniae*, ed. David Wilkins, 4 vols. (London: Bowyer, Richardson, Purser, 1737)
DNB	*Oxford Dictionary of National Biography*, *http://www.oxforddnb.com .ezp1.harvard.edu/subscribed/*
EEBO	Early English Books Online, *http://eebo.chadwyck.com.ezp1 .harvard.edu/home*
EETS	Early English Text Society
JEH	*Journal of Ecclesiastical History*
L&P Henry VIII	*Letters and Papers, Foreign and Domestic, of the Reign of Henry VIII* . . . calendared by J. S. Brewer et al., 21 vols. in 33 (London: Longman, Green, Longman and Roberts, 1862–1910)
RSTC	*A Short-Title Catalogue of Books Printed in England, Scotland and Ireland and of English Books Printed Abroad 1475–1640*, ed. A. W. Pollard and G. R. Redgrave, 2nd ed. rev. W. A. Jackson et al., 3 vols. (London: Bibliographical Society, 1976–1791)
SR	*Statutes of the Realm*, ed. T. E. Tomlins et al., 11 vols. (London: Dawsons, 1810–1828; reprinted 1963)

Notes

Introduction

1. "Soteriology" derives from the Greek *soteria* (deliverance, means of safety) and *logos* (reflection, thought).
2. I am indebted to Laura Ashe for crisp formulation of this insight.
3. See Max Weber, *The Protestant Ethic and the Spirit of Capitalism*, trans. Talcott Parsons (New York: Scribner, 1958; first published in German, 1904), p. 172.
4. For an understanding of More's modernity, I am indebted to Tom Betteridge, *Writing Faith and Telling Tales: Sir Thomas More and the English Reformation* (forthcoming, University of Notre Dame Press).
5. For more extensive discussion of this point, see James Simpson, "Diachronic History and the Shortcomings of Medieval Studies," in *Reading the Medieval in Early Modern England*, ed. David Matthews and Gordon McMullan (Cambridge: Cambridge University Press, 2007), pp. 17–30.
6. See Diarmaid MacCulloch, *Reformation: Europe's House Divided* (London: Allen Lane, 2003), p. xx, for a wider discussion and the same choice of "evangelical."
7. For an argument that also sees early twentieth-century fundamentalism as the resurgence of sixteenth-century practice, see David S. Katz, *God's Last Words: Reading the English Bible from the Reformation to Fundamentalism* (New Haven: Yale University Press, 2006), p. 315.

1. Two Hundred Years of Biblical Violence

1. For the likelihood of Tyndale's authorship of these books, see William Tyndale, *Tyndale's Old Testament*, ed. David Daniell (New Haven: Yale University Press, 1992), pp. xxiv–xxvi.

2. Ibid., p. 537.

3. Thomas Cranmer, "Speech at the Coronation of Edward VI," in *Miscellaneous Writings and Letters of Thomas Cranmer*, ed. John E. Cox (Cambridge: Cambridge University Press, 1846), pp. 126–127 (at p. 127). For the common mid-sixteenth-century comparison between Edward VI and Josiah, see Margaret Aston, *The King's Bedpost: Reformation Iconography in a Tudor Group Portrait* (Cambridge: Cambridge University Press, 1993), pp. 26–36; and Diarmaid MacCulloch, *Tudor Church Militant: Edward VI and the Protestant Reformation* (London: Allen Lane, 1999), pp. 57–104.

4. William Tyndale, *The Obedience of a Christian Man*, ed. David Daniell (London: Penguin, 2000), p. 6. I continue to cite Daniell's easily accessible modern edition of this text in favor of the less accessible standard edition, in William Tyndale, *Doctrinal Treatises and Introductions to Different Portions of the Holy Scriptures*, ed. Henry Walter, Parker Society (Cambridge: Cambridge University Press, 1848), pp. 127–344.

5. *Visitation Articles and Injunctions*, ed. Walter Howard Frere and William McClure Kennedy, 3 vols. (London: Longmans, Green, 1910), 1: 126. Further references will be made by volume and page number in the body of the text. For the larger history of English Reformation iconoclasm, see Margaret Aston, *England's Iconoclasts*, vol. 1: *Laws Against Images* (Oxford: Clarendon Press, 1988).

6. "For, as mild Iosias plucked down the hill altars, cut down the groves, and destroyed all monuments of idolatry in the Temple: the like corruptions, dross, and deformities of popish idolatry crept into the Church of Christ of long time, this evangelical Iosias King Edward removed, and purged the true Temple of the Lord." John Foxe, *Acts and Monuments* [. . .] (1570 edition), [online]. (hriOnline, Sheffield). Available from *http://www.hrionline.ac.uk/johnfoxe*, Book 9, p. 1484.

7. The image is frequently reproduced. For one example, see James Simpson, "The Rule of Medieval Imagination," *Images, Idolatry, and Iconoclasm in Late Medieval England*, ed. Jeremy Dimmick, James Simpson, and

Nicolette Zeeman (Oxford: Oxford University Press, 2002), pp. 4–24 (Figure 2).

8. Foxe, *Acts and Monuments* (1570 edition), Book 9, p. 1483.

9. For a survey of pre-Reformation Biblical translation and its repression, see Margaret Deanesly, *The Lollard Bible and Other Medieval Biblical Versions* (New York: AMS Press, 1978; first published 1920).

10. See William M. Schniedewind, *How the Bible Became a Book: The Textualization of Ancient Israel* (Cambridge: Cambridge University Press, 2004), p. 17.

11. The classic study remains Elizabeth Eisenstein, *The Printing Press as an Agent of Change*, 2 vols. in 1 (Cambridge: Cambridge University Press, 1979), especially Part 2: 4, "The Scriptural Tradition Recast," pp. 303–452. For likely literacy rates of 10–15 percent of English people in the 1530s, see Ian Green, *Print and Protestantism in Early Modern England* (Oxford: Oxford University Press, 2000), p. 26. See also David Cressy, *Literacy and the Social Order: Reading and Writing in Tudor and Stuart England* (Cambridge: Cambridge University Press, 1980), who paints a nuanced picture of rising literacy rates in the 1520s and 1530s, with a slowdown in the reigns of Edward and Mary (pp. 164–167).

12. Of course there was a competition between these two forms of authority. For Luther's attacks on contemporary prophets whose revelations are unscriptural, see Martin Luther, *Schmalkald Articles*, in William R. Russell, *Luther's Theological Testament: The Schmalkald Articles* (Minneapolis: Fortress Press, 1995), Appendix A, p. 145. See also Paul Althaus, *The Theology of Martin Luther*, trans. Robert C. Schultz (Philadelphia: Fortress Press, 1966; first published 1962), p. 36.

13. All the following mini-histories of the Reformation centuries in western Europe are drawn from Diarmaid MacCulloch, *Reformation: Europe's House Divided* (London: Allen Lane, 2003) (here p. 158).

14. Martin Luther, *Against the Robbing and Murderous Hordes*, in *Luther's Works*, 46, *The Christian in Society*, 3, ed. Robert C. Schultz (Philadelphia: Fortress Press, 1967), pp. 49–55.

15. Ibid., p. 50.

16. MacCulloch, *Reformation*, p. 275.

17. Ibid., p. 485.

18. Ibid., pp. 194, 306–307, 471–472, 670.

19. Ibid., pp. 311–313.

20. Ibid., p. 337.

21. Ibid., p. 285.

22. Cited from *DNB*, "Oliver Cromwell," under "Cromwell in Ireland, 1649–1650."

23. Ibid.

24. *The Letters and Speeches of Oliver Cromwell*, ed. T. Carlyle and S. C. Lomas, 3 vols. (London: Methuen, 1904), letter 105, 17 September 1649. Cited from *DNB*, "Oliver Cromwell," under "Cromwell in Ireland, 1649–1650."

25. Cited from ibid.

26. Some landmarks in the history of European and American toleration within states are as follows: 1598 (the Edict of Nantes [France]), 1689 (Toleration Act [England]), 1778 (Catholic Relief Act [Britain]), 1791 (Bill of Rights [United States]), 1829 (Catholic Emancipation Act [Britain]). For a scholarly history of studies of toleration, see Alexandra Walsham, *Charitable Hatred: Tolerance and Intolerance in England, 1500–1700* (Manchester: Manchester University Press, 2006), pp. 6–13. See also Perez Zagorin, *How the Idea of Religious Toleration Came to the West* (Princeton, N.J.: Princeton University Press, 2003). I thank Earl Havens for this reference.

27. See Walsham, *Charitable Hatred*, pp. 40–49.

28. William Roper, *The Life of Sir Thomas More*, in *Two Early Tudor Lives*, ed. Richard S. Sylvester and Davis P. Harding (New Haven: Yale University Press, 1962), p. 216.

29. "An Open Letter to Leo X," in *Reformation Writings of Martin Luther*, trans. Bertram Lee Woolf, 2 vols. (New York: Philosophical Library, 1953), 1: 333–347 (at p. 337).

30. Martin Luther, *On the Bondage of the Will*, in *Luther and Erasmus: Free Will and Salvation*, trans. E. Gordon Rupp, A. N. Marlow, Philip S. Watson, and B. Drewery (Philadelphia: Westminster Press, 1969), p. 128.

31. Ibid., p. 129.

32. Desiderius Erasmus, *A dialogue or communication intituled [the] pylgremage of pure deuotyon* (London, 1540), RSTC, 10454.

33. For a parallel list, see Tyndale, *Obedience*, ed. Daniell, p. 82.

34. Martin Luther, *The Babylonian Captivity of the Church*, in *Luther's Works*, 36, *Word and Sacrament*, 2, ed. Abdel Ross Wentz (Philadelphia: For-

tress Press, 1959), pp. 11–126 (at p. 72). For the theme of liberty as expressed by English evangelicals in the early sixteenth century, see Alec Ryrie, "Counting Sheep, Counting Shepherds: The Problem of Allegiance in the English Reformation," in *The Beginnings of English Protestantism* (Cambridge: Cambridge University Press, 2002), pp. 84–110 (at pp. 103–105).

35. Herbert Butterfield, *The Whig Interpretation of History* (London: Bell and Sons, 1931), pp. 11–12.

36. *L&P Henry VIII*, 14.2, 796.

37. The text was republished in the following year; RSTC, 23207, 23208. All further references will be made by image number in the body of the text.

38. J. J. Scarisbrick, *The Reformation and the English People* (Oxford: Blackwell, 1984); *The English Reformation Revised*, ed. Christopher Haigh (Cambridge: Cambridge University Press, 1987); Eamon Duffy, *The Stripping of the Altars: Traditional Religion in England, 1400–1580* (New Haven: Yale University Press, 1992).

39. Duffy, *The Stripping of the Altars*, p. 80.

40. Ibid., p. 530.

41. Ibid., p. 586.

42. See David Daniell, *William Tyndale, A Biography* (New Haven: Yale University Press, 1994), and David Daniell, *The Bible in English: Its History and Influence* (New Haven: Yale University Press, 2003), pp. 133–159. See also Brian Moynahan, *God's Bestseller: William Tyndale, Thomas More, and the Writing of the English Bible—A Story of Martyrdom and Betrayal* (New York: St. Martin's Press, 2002). This last book is not a work of scholarship; it tells Daniell's story with Daniell's sympathies.

43. Thus, for example, "Paul's Epistle to the Romans, in particular, spells out the heart of Christian theology, with its strong emphasis on justification by faith"; Daniell, *The Bible in English*, p. 145.

44. Anne Richardson, "William Tyndale and the Bill of Rights," in *William Tyndale and the Law*, ed. John A. R. Dick and Anne Richardson (Kirksville, Mo.: Sixteenth Century Journal Publishers, 1994), pp. 11–29 (at p. 29).

45. Daniell, *The Bible in English*, p. 233.

46. Ibid., p. 234.

47. Ibid., p. 160.

48. The position is a subset of the Norman Yoke narrative of English history, for which see Linda Georgianna, "Coming to Terms with the Norman Conquest: Nationalism and English Literary History," in *REAL: Yearbook of Research in English and American Literature,* 14 *(Literature and the Nation),* ed. Brook Thomas (Tübingen: Gunter Narr, 1998), pp. 33–53. For the relation of English nationalism and Protestantism, see Patrick Collinson, *The Birthpangs of Protestant England: Religious and Cultural Change in the Sixteenth and Seventeenth Centuries* (London: Macmillan, 1988), chap. 1.

49. Daniell, *The Bible in English,* p. 136. One of the reasons late medieval English prose looks dead on Daniell's page is that Daniell unaccountably inserts ampersands into words (e.g., pp. 77, 79, 88) when he needs the antiquated letter form "yogh," or, better, its modern equivalent "gh."

50. Daniell, *The Bible in English,* pp. 60–61. On p. 12 Daniell remarks that the English language is "particularly friendly to neighbouring tongues"; the same cannot, clearly, be said for Daniell himself.

51. For the larger tradition of English nationalist, Protestant historiography, see Rosemary O'Day, *The Debate on the English Reformation* (London: Methuen, 1986). See, for example, her comments on J. A. Froude's *The History of England from the Fall of Wolsey to the Spanish Armada,* 12 vols. (1856–1870): "In his history Froude portrayed the English Reformation as a moral victory in the struggle for human freedom and intellectual honesty" (p. 91). See also Georgianna, "Coming to Terms with the Norman Conquest."

52. Daniell's counts for, and characterizations of, non-Latin vocabulary are, for example, frequently wrong. He quotes (*The Bible in English,* p. 138) a sentence from *Hamlet* ("This fell sergeant, death, / Is strict in his arrest") in order to show a "plain Saxon base in vocabulary"; the line has three Latin-derived words. On the same page he declares that a given passage from Tyndale has only five "Latinist" words (of which one, "agony," is in fact Greek), when in fact the passage cited has ten Latin-derived words. Daniell misses "place," "apart," "face," "prayed," "pass," "hour." On p. 158 we are told that Tyndale's "vocabulary was predominantly Saxon"; the first paragraph exemplifying this point, on p. 159, has no fewer than eleven Latin-derived words. See further Chapter 4 below.

53. Daniell, *The Bible in English,* pp. 270–272.

54. Ibid., p. 271.
55. Ibid., p. 126.
56. Richard Hooker, *Of The Laws of Ecclesiastical Polity*, ed. A. S. McGrade and Brian Vickers (London: Sigdwick and Jackson, 1975), 2: 6, p. 183.
57. The schismatic future of evangelical reading habits is not part of the subject of this book. The best treatment of the subject I know is Anthony Kemp, *The Estrangement of the Past: A Study in the Origins of Modern Historical Consciousness* (New York and Oxford: Oxford University Press, 1991), chap. 3.
58. See the penetrating study by John Stachniewski, *The Persecutory Imagination: English Puritanism and the Literature of Religious Despair* (Oxford: Clarendon Press, 1991).
59. Daniell, *The Bible in English*, p. 131.
60. The evangelical tradition of rejecting More is long; it starts with Tyndale, and includes John Foxe's *Actes and Martyrs*. The most recent member of the tradition is David Daniell: see Daniell, *William Tyndale*, p. 4, and Daniell, *The Bible in English*, p. 243. For the tradition of those who admire More as humanist but see him losing his poise as he broaches heresy, see, for example, Alistair Fox, *Thomas More, History and Providence* (Oxford: Blackwell, 1982). For the secular hagiographic tradition, see R. W. Chambers, *Thomas More* (New York: Harcourt Brace, 1935). A newer tradition sees continuities between More the humanist and More the persecutor of heretics: both are authoritarian. See, for example, Richard Marius, *Thomas More: A Biography* (London: Dent, 1984): More's fury against Protestants was "almost the essence of the man" (p. xxiv). For the reception of More as heresy hunter by scholars writing from very different positions, see John Guy, *Thomas More* (London: Arnold, 2000), pp. 106–114.
61. In Chapter 8 I discuss the way the Catholic More became his enemy, rather than the way in which evangelicals became theirs. For a brilliant start on that second history, see Brian Cummings, "Iconoclasm and Bibliophobia in the English Reformations," in *Images, Idolatry, and Iconoclasm*, ed. Dimmick, Simpson, and Zeeman, pp. 185–206.

2. Good Bible News

1. For the introduction of the English Bible, see also David Scott Kastan, "'The noyse of the new Bible': Reform and Reaction in Henrician Eng-

land," in *Religion and Culture in Renaissance England,* ed. Claire McEachern and Debora Shuger (Cambridge: Cambridge Unversity Press, 1997), pp. 46–68.

2. William Tyndale, *Tyndale's Old Testament,* ed. David Daniell (New Haven: Yale University Press, 1992), p. 4. The biographical account of Tyndale is dependent on David Daniell, *William Tyndale, A Biography* (New Haven: Yale University Press, 1994); David Daniell, *The Bible in English: Its History and Influence* (New Haven: Yale University Press, 2003), pp. 133–159; and *DNB,* "William Tyndale," also written by David Daniell.

3. Tyndale, *Old Testament,* ed. Daniell, p. 5.

4. See *Records of the English Bible: The Documents Relating to the Translation and Publication of the English Bible, 1525–1611,* ed. Alfred W. Pollard (London: Oxford University Press, 1911), p. 133. For anti-Lutheran censorship in England from 1520, see D. M. Loades, "Illicit Presses and Clandestine Printing in England, 1520–90," in his *Politics, Censorship, and the English Reformation* (London: Pinter, 1991), pp. 109–126.

5. For sixteenth-century censorship in England more generally, see D. M. Loades, "The Theory and Practice of Censorship in Sixteenth-Century England," in Loades, *Politics, Censorship, and the English Reformation,* pp. 96–108.

6. For skepticism, though not outright dismissal, of the entire story of official Bible buying, see Daniell, *The Bible in English,* p. 145.

7. This paragraph is dependent on *DNB,* "William Tyndale."

8. Cited from *DNB,* "William Tyndale," under "Inquisition."

9. Tyndale, *Old Testament,* ed. Daniell, p. 6.

10. *Records of the English Bible,* ed. Pollard, p. 170.

11. Ibid., pp. 170–171.

12. *The Psalter of Dauid in Englishe purely a[n]d faithfully tra[n]slated aftir the texte of Feline* (Antwerp, 1530), RSTC, 2370; *The prophete Isaye, translated into englysshe, by George Ioye* (Antwerp, 1531), RSTC, 2777; and *Ieremy the prophete, translated into Englisshe: by George Ioye* (Antwerp, 1534), RSTC, 2778. For these translations, see Orlaith O'Sullivan, "The Bible Translations of George Joye," in *The Bible as Book: The Reformation,* ed. Orlaith O'Sullivan and Ellen Herron (London: The British Library, 2000), pp. 25–38.

13. See Daniell, *The Bible in English,* pp. 173–189 (at p. 174).

14. *Concilia*, ed. Wilkins, 3:815. For a slight uncertainty regarding the precise date of this injunction, see *Records of the English Bible*, ed. Pollard, p. 262, note 1.
15. *Records of the English Bible*, ed. Pollard, p. 262, note 1.
16. *Tudor Royal Proclamations*, ed. P. L. Hughes and J. F. Larkin (3 vols.), vol. 1: *The Early Tudors (1485–1553)* (New Haven: Yale University Press, 1964), pp. 286–287. For a fuller narrative of the rather painful birth of the Great Bible, see Daniell, *The Bible in English*, pp. 200–204.
17. *Tudor Royal Proclamations*, ed. Hughes and Larkin, pp. 296–298.
18. See Daniell, *The Bible in English*, pp. 844–845, for a complete list of Biblical production in the period covered by this book.
19. For the production of catechetical material in England from 1530, see Ian Green, *The Christian's ABC: Catechisms and Catechizing in England c. 1530–1740* (Oxford: Oxford University Press, 1996), especially pp. 51 and 59–62. The table on p. 51 lists twenty catechisms or catechetical works published between 1530 and 1549. See also Philippa Tudor, "Religious Instruction for Children and Adolescents in the Early English Reformation," *Journal of Ecclesiastical History*, 35 (1984): 391–413. For the Book of Common Prayer, see Ramie Targoff, *Common Prayer: The Language of Devotion in Early Modern England* (Chicago: University of Chicago Press, 2001).
20. See *DNB*, "John Frith."
21. John Frith, *The Articles wherefore John Frith dyed* (Antwerp, 1533), RSTC, 11381.
22. *DNB*, under "Robert Barnes."
23. *DNB*, under "Patrick Hamilton."
24. *DNB*, under "Thomas Bilney."
25. *DNB*, under "John Rogers."
26. *DNB*, under "Miles Coverdale."
27. *DNB*, under "Thomas Cromwell."
28. *DNB*, under "Thomas Cranmer."
29. John Fisher, *Sermon Made Agayn the Perncyous Doctryn of Martin Luther*, in *The English Works of John Fisher*, ed. John E. B. Major, Early English Text Society, extra series 27 (London: Trübner, 1876), pp. 311–348 (at p. 339). Further references to this sermon in this chapter will be made by page number in the body of the text.
30. Thomas More, *A Dialogue Concerning Heresies*, ed. T. M. C. Lawler,

Germain Marc'hadour, and Richard Marius, 2 Parts, in *The Complete Works of St. Thomas More*, 6 (New Haven: Yale University Press, 1981), 1: 37/28–29.

31. John Fisher, *A sermon had at Paulis by the co[m]mandment of the most reuerend father in god my lorde legate, and sayd by Ioh[a]n the bysshop of Rochester* (London, 1526), RSTC, 10892, image 4. Further reference to this sermon will be made by image number in the body of the text.

32. For Fisher's more conciliatory approach, and its reality, see C. W. D'Alton, "The Suppression of Lutheran Heretics in England, 1526–1529," *JEH*, 54 (2003): 728–753. See also Richard Rex, *The Theology of John Fisher* (Cambridge: Cambridge University Press, 1991).

33. D'Alton, "The Suppression of Lutheran Heretics in England."

34. For a survey of More's career as polemicist, see Luis A. Schuster, "Thomas More's Polemical Career, 1523–1533," in Thomas More, *The Confutation of Tyndale's Answer*, ed. Louis A. Schuster, Richard Marius, James P. Lusardi, and Richard J. Schoeck, in *The Complete Works of St. Thomas More*, 8, 3 Parts (New Haven: Yale University Press, 1973), 3: 1135–1268.

35. See Thomas More, *In Defense of Humanism: Letter to Martin Dorp, Letter to the University of Oxford, Letter to Edward Lee, Letter to a Monk*, ed. Daniel Kinney, in *The Complete Works of St. Thomas More*, 15 (New Haven: Yale University Press, 1986), p. xxiii.

36. More, *Letter to Martin Dorp*, ed. Kinney, p. 71.

37. Ibid., p. 75.

38. Thomas More, *Responsio ad Lutherum*, ed. John M. Headley, in *The Complete Works of St. Thomas More*, 5, 2 Parts (New Haven: Yale University Press, 1969), 1: 61.

39. More, *A Dialogue Concerning Heresies*, ed. Lawler et al., 1: 416/7–9.

40. Ibid., 1: 433.

41. D'Alton, "The Suppression of Lutheran Heretics in England."

42. Wolsey circulated a first list of Lutheran errors in 1521; see *Concilia*, ed. Wilkins, 3: 690–693. See Loades, "Illicit Presses and Clandestine Printing in England" (at pp. 110–111).

43. See *Concilia*, ed. Wilkins, 3: 711, and, for lists of proscribed books, 3: 706–707 (1526); 719–720 (1529); 727–737 (1530); and 737–739 (1530).

44. *Tudor Royal Proclamations*, ed. Hughes and Larkin, pp. 181–186. The

date given (6 March 1529) for item 122 ("Enforcing Statutes against Heresy: Prohibiting Unlicensed preaching, heretical Books") is incorrect; it should read 1530. See G. R. Elton, *Policy and the Police* (Cambridge: Cambridge University Press, 1972), p. 218, note 5.

45. *Tudor Royal Proclamations,* ed. Hughes and Larkin, pp. 196–197.
46. Ibid., p. 196.
47. Ibid., p. 197.
48. *Concilia,* ed. Wilkins, 3: 711–712.
49. *DNB,* "Thomas More," under "Opposition to the Royal Divorce." See Chapter 8 below.
50. For More's weariness, see Stephen Greenblatt, "The Word of God in an Age of Mechanical Reproduction," in *Renaissance Self-Fashioning, from More to Shakespeare* (Chicago: University of Chicago Press, 1980), pp. 74–114 (at p. 82).
51. More, *Responsio ad Lutherum,* ed. Headley, p. 85.
52. Ibid., p. 313.
53. See James Simpson, *Reform and Cultural Revolution* (Oxford: Oxford University Press, 2002), p. 450.
54. By the "Wycliffite" Bible, I mean the two versions of the entire Bible produced in the last two decades of the fourteenth century. Translators working broadly within the movement that soon after came to be known as "Lollardy" produced these two versions, translated from the Latin Vulgate Bible of Jerome (fourth century). The first was a strictly translated version, so strict as to obstruct easy access; the second offered the same text in a more syntactically flexible rendering. No fewer than 250 manuscripts of this translation survive, containing part or, in 21 instances, the whole Bible. (Daniell, *The Bible in English,* erroneously states the figure at 230 on p. xiv. He gives the correct figure on p. 92.) For the text, see *The Holy Bible . . . made from the Vulgate by John Wycliffe and His Followers,* ed. Josiah Forshall and Frederic Madden, 4 vols. (Oxford: Oxford University Press, 1850). For a survey of scholarship on the Wycliffite Bible, see Anne Hudson, *The Premature Reformation: Wycliffite Texts and Lollard History* (Oxford: Clarendon Press, 1988), pp. 228–247. See also David Lawton, "Englishing the Bible," in *The Cambridge History of Medieval English Literature,* ed. David Wallace (Cambridge: Cambridge University Press, 1999), and, most recently, the important book by Mary Dove, *The First English Bible: The Text and*

Context of The Wycliffite Versions (Cambridge: Cambridge University Press, forthcoming 2007). I am grateful to Dr. Dove for allowing me to see the typescript of this book, even if its existence came to my notice too late for incorporation in the argument of the present book.

55. More, *A Dialogue Concerning Heresies*, ed. T. M. C. Lawler, 1: 337. For a summary of More's views on the appropriateness of a vernacular Bible, see Heinz Holeczek, *Humanistische Bibelphilologie als Reformproblem bei Erasmus von Rotterdam, Thomas More und William Tyndale* (Leiden: Brill, 1975), pp. 359–394.

56. More, *A Dialogue Concerning Heresies*, ed. T. M. C. Lawler, 1: 337.

57. Ibid., 1: 338.

58. *Records of the English Bible*, ed. Pollard, p. 109.

59. Ibid., pp. 122–123.

60. Ibid., p. 159.

61. Ibid., p. 163.

62. Ibid., p. 177.

63. Stephen Gardiner seems to have finished his section (Luke and John); see *Records of the English Bible*, ed. Pollard, p. 196, note 2.

64. Ibid., pp. 197–198.

65. For Luther's continental opponents also dismissing the laity from serious engagement in the debate, see David V. N. Bagchi, *Luther's Earliest Opponents: Catholic Controversialists, 1518–1525* (Minneapolis: Fortress Press, 1989), pp. 89–90.

66. For the Latin text, see *Enchiridion Symbolorum, Definitionum et Declarationum de rebus Fidei et Morum*, ed. Henricus Denzinger and Adolfus Schönmetzer (Barcelona: Herder, 1967), p. 366. The translation is mine.

67. Diarmaid MacCulloch, *Reformation: Europe's House Divided* (London: Allen Lane, 2003), p. 406.

68. *SR*, ed. Tomlins, 34 Henry 8, 3: 894.

69. Ibid., 34 Henry 8, 3: 896.

70. For the medieval Church's prohibitions on scripture in the vernacular, see Margaret Deanesly, *The Lollard Bible and Other Medieval Biblical Versions* (Cambridge: Cambridge University Press, 1920; rpt. 1966), chaps. 2–4.

71. For both these Bible projects, see Jerry H. Bentley, *Humanists and Holy*

Writ: New Testament Scholarship in the Renaissance (Princeton: Princeton University Press, 1983).

72. See "Continental Versions to c. 1600," in *The Cambridge History of the Bible*, ed. S. L. Greenslade, 3 vols. (Cambridge: Cambridge University Press, 1963), vol. 2: *From the West to the Present Day*, pp. 94–140.

73. See "The Printed Bible," in *The Cambridge History of the Bible*, vol. 2, ed. Greenslade, pp. 423–441. For the Italian translations, see Gigliola Fragnito, *La Bibbia al Rogo: La Censura Ecclesiastica e I Volgarizzamenti della Scrittura, 1471–1605* (Bologna: Il Mulino, 1997), pp. 23–74. See also Jean-François Gilmont, "Protestant Reformations and Reading," in *A History of Reading in the West*, ed. Guiglielmo Cavallo and Roger Chartier, trans. Lydia G. Cochrane (Cambridge: Polity Press, 1999), pp. 213–237.

74. William Barlow, *A dyaloge describing the originall grou[n]d of these Lutheran faccyons, and many of theyr abusys, compyled by syr wyllyam Barlow chanon* (London, 1531), RSTC, 1461 (at image 77). A facsimile text is available in *William Barlowe's Dialogue on the Lutheran Factions*, introduction by Andrew McClean (Appleford, Oxon.: Sutton Courtenay Press, 1981); this passage from p. 108.

75. Barlow, *A dyaloge describing the originall grou[n]d of these Lutheran faccyons*, image 84 (*William Barlowe's Dialogue*, ed. McClean, p. 116).

76. More, *A Dialogue Concerning Heresies*, ed. Lawler et al., 1: 34/6–7.

77. Tyndale, "The Preface . . . that he made before . . . Genesis," in *Old Testament*, ed. Daniell, p. 8.

78. John Foxe, *Acts and Monuments* [. . .] (1563 edition), [online]. (hriOnline, Sheffield). Available from http://www.hrionline.ac.uk/johnfoxe, *Acts and Monuments*, Part 3, p. 468.

79. *Records of the English Bible*, ed. Pollard, p. 173.

80. For further conversion narratives centered on reading experience, see Alec Ryrie, *The Gospel and Henry VIII: Evangelicals in the Early English Reformation* (Cambridge: Cambridge University Press, 2003), pp. 157–159, and also pp. 201–252 for different loci that warmly embraced reading of the vernacular Bible. See also Peter Marshall, "Evangelical Conversion in the Reign of Henry VIII," in *The Beginnings of English Protestantism* (Cambridge: Cambridge University Press, 2002), pp. 14–37.

81. For the figure of fifty thousand copies of the Tyndale and Coverdale

Bibles sold before 1539, see the plausible calculations of Daniell, *The Bible in English*, p. 135, note 9. See also Ian Green, *Print and Protestantism in Early Modern England* (Oxford: Oxford University Press, 2000), pp. 50–52.

82. See Gilmont, "Protestant Reformations and Reading," p. 216.

83. George Joye, *A present consolation for the sufferers of persecucion for ryghtwysenes* (Antwerp, 1544), RSTC, 14828, image 3. All further citations will be made by image number in the body of the text.

84. *Paraclesis*, in *Novum Instrumentum* (Basel, 1516), facsimile edition, ed. Heinz Holeczek (Stuttgart: Fromann, 1986), aaa3v–aaa6v. The first English translation was published in 1529: *An exhortation to the diligent studye of scripture, made by Erasmus Roterodamus* (Antwerp, 1529), RSTC, 10493. All further citations will be made by image number in the body of the text.

85. William Tyndale, *The Obedience of a Christian Man*, ed. David Daniell (London: Penguin, 2000), p. 16. Further references are made by page number in the body of the text.

86. For an overview of pre-Wycliffite scriptural translation and adaption, see Geoffrey Shepherd, "English Versions of the Scriptures Before Wyclif," in *Poets and Prophets: Essays in Medieval Studies by G. T. Shepherd*, ed. T. A. Shippey and John Pickles (Cambridge: Brewer, 1990), pp. 59–83. For a wider survey, see Lawton, "Englishing the Bible," pp. 454–482.

87. RSTC, 2070. For the text, see Thomas Cranmer, "A Prologue or Preface," in *Miscellaneous Writings and Letters of Thomas Cranmer*, ed. John E. Cox (Cambridge: Cambridge University Press, 1846), pp. 118–125. Further references will be made by page number in the body of the text.

88. Martin Luther, *To the Christian Nobility of the German Nation*, in *Luther's Works*, 44, *The Christian in Society*, 1, ed. James Atkinson (Philadelphia: Fortress Press, 1966), pp. 123–217 (at p. 133).

89. Tyndale, *Obedience*, ed. Daniell, p. 20.

90. Ibid., p. 23.

91. William Tyndale, *The Parable of the Wicked Mammon*, in *Doctrinal Treatises and Introductions to Different Portions of The Holy Scriptures by William Tyndale*, ed. Henry Walter (Cambridge: Cambridge University Press, 1848), pp. 37–126.

92. Tyndale, *The Parable of the Wicked Mammon*, ed. Walter, p. 42. All subsequent references in this chapter will be by page number in the body of the text.

93. For the Book of Jonah's popularity among evangelicals, see Tyndale, *Old Testament*, ed. David Daniell, p. xxvi.

94. Tyndale, *Old Testament*, ed. Daniell, p. 628. All further references to the Prologue to Jonah in this chapter will be made by page number in the body of the text.

95. William Tyndale, *Tyndale's New Testament*, ed. David Daniell (New Haven: Yale University Press, 1989), p. 290. For evangelical readiness to suffer death, see Brad S. Gregory, *Salvation at Stake: Christian Martyrdom in Early Modern Europe* (Cambridge, Mass.: Harvard University Press, 1999), p. 109.

3. Salvation, Reading, and Textual Hatred

1. For simplistic, exceptionally repetitive, and sometimes inaccurate discussions of Tyndale's style, see David Daniell, *The Bible in English: Its History and Influence* (New Haven: Yale University Press, 2003), pages listed in the index under "Tyndale, and simplicity of style." See further Chapters 1 above and 4 below. See also Gerald Hammond, *The Making of the English Bible* (Manchester: Carcanet, 1982). For a much more sophisticated discussion of style that recognizes the full range of claims being made by a style, see Janel M. Mueller, *The Native Tongue and the Word: Developments in English Prose Style 1380–1580* (Chicago: University of Chicago Press, 1984), pp. 177–201. For sixteenth-century defenses of the plain style, see John N. King, *English Reformation Literature: The Tudor Origins of the Protestant Tradition* (Princeton: Princeton University Press, 1982), pp. 138–144. For a penetrating discussion of the difference between what sixteenth-century translators say about their style and the functions of that style, see Richard Duerden, "Equivalence or Power? Authority and Reformation Bible Translation," in *The Bible as Book: The Reformation*, ed. Orlaith O'Sullivan and Ellen Herron (London: The British Library, 2000), pp. 9–23. In this chapter and the next I take my cue from this point by Duerden: "The Bible is still treated in a separate realm of aesthetics and language. We discuss philological accuracy and stylistic beauty, while all

about and through these texts swirl the perils and promises of conviction—both kinds—and of ideology, authority, and power" (p. 9).

2. Miles Coverdale, *Biblia the Bible, that is, the holy Scripture of the Olde and New Testament, faithfully and truly translated out of Douche and Latyn in to Englishe* (Antwerp, 1535), RSTC, 2063.3, image 7. All further references to this prologue in this chapter will be made by image number in the body of the text.

3. *Biblia Sacra iuxta Vulgatam Clementinam*, 5th ed., ed. Alberto Colunga and Laurentio Turrado (Madrid: Biblioteca de Autores Cristianos, 1977). Christ says exactly the same thing in Matthew 4:17.

4. Both versions of the Wycliffite Bible have this reading.

5. William Tyndale, *Tyndale's New Testament*, ed. David Daniell (New Haven: Yale University Press, 1989), p. 23.

6. *Erasmus von Rotterdam, Novum Instrumentum* (Basel, 1516), facsimile edition, ed. Heinz Holeczek (Stuttgart: Fromann, 1986), p. 5.

7. Ibid., p. 241.

8. William Tyndale, *An Answer unto Sir Thomas Mores Dialogue*, ed. Anne M. O'Donnell and Jared Wicks (Washington: The Catholic University of America Press, 2000), p. 22.

9. Ibid., p. 21. See also the pages headed "Of Penance" in William Tyndale, *The Obedience of a Christian Man*, ed. David Daniell (London: Penguin, 2000), pp. 115–116.

10. Thomas More, *The Confutation of Tyndale's Answer*, ed. Louis A. Schuster, Richard Marius, James P. Lusardi, and Richard J. Schoeck, in *The Complete Works of St. Thomas More*, 8, 3 Parts (New Haven: Yale University Press, 1973), 1: 212.

11. For its consequences in England, see Marjorie Curry Woods and Rita Copeland, "Classroom and Confession," in *The Cambridge History of Medieval English Literature*, ed. David Wallace (Cambridge: Cambridge University Press, 1999), pp. 376–406.

12. Coverdale, *Biblia the Bible*, image 477.

13. Coverdale actually does use the word "penance" in his New Testament translation. At Acts 3:19, for example, his translation reads "Do penaunce therefore now and turn you" (see Coverdale, *Biblia the Bible*, image 528). Tyndale's translation (1534) reads: "Repent ye therefore and turn" (Tyndale, *New Testament*, ed. Daniell, p. 168).

14. Tyndale also has a passage devoted to translation of the word "repen-

tance" in the prologue to his 1534 edition of the New Testament; see Tyndale, *New Testament*, ed. Daniell, pp. 9–10. Tyndale nowhere allows "penance" as a possible translation, and he is more forthright in Lutheran dismissal of the Catholic sacrament of penance: confession is necessary for repentance, but "not in the priest's ear, for that is but man's invention, but to God in the heart and before all the congregation of God, how that we be sinners and sinful, and that our whole nature is corrupt and inclined to sin and all unrighteousness, and therefore evil, wicked and damnable . . . even so faith in Christ's blood is counted righteousness and a purging of all sin before God" (pp. 9–10).

15. For a crisp summation of Erasmus's sense of the importance of inner piety and his lesser emphasis on the sacraments, see Alister E. McGrath, *Reformation Thought: An Introduction*, 3rd ed. (Oxford: Blackwell, 1999), p. 53. For the Erasmian program in its English context, see James Kelsey McConica, *English Humanists and Reformation Politics under Henry VIII and Edward VI* (Oxford: Clarendon Press, 1965), though McConica too readily describes Lutheran policies as Erasmian.

16. Luther, *Ninety-five Theses*, in *Luther's Works*, 31, ed. Grimm, p. 30.

17. Ibid., p. 25. There are other, more far-reaching theses that leap out from this mercurial, witty text (e.g., 58, 60).

18. Luther's Latin text reads: "Dominus et magister noster Iesus Christus dicendo 'Penitentiam agite &c.' omnem vitam fidelium penitentiam esse voluit." Cited from online edition of the Weimar edition of Luther's works, *Luther's Werke* (*http://luther.chadwyck.com*), *Schriften*, 1: 233.

19. Martin Luther, *The Babylonian Captivity of the Church*, in *Luther's Works*, 36, *Word and Sacrament*, 2, ed. Abdel Ross Wentz (Philadelphia: Fortress Press, 1959), p. 84.

20. Ibid., p. 84.

21. "Eyn Christen mensch ist eyn freyer herr ueber alle ding, und niemandt unterthan. Eyn Christen mensch ist eyn dienstpar knecht aller ding, und yderman unterthan." Cited from Martin Luther, *Von der Freiheit eines Christenmenschen*, in *Luther's Werke* (*http://luther.chadwyck.com*), *Schriften*, 7: 21. English translation taken from *The Freedom of a Christian*, in *Luther's Works*, 31, *Career of the Reformer*, 1, ed. Harold Grimm (Philadelphia: Muhlenberg Press, 1957), pp. 327–377 (at p. 344).

22. Luther, *The Freedom of a Christian*, ed. Grimm, pp. 346–347.

23. For the profile of despair in English Puritan culture more generally, see John Stachniewski, *The Persecutory Imagination: English Puritanism and the Literature of Religious Despair* (Oxford: Oxford University Press, 1991).

24. For historical perspective on Luther's theology, see Alister E. McGrath, *Iustitia Dei: A History of the Christian Doctrine of Justification*, 2 vols. (Cambridge: Cambridge University Press, 1986), vol. 1: *From the Beginnings to 1500*. See also Heiko A. Oberman, *The Harvest of Medieval Theology: Gabriel Biel and Late Medieval Nominalism* (Cambridge, Mass.: Harvard University Press, 1963).

25. The history of individuality or, more recently, subjectivity in the West, routinely part of a progressivist narrative, tends to ignore this negative aspect of "subjectivity." The seminal work is Jacob Burckhardt, *The Civilization of the Renaissance in Italy*, trans. S. G. C. Middlemore (New York: Harper, 1958; first published in German, 1860), Part 2, "The Development of the Individual." The more recent history of the concept in literary studies derives from an important article by Thomas M. Greene, "The Flexibility of the Self in Renaissance Literature," in *The Disciplines of Criticism: Essays in Literary Theory, Interpretation, and History*, ed. Peter Demetz, Thomas Greene, and Lowry Nelson Jr. (New Haven: Yale University Press, 1968), pp. 241–264. The great exception to placement of early modern subjectivity in a progressivist, enlightened narrative is Stephen Greenblatt's *Renaissance Self-Fashioning* (Chicago: University of Chicago Press, 1980); see especially Greenblatt's comments about subjectivity in Tyndale (p. 85). For a critique of the simplistic way in which this view is almost always underwritten by a conviction that medieval subjectivity was both stable and conceivable only within larger collectivities, see David Aers, "A Whisper in the Ear of the Early Modernists, or Reflections on Literary Critics Writing the 'History of the Subject,'" in *Culture and History 1350–1600: Essays on English Communities, Identities, and Writing*, ed. David Aers (Detroit: Wayne State University Press, 1992), pp. 177–202.

26. For Luther's rejection of contemporary Biblical prophecy, see Martin Luther, *Against the Heavenly Prophets in the Matter of Images and Sacraments*, ed. Conrad Bergendorff, in *Luther's Works*, ed. Helmut T. Lehmann (Philadelphia: Muhlenberg Press, 1958), vol. 40, pp. 79–223.

27. Luther, *The Freedom of a Christian*, ed. Grimm, p. 346.

28. For the medieval tradition of applied ethical readings, see Winthrop Wetherbee, "The Study of Classical Authors: From Late Antiquity to the Twelfth Century," and Vincent Gillespie, "The Study of Classical Authors: From the Twelfth Century to c. 1450," both in *The Cambridge History of Literary Criticism*, vol. 2, *The Middle Ages*, ed. Alastair Minnis and Ian Johnson (Cambridge: Cambridge University Press, 2005), pp. 99–144 and 145–238.

29. Luther, *The Freedom of a Christian*, ed. Grimm, p. 348.

30. See *Der Durchbruch: Neuere Untersuchungen*, ed. Bernhard Lohse (Stuttgart: F. Steiner, 1988).

31. The English translation is cited from Martin Luther, *Preface to the Complete Edition of Luther's Latin Writings, 1545*, in *Luther's Works*, 34, *Career of the Reformer 4*, ed. Lewis W. Spitz (Philadelphia: Muhlenberg Press, 1960), pp. 327–343 (at pp. 336–338). The Latin text is cited from *Luther's Werke* (*http://luther.chadwyck.com*), *Schriften* 54, pp. 185–186.

32. For the grammatical issues underlying sixteenth-century theology, see the profound work by Brian Cummings, *The Literary Culture of the Reformation: Grammar and Grace* (Oxford: Oxford University Press, 2002). For discussion of Luther's "breakthrough," see pp. 57–68.

33. Grammarians would use the distinction between the objective and subjective genitive. In cases of the objective genitive, the noun modified by the genitive is affected by the word in the genitive ("the [recognized, common standard of] justice that God practices"). In cases of the subjective genitive, the noun modified by the genitive word is the source of the thing designated by the genitive word ("the justice that belongs wholly to God").

34. Luther, *The Freedom of a Christian*, ed. Grimm, p. 348.

35. Luther, *Preface to the Complete Edition of Luther's Latin Writings*, in *Luther's Werke* (*http://luther.chadwyck.com*), *Schriften* 54, p. 186.

36. William Tyndale, *Tyndale's Old Testament*, ed. David Daniell (New Haven: Yale University Press, 1992), p. 193.

37. I owe this observation to Frances Whistler.

38. The English text is available as *The Pathway into the Holy Scripture*, in William Tyndale, *Doctrinal Treatises and Introductions to Different Portions of the Holy Scriptures*, ed. Henry Walter (Cambridge: Cambridge University Press, 1848), pp. 7–28. The *Pathway* is a revision of the 1525 prologue. All further references to this text in this chapter will be made

by page number in the body of the text. An English translation of Luther's prologue to his 1522 New Testament is available in Martin Luther, *Prefaces to the New Testament*, in *Luther's Works*, 35, *Word and Sacrament*, 1, ed. E. Theodore Bachmann (Philadelphia: Muhlenberg Press, 1960), pp. 357–362.

39. The passages in square brackets did not appear in the 1525 Prologue, and were added to the 1530 edition of the *Pathway*.

40. David Daniell, *William Tyndale, A Biography* (New Haven: Yale University Press, 1994), pp. 131–132.

41. Ibid., pp. 131–133.

42. Tyndale, *New Testament*, ed. Daniell, p. 3. All further references to the Prologue to the 1534 New Testament in this chapter will be made by page number in the body of the text.

43. See, for example, Paul Althaus, *Die Theologie Martin Luthers* (Gütersloh: Gerd Mohn, 1962), pp. 75–77.

44. Citation from "A Fruitful Exhortation to the Reading and Knowledge of Holy Scripture," in *"Certain Sermons or Homilies" (1547) and "A Homily against Disobedience and Wilful Rebellion" (1570)*, ed. Ronald B. Bond (Toronto: University of Toronto Press, 1987), pp. 61–67 (at p. 62).

45. *A Christmas Banquet*, in *The Early Works of Thomas Becon*, ed. John Ayre (Cambridge: Cambridge University Press, 1843), pp. 63–84 (at pp. 63–65).

46. For the question of Tyndale's agreement or disagreement with Luther regarding works, see William A. Clebsch, *England's Earliest Protestants, 1520–1535* (New Haven: Yale University Press, 1964), and Carl Trueman, *Luther's Legacy: Salvation and English Reformers, 1525–1556* (Oxford: Clarendon Press, 1994). Both Clebsch and Trueman argue that Tyndale adopted a covenant doctrine concerning the Christian's relationship with God. Such a doctrine is at odds with Luther's repudiation of any pact whatsoever, since a pact would constrain God's wholly unbounded prerogative. Clebsch argues that the repudiation of Luther is complete by 1530, by which time Tyndale had rejected God's *opus alienum* and instead domesticated the law (p. 155). It is true that, in the 1534 New Testament prologue, Tyndale does stress the importance of works within a "general covenant" (p. 4). The prologue as a whole, however, offers no resolution between that non-Lutheran accent and the distinctively Lutheran statements made elsewhere in the same prologue.

47. Desiderius Erasmus, *De Libero Arbitrio* (*On the Freedom of the Will*), in *Luther and Erasmus: Free Will and Salvation*, trans. E. Gordon Rupp, A. N. Marlow, Philip S. Watson, and B. Drewery (Philadelphia: Westminster Press, 1969), pp. 35–97 (at p. 65).

48. Ibid., p. 65.

49. Martin Luther, *On the Bondage of the Will*, in *Luther and Erasmus*, trans. Rupp et al., pp. 101–334. For subtle discussion of the Erasmus/Luther confrontation, see Cummings, *The Literary Culture of the Reformation*, pp. 144–183.

50. Luther, *On the Bondage of the Will*, trans. Rupp et al., p. 223.

51. Ibid., p. 230.

52. Ibid.

53. Luther's position on Pharaoh is taken directly from Paul, Romans 9:17: "For the scripture saith unto Pharaoh: Even for this same purpose I have stirred thee up, to show my power on thee."

54. Tyndale, *Old Testament*, ed. Daniell, p. 179 (Leviticus 20:24).

55. Thomas Cranmer, "A Prologue or Preface," in *Miscellaneous Writings and Letters of Thomas Cranmer*, ed. John E. Cox (Cambridge: Cambridge University Press, 1846), pp. 118–125 (at p. 118). All further references to this Prologue in this chapter will be made by page number in the body of the text.

56. Discussed in Chapters 2 and 5.

57. Thomas Cranmer, *Catechismus, that is to say, a shorte instruction into Christian religion for the synguler commoditie and profyte of childre[n] and yong people* (London, 1548), RSTC, 5993.

58. Ibid., image 128.

4. *The Literal Sense and Predestination*

1. This and the following two paragraphs are based on James Simpson, *Reform and Cultural Revolution* (Oxford: Oxford University Press, 2002), pp. 458–459.

2. John Foxe, *Acts and Monuments* [. . .] (1570 edition), [online]. (hriOnline, Sheffield). Available from *http://www.brionline.ac.uk/johnfoxe*, *Acts and Monuments*, 8: 1230.

3. John Foxe, *Acts and Monuments* [. . .] (1570 edition), 8: 1230.

4. Ibid., 8: 1225.

5. Ibid., 8: 1228.

6. Ibid., 8: 1226.

7. My argument parallels that of the excellent book by Thomas Betteridge, *Tudor Histories of the English Reformations, 1530–1583* (Aldershot, Hants.: Ashgate, 1999), especially p. 21.

8. Martin Luther, *On the Bondage of the Will*, in *Luther and Erasmus: Free Will and Salvation*, trans. E. Gordon Rupp, A. N. Marlow, Philip S. Watson, Paul Althaus, and B. Drewery (Philadelphia: Westminster Press, 1969), pp. 110–111. See also Paul Althaus, *The Theology of Martin Luther*, trans. Robert C. Schultz (Philadelphia: Fortress Press, 1966; first published 1962), pp. 75–77.

9. "The Preface of Master William Tyndale that he made before the Five Books of Moses called Genesis," in William Tyndale, *Tyndale's Old Testament*, ed. David Daniell (New Haven: Yale University Press, 1992), pp. 3–4.

10. "A Prologue into the Second Book of Moses called Exodus," in *Tyndale's Old Testament*, ed. Daniell, p. 84.

11. "A Prologue into the Third Book of Moses called Leviticus," in *Tyndale's Old Testament*, ed. Daniell, p. 148.

12. William Tyndale, *The Obedience of a Christian Man*, ed. David Daniell (London: Penguin, 2000), p. 156. Further references to the *Obedience* in this chapter will be made by page number in the body of the text.

13. For histories of the literal sense, see the following works by Rita Copeland: *Rhetoric, Hermeneutics, and Translation in the Middle Ages: Academic Traditions and Vernacular Texts*, Cambridge Studies in Medieval Literature, 11 (Cambridge: Cambridge University Press, 1991); and her *Pedagogy, Intellectuals, and Dissent in the Later Middle Ages: Lollardy and Ideas of Learning* (Cambridge: Cambridge University Press, 2001). See also Gilbert Dahan, *L'Exégèse Chrétienne de la Bible en Occident Médiéval, XII–XIV siècle* (Paris: Cerf, 1999), pp. 243–271.

14. See, for example, Thomas Aquinas (d. 1274): "Holy Scripture sets up no confusion, since all meanings are based on one, namely the literal sense. From this alone can arguments be drawn, and not . . . from the things said by allegory." See St. Thomas Aquinas, *Summa Theologiae*, ed. Thomas Gilby, 60 vols. (London: Eyre and Spottiswoode, 1968), 1a.1,10, 1:39.

15. For the history of late antique and medieval Biblical scholarship, see Henri de Lubac, *Exégèse médiévale: les quatres sens de l'Écriture*, vols. 41, 42,

and 59 of *Théologie*, 2 vols. in 4 (Paris: Aubier, 1959–1964); Beryl Smalley, *The Study of the Bible in the Middle Ages* (Notre Dame: University of Notre Dame Press, 1964); and Dahan, *L'Exégèse Chrétienne*. Dahan remarks that in practice the system was much more flexible than it sounds: exegetes did not attempt a consistent application of the fourfold system to each text; and most exegetes between the twelfth and fourteenth centuries insist on the fundamental importance of the literal sense and its richness (p. 436).

16. See especially Barbara Kiefer Lewalski, *Protestant Poetics and the Seventeenth-Century Religious Lyric* (Princeton: Princeton University Press, 1979), pp. 111–144.

17. William Tyndale, *Tyndale's New Testament*, ed. David Daniell (New Haven: Yale University Press, 1989), p. 279. Further references to Tyndale's New Testament in this chapter will be made by page number in the body of the text. Erasmus's *Novum Instrumentum* has "allegoriam"; *Erasmus von Rotterdam, Novum Instrumentum* (Basel, 1516), facsimile edition, ed. Heinz Holeczek (Stuttgart: Fromann, 1986), p. 80.

18. The words are those of Nicholas Udall, in his translation of Erasmus's Paraphrase of the New Testament; see Desiderius Erasmus, *The first tome or volume of the Paraphrase of Erasmus upon the newe testamente* (London, 1548), RSTC, 2854.4, image 10.

19. See Aquinas, *Summa Theologiae*, ed. Gilby, 1a.1,10, 1:40.

20. Tyndale frequently refers to the text of the heart. See, for example, the Prologue to Jonas: ". . . which two points I say, if they be written in thine heart, are the keys which so open all the scripture unto thee, that no creature can lock thee out" (*Tyndale's Old Testament*, ed. Daniell, p. 638).

21. Martin Luther, *Predigten, 1533–4*, in *Luther's Werke* (http://luther.chadwyck.com), 37: 246; translation cited from Joseph Leo Koerner, *The Reformation of the Image* (Chicago: University of Chicago Press), pp. 305–306.

22. Cited from "A Fruitful Exhortation to the Reading and Knowledge of Holy Scripture," in *"Certain Sermons or Homilies" (1547) and "A Homily against Disobedience and Wilful Rebellion" (1570)*, ed. Ronald B. Bond (Toronto: University of Toronto Press, 1987), pp. 61–67 (at p. 63).

23. Martin Luther, *Prefaces to the New Testament*, in *Luther's Works*, 35, *Word and Sacrament*, 1, ed. E. Theodore Bachmann (Philadelphia: Muhlenberg Press, 1960), pp. 361–362.

24. Ibid., p. 362.
25. Ibid.
26. ". . . per sese certissima, facillima, apertissima, sui ipsius interpres, omnium omnia probans, iudicans et illuminans." *Assertio omnium articulorum per bullam Leonis X. novissimam damnatorum,* in Luther's *Werke (http://luther.chadwyck.com),* 7: 94–151 (at p. 97). For the idea of Scripture interpreting itself elsewhere in Luther's works, see Paul Althaus, *Die Theologie Martin Luthers* (Gütersloh: Gerd Mohn, 1962), pp. 75–77. See also Walter Mostert, "Scriptura Sui Ipsius Interpres. Bemerkungen zum Verständnis der heligen Schrift durch Luther," *Luther-Jahrbuch,* 46 (1979): 60–96.
27. Tyndale gives a brief but inaccurate account of the four senses; he says that "the allegory is appropriate to faith" (Tyndale, *The Obedience of a Christian Man,* ed. Daniell, p. 156). With perhaps less excuse, David Daniell repeats this cardinal error in his own account of the fourfold scheme. His definition of the allegorical sense is given as follows: "speaking to some belief" (*The Bible in English: Its History and Influence* [New Haven: Yale University Press, 2003], p. 128). Daniell reserves one inaccurate paragraph for "questions of exegesis" in his discussion of the Protestant Bible (ibid., pp. 127–128).
28. Daniell, *The Bible in English,* p. 160.
29. Ibid., pp. 60–61.
30. Thus, for example, "in 1526, a few local documents were beginning to be expressed in English" (ibid., p. 136). For the change to English for official documents in the early fifteenth century, see John H. Fisher, "A Language Policy for Lancastrian England," *PMLA,* 107 (1992): 1168–1180.
31. For Daniell's inaccurate word-counts, see Chapter 1.
32. In Daniell, *The Bible in English,* p. 253, we are given an example of prose (1660) from the Royal Society, designed to show how "St. Paul's stylistic artistry" found its way into English scientific prose; the features we are asked to attend to are the "Saxon words and order, the parataxis, the short units, of the best plain style." The single paragraph of seven lines cited contains 17 Latin-derived words; its first sentence contains four main clauses, each joined by "and," but within those main clauses there are three subordinate clauses, one of which itself contains a further subordinate clause.
33. William Tyndale, *An Answer unto Sir Thomas Mores Dialogue,* ed. Anne

M. O'Donnell and Jared Wicks (Washington: Catholic University of America Press, 2000), p. 23.

34. For the later medieval history of written legal and theological documents impersonally applied, see Brian Stock, *The Implications of Literacy: Written Language and Models of Interpretation in the Eleventh and Twelfth Centuries* (Princeton: Princeton University Press, 1983); M. T. Clanchy, *From Memory to Written Record: England 1066–1307,* 2nd ed. (Oxford: Blackwell, 1993); and Richard Firth Green, *A Crisis of Truth: Literature and Law in Ricardian England* (Philadelphia: University of Pennsylvania Press, 2002).

35. See Elizabeth Eisenstein, *The Printing Press as an Agent of Change,* 2 vols. (Cambridge: Cambridge University Press, 1979).

36. William Tyndale, *The Pathway into the Holy Scripture,* in Tyndale, *Doctrinal Treatises and Introductions to Different Portions of the Holy Scriptures,* ed. Henry Walter, Parker Society (Cambridge: Cambridge University Press, 1848), p. 28.

37. Martin Luther, "Luther at the Diet of Worms, 1521," in *Luther's Works,* 32, *Career of the Reformer,* 2, ed. George W. Forell (Philadelphia: Muhlenberg Press, 1958), pp. 101–132 (at p. 111). The original Latin can be found in *Luther's Werke (http://luther.chadwyck.com),* 7: 832a–857a.

38. Luther, "Luther at the Diet of Worms, 1521," ed. Forell, p. 111.

39. "Ich kan nicht anderst, hie stehe ich, Got helff mir, Amen." Ibid., p. 113. For the German insertion, see *Luther's Werke (http://luther .chadwyck.com),* 7: 838a.

40. For Luther's rejection of Penance, see Alister E. McGrath, *Reformation Thought,* 3rd ed. (Oxford: Blackwell, 1999), p. 175.

41. For all these positions, see Martin Luther, *The Babylonian Captivity of the Church,* in *Luther's Works,* 36, *Word and Sacrament,* 2, ed. Abdel Ross Wentz (Philadelphia: Fortress Press, 1959), pp. 11–126.

42. Ibid., p. 58.

43. All points made in the introductory essay of Tyndale's *Answer to More;* see Tyndale, *An Answer unto Sir Thomas Mores Dialogue,* ed. O'Donnell and Wicks, pp. 5–78.

44. Thomas More, *A Dialogue Concerning Heresies,* ed. T. M. C. Lawler, Germain Marc'hadour, and Richard Marius, 2 Parts, in *The Complete Works of St. Thomas More,* 6 (New Haven: Yale University Press, 1981), 1: 433/23–28.

45. For these symptoms, see Betteridge, *Tudor Histories of the English Re-*

formations, especially p. 119: for evangelicals, only the Word of God could be trusted, "provided this Word was first mediated, explained, glossed, cleaned [and] explicated . . . by the *veritas*-producing author within whose works the Word of God could be found." See also Richard L. Gawthrop and Gerald Strauss, "Protestantism and Literacy in Early Modern Germany," *Past and Present,* 104 (1984): 31–55. They argue that until 1525, Luther favored "everyman as his own Bible reader; thereafter he falls silent and effectively discouraged the unmediated encounter between sacred scripture and the untrained lay mind" (p. 34).

46. For discussion of this feature of Christian hermeneutics in the larger history of interpretation, see James Simpson, "Faith and Hermeneutics: Pragmatism versus Pragmatism," *Journal of Medieval and Early Modern Studies,* 33 (2003): 215–239.

47. William Tyndale, *An exposicion vppon the v. vi. vii. chapters of Mathew which thre chaptres are the keye and the dore of the scripture* (London, 1536; first published 1533), RSTC, 24441.3. Further references to this text in this chapter will be made by image number in the body of the text, unless otherwise specified.

48. For discussion of the *topos* of writing on the heart, I am much indebted to Milad Doueihi. See also his *A Perverse History of the Human Heart* (Cambridge, Mass.: Harvard University Press, 1997).

49. Desiderius Erasmus, *De Libero Arbitrio (On the Freedom of the Will),* in *Luther and Erasmus: Free Will and Salvation,* trans. E. Gordon Rupp, A. N. Marlow, Philip S. Watson, and B. Drewery (Philadelphia: Westminster Press, 1969), p. 43. Thomas More makes exactly the same point (no doubt drawn from Erasmus), in *The Confutation of Tyndale's Answer,* ed. Louis A. Schuster, Richard Marius, James P. Lusardi, and Richard J. Schoeck, *The Complete Works of St. Thomas More,* 8, 3 Parts (New Haven: Yale University Press, 1973), 2: 658/10–15.

50. "A Prologue into the Second Book of Moses called Exodus," in *Tyndale's Old Testament,* ed. Daniell, p. 85.

51. For the endemic Protestant practice of breaking up Scripture into more digestible units, see Peter Stallybrass, "Books and Scrolls: Navigating the Bible," in *Books and Readers in Early Modern England: Material Studies,* ed. Jennifer Anderson and Elizabeth Sauer (Philadelphia: University of Philadelphia Press, 2002), pp. 42–79.

52. ". . . Der rechte kern und marck unter allen buchern," in Martin Luther, "Vorrede auf das Neue Testament." See *Luther's Werke* (http://luther.chadwyck.com), 6: 10.

53. Luther, "Preface to the Epistle of Paul to the Romans," in Martin Luther, *Prefaces to the New Testament*, in *Luther's Works*, 35, *Word and Sacrament*, 1, ed. Bachmann, pp. 365–380 (at p. 365).

54. "A Prologue into the Fifth Book of Moses called Deuteronomy," in *Tyndale's Old Testament*, ed. Daniell, p. 254.

55. Luther, *Prefaces to the New Testament*, in *Luther's Works*, 35, *Word and Sacrament*, 1, ed. Bachmann, p. 362.

56. Tyndale takes especial care to reinterpret James's remarks about works within a Lutheran optic. See *Tyndale's New Testament*, ed. Daniell, pp. 361–362.

57. For Luther's theology in its historical perspective, see Alister E. McGrath, *Iustitia Dei: A History of the Christian Doctrine of Justification*, 2 vols. (Cambridge: Cambridge University Press, 1986), vol. 2: *From 1500 to the Present Day*, especially p. 199.

58. Luther, *Prefaces to the New Testament*, in *Luther's Works*, 35, *Word and Sacrament*, 1, ed. Bachmann, p. 357.

59. On this see Heinrich Bornkamm, *Luther and the Old Testament*, trans. Eric W. Gritsch and Ruth C. Gritsch (Philadelphia: Fortress Press, 1969), pp. 82–86, and Althaus, *Die Theologie Martin Luthers*, pp. 83–86.

60. The profoundly influential source text for Luther's concept of God as the *deus alienus* is Isaiah 28:21: "For the Lord will rise up as in Mount Perazim, he will rage as in the valley of Gibeon; to do his deed—strange is his deed! And to work his work—alien is his work!" (cited from *The Holy Bible, New Revised Standard Version* [Oxford: Oxford University Press, 1989]). For the theology of God's justice as alien to humanity, see Althaus, *Die Theologie Martin Luthers*, pp. 197–203, and McGrath, *Iustitia Dei*, 2: 199.

61. Thus, for example, twelfth-century Neo-Platonist writers who accented the utterly transcendent nature of God also accented the impossibility of language to designate God. See James Simpson, *Sciences and the Self in Medieval Poetry: Alan of Lille's "Anticlaudianus" and John Gower's "Confessio amantis"* (Cambridge: Cambridge University Press, 1995), pp. 66–74.

62. Thomas Becon, *News out of Heaven* (London, 1541), RSTC, 1740. "He

that shall make this book his companion shall here find in few leaves that the whole bible and commentaries of the ancient doctors do teach of Christ in many." Cited from Thomas Becon, *News out of Heaven*, in *The Early Works*, ed. John Ayre (Cambridge: Cambridge University Press, 1843), pp. 37–58 (at p. 43).

63. See further Douglas H. Parker, "Tyndale's Biblical Hermeneutics," in *Word, Church and State: Tyndale Quincentenary Essays*, ed. John T. Day, Eric Lund, and Anne M. O'Donnell (Washington: Catholic University Press of America, 1998), pp. 87–101.

64. For the production of catechetical material in Protestant England, see Ian Green, *The Christian's ABC: Catechisms and Catechizing in England c. 1530–1740* (Oxford: Oxford University Press, 1996).

65. For the bitter Eucharistic divisions between Lutheran and Reformed (that is, broadly, Calvinist) Protestants in the sixteenth century, see Diarmaid MacCulloch, *Reformation: Europe's House Divided* (London: Allen Lane, 2003), pp. 248–253.

66. Erasmus, *De Libero Arbitrio*, in *Luther and Erasmus*, trans. Rupp et al., pp. 44–45.

67. Ibid., p. 46. See further C. Augustin, "Hyperaspistes I: La doctrine d'Érasme et de Luther sur la *claritas scripturae*," in *Colloquiua Erasmiana Turonensia*, 2 vols. (Paris: Vrin, 1972), 2: 737–748.

68. Tyndale, *An Answer unto Sir Thomas Mores Dialogue*, ed. O'Donnell and Wicks, p. 159. For Luther's hostility to councils, see, for example, Luther, *On the Bondage of the Will*, in *Luther and Erasmus: Free Will and Salvation*, trans. Rupp et al., pp. 154–158.

69. Tyndale elsewhere attacks Church councils; see, for example (for attacks on councils), William Tyndale, *The practyse of prelates. Compyled by the faythfull and godly learned man, Wyllyam Tyndale* (London, 1548), image 42, and Tyndale, *An exposicion vppon the v. vi. vii. chapters of Mathew*, image 44.

70. The citation is from Stephen Gardiner, *A declaration of suche true articles as George Ioye hath gone about to confute as false* (London, 1546), RSTC, 11589, image 86.

71. Daniell, *The Bible in English*, p. 268. Some of Britain's imperial subjects may not have felt quite so enthusiastic about the spread of English individualism "worldwide." I cite from *The Daily Telegraph* (U.K.), 9 February 2006, reporting on the Anglican Synod's apology for slave own-

ership in the eighteenth century: "The Church's missionary arm, the Society for the Propagation of the Faith in Foreign Parts, owned the Codrington plantation in Barbados and slaves had the word 'Society' branded on their chests with red-hot irons." Daniel himself cites American defenses of slavery on Biblical grounds (especially Paul's defense of slavery in 1 Timothy 6:1–2, where Paul's word is *doulos*, meaning "slave"); see Daniel, *The Bible in English*, pp. 708–710.

72. Daniell, *The Bible in English*, p. 130.

73. Ibid., p. 161.

74. Tyndale, *An exposicion vppon the v. vi. vii. chapters of Mathew*, image 129.

75. For Luther's commitment to predestination, see, for example, his Preface to Romans, in Luther, "Preface to the Epistle of Paul to the Romans," in Martin Luther, *Prefaces to the New Testament*, in *Luther's Works*, 35, *Word and Sacrament*, 1, ed. Bachmann, p. 378. For Tyndale's early commitment to predestination, see, for example, Tyndale, *The Pathway into the Holy Scripture*, in Tyndale, *Doctrinal Treatises*, ed. Walter, p. 14. For Luther's predestinarianism, see also Gordon Rupp, *The Righteousness of God: Luther Studies* (London: Hodder and Stoughton, 1953), pp. 186–191. For Tyndale's distancing from Luther's utter repudiation of works, see William A. Clebsch, *England's Earliest Protestants, 1520–1535* (New Haven: Yale University Press, 1964), chaps. 9 and 10; for Tyndale's reticence regarding predestination, see Carl Trueman, *Luther's Legacy: Salvation and English Reformers, 1525–1556* (Oxford: Clarendon Press, 1994), p. 85.

76. Tyndale frequently makes reference to predestination and the "elect" in, for example, *The Parable of the Wicked Mammon* (1528); see William Tyndale, *The Parable of the Wicked Mammon*, in *Doctrinal Treatises and Introductions to Different Portions of The Holy Scriptures by William Tyndale*, ed. Henry Walter (Cambridge: Cambridge University Press, 1848), p. 65: the true believer "in Christ was predestinate, and ordained unto eternal life, before the world began"; and p. 89: "Now may not we ask why God chooseth one and not another; either think that God is unjust to damn us afore we do any actual deed . . . our darkness cannot perceive his light." In the 1534 Prologue to Romans, Tyndale directly translates Luther's comments about the fact that God's predestination is "the most necessary of all" (Tyndale, "The Prologue to Romans," in *Tyndale's New Testament*, ed. Daniel, p. 221). Tyndale follows Luther in

trying to warn readers away from thinking overmuch about the terrors of predestination.

77. Tyndale, *The Pathway into the Holy Scripture*, in Tyndale, *Doctrinal Treatises*, ed. Walter, p. 14.

78. Tyndale, *The Parable of the Wicked Mammon*, in Tyndale, *Doctrinal Treatises*, ed. Walter, p. 80.

79. Tyndale, *An Answer unto Sir Thomas Mores Dialogue*, ed. O'Donnell and Wicks, p. 25.

80. Ibid., p. 47.

81. Thomas More himself remarks on the beauty of this passage; after calling Tyndale "our young eagle," he drops his guard momentarily: "These words walk, lo, very goodly by the hearer's ear, and they make a man amazed in a manner, and somewhat to study and muse, when he heareth so strange a tale told of such holy elects, so spying out the foot where the soil receiveth no footing" (see More, *Confutation of Tyndale's Answer*, ed. Schuster et al., 2: 724–725).

82. Tyndale, "A Prologue into the Second Book of Moses called Exodus," in *Tyndale's Old Testament*, ed. Daniell, p. 87.

83. Gardiner, *A declaration of suche true articles as George Ioye hath gone about to confute as false*, image 86.

84. For the terrible ambiguity of the signs of both election and reprobation in Puritan culture, see John Stachniewski, *The Persecutory Imagination: English Puritanism and the Literature of Religious Despair* (Oxford: Oxford University Press, 1991), pp. 89–90.

85. Tyndale, *The Parable of the Wicked Mammon*, in *Doctrinal Treatises and Introductions to Different Portions of The Holy Scriptures by William Tyndale*, ed. Walter, p. 85.

86. For the Protestant fascination with portents, see David Hall, *Worlds of Wonder, Days of Judgment: Popular Religious Belief in Early New England* (New York: Knopf, 1989).

5. Bible Reading, Persecution, and Paranoia

1. Peter R. Moore, "The Heraldic Charge Against the Earl of Surrey, 1546–47," *English Historical Review*, 116 (2001): 557–583, at p. 559.

2. Ibid., p. 562.

3. Susan Brigden, "Henry Howard, Earl of Surrey and the 'Conjured League,'" *The Historical Journal*, 37 (1994): 507–537, at p. 536.
4. Moore, "The Heraldic Charge," p. 581.
5. Brigden, "Henry Howard, Earl of Surrey," pp. 536–537.
6. *Certayne chapters of the proverbes of Salomon drawen into metre by Thomas Sternholde* (London, 1550), RSTC, 2760.
7. Examples are legion. Thus Isaiah 2:8; Jeremiah 44:15; Ezekiel 16.
8. All citations of the Psalms refer to the Vulgate numbering.
9. There are numerous other examples. I find the characteristic voice of the lonely and betrayed speaker in the following psalms: 2, 3, 5, 9b, 11, 16, 17, 30, 34, 35, 37, 43, 53, 54, 55, 58, 63, 68, 87, 108, 118, 139, 141. Though far less often than the prophets, some psalms also attack the idolatry of surrounding nations: for example, 39, 80, 105, 134.
10. Thomas Becon, *The new pollecye of warre . . . lately deuised by Theodore Basille* (London, 1542), RSTC, 1735. The text is available in Thomas Becon, *The Policy of War*, in *The Early Works*, ed. John Ayre (Cambridge: Cambridge University Press, 1843), pp. 232–261 (this citation at p. 243).
11. Becon, *The Policy of War*, ed. Ayre, p. 240.
12. For the tautness of Wyatt's theological and, therefore, linguistic predicament in his *Penitential Psalms*, see Brian Cummings, *The Literary Culture of the Reformation: Grammar and Grace* (Oxford: Oxford University Press, 2002), pp. 223–231.
13. The following three paragraphs are based on James Simpson, *Reform and Cultural Revolution* (Oxford: Oxford University Press, 2002), pp. 323–324.
14. Thomas More, *The Apology*, ed. J. B. Trapp, in *The Complete Works of St. Thomas More*, 9 (New Haven: Yale University Press, 1979), p. 9/22–23.
15. Citation of Wyatt's poetry is from *Sir Thomas Wyatt, The Complete Poems*, ed. R. A. Rebholz (London: Penguin, 1978). Further references to Wyatt's *Paraphrase of the Penitential Psalms* will be made by line number in the body of the text.
16. The text is available in *Narratives of the Days of the Reformation*, ed. John Gough Nichols, Camden Society 77 (London: Camden Society, 1859), pp. 52–56.

17. William Tyndale, *The Obedience of a Christian Man*, ed. David Daniell (London: Penguin, 2000), p. 39.

18. Ibid., pp. 41–42.

19. Ibid., p. 57.

20. For a brilliant and penetrating account of the relation between evangelical soteriology and absolutist politics in Tyndale's thought, see Richard Y. Duerden, "Justice and Justification: King and God in Tyndale's *The Obedience of a Christian Man*," in *William Tyndale and the Law*, ed. John A. R. Dick and Anne Richardson (Kirksville, Mo.: Sixteenth Century Journal Publishers, 1994), pp. 69–80; both the politics and the soteriology are motivated by a "sense of intolerable burdens and a longing for deliverance" (p. 73). See also the penetrating reading of Stephen Greenblatt, "The Word of God in an Age of Mechanical Reproduction," in *Renaissance Self-Fashioning, from More to Shakespeare* (Chicago: University of Chicago Press, 1980), pp. 74–114 (at pp. 91–92).

21. For the charges against Surrey and his imprisonment and execution, see W. A. Sessions, *Henry Howard: The Poet Earl of Surrey. A Life* (Oxford: Oxford University Press, 1999), pp. 358–387; and Moore, "The Heraldic Charge."

22. For arguments about dating each of these three psalm translations to this period, see (in addition to Sessions, *Henry Howard*), Rivkah Zim, *English Metrical Psalms: Poetry as Praise and Prayer 1535–1601* (Cambridge: Cambridge University Press, 1987), pp. 88–91.

23. C. A. Huttar, "Poems by Surrey and Others in a Printed Miscellany, c. 1550," *Miscellany*, 16 (1965): 9–18, argues (at pp. 11–15) that two of the translations (Psalms Vulgate 30 and 50) in *Certayne chapters of the proverbes of Salomon drawen into metre by Thomas Sternholde* (1550) were by Surrey.

24. Sessions, *Henry Howard*, pp. 354–357.

25. Citations from Surrey's Biblical translations are taken from *The Poems of Henry Howard Earl of Surrey*, ed. Frederick Morgan Padelford, revised edition (Seattle: University of Washington Press, 1928). Texts will be numbered in the body of the text by Biblical locus; number in Padelford edition; and line number. Padelford cites psalms by the King James numbering; I have altered these to Vulgate numbers. I have modernized spelling and made minor, unmarked emendations to Padelford's texts in matters of accidentals. References to any non-Bib-

lical texts by Surrey will also be made in the body of the text, and will also be drawn from the Padelford edition, by number in Padelford edition, and line number. See also *Henry Howard, Earl of Surrey, Poems,* ed. Emrys Jones (Oxford: Clarendon Press, 1964).

26. Sessions, *Henry Howard,* p. 146. For further discussion of Surrey's defiance toward Henry VIII as expressed by the Ecclesiastes paraphrases, see Greg Walker, *Writing Under Tyranny: English Literature and the Henrician Reformation* (Oxford: Oxford University Press, 2005), pp. 400–407.

27. *The Examinations of Anne Askew,* ed. Elaine V. Beilin (Oxford: Oxford University Press, 1996), p. 150, lines 41–48; I have repunctuated the text. See Sessions, *Henry Howard,* pp. 353–357 for Askew's borrowing from Surrey.

28. For Henry VIII's appropriation of the voices of both Solomon and David, see Pamela Tudor-Craig, "Henry VIII and King David," in *Early Tudor England: Proceedings of the 1987 Harlaxton Symposium,* ed. Daniel Williams (Woodbridge, Suffolk: Brewer, 1989), pp. 183–205.

29. Respectively, Padelford 35 and 36. For the positions of influence occupied by Denny and Blage, see Susan Brigden, "Henry Howard, Earl of Surrey," pp. 533–534. See also the discussion in Walker, *Writing Under Tyranny,* pp. 410–412.

30. The same psalm was also translated, in an equally vengeful spirit, by (?)John Dudley, Earl of Warwick, while in the Tower between 1553 and 1554. See *The Arundel Harrington Manuscript of Tudor Poetry,* ed. Ruth Hughey, 2 vols. (Columbus: Ohio State University Press, 1960), no. 289, and 2:433–435 for notes. Psalm 54, along with others, was also translated in the Tower by Sir Thomas Smith in 1549; see John N. King, *English Reformation Literature: The Tudor Origins of the Protestant Tradition* (Princeton: Princeton University Press, 1982), pp. 233–234. For courtly evangelical culture in Henrician England, see Alec Ryrie, *The Gospel and Henry VIII: Evangelicals in the Early English Reformation* (Cambridge: Cambridge University Press, 2003), pp. 201–205.

31. See also the comment in *L&P Henry VIII,* 21.2.287, a letter dated 19 October 1546, from Surrey to Paget, in which Surrey says that the cloister and dorter of Christ Church Norwich is of no use "saving for a memory of the old superstition." That Surrey did adopt an evangelical spirituality has not by any means always been accepted. The deci-

sive turning point was made by H. A. Mason, *Humanism and Poetry in the Early Tudor Period* (London: Routledge and Kegan Paul, 1959), pp. 240–247. For a subtle discussion of Surrey's evangelical accents, suggesting that they could themselves be politically strategic, see Elizabeth Heale, *Wyatt, Surrey, and Early Tudor Poetry* (Harlow, Essex: Longman, 1998), pp. 175–176. See also the finely nuanced account in Andrew Taylor, "Psalms and Early Tudor Humanism," Ph.D. dissertation, University of Cambridge, 2002. Walker, *Writing Under Tyranny*, pp. 397–398, urges caution in assuming that "Surrey was necessarily consistently Lutheran in his beliefs."

32. Padelford 36.

33. Brigden, "Henry Howard, Earl of Surrey," p. 525.

34. The text is printed in *The Life and Letters of Sir Thomas Wyatt*, ed. Kenneth Muir (Liverpool: University of Liverpool Press, 1963), Appendix C, pp. 273–276. Further citations are made in the body of the text by page number (Muir does not give line numbers).

35. See note 22 above.

36. Brad S. Gregory, *Salvation at Stake: Christian Martyrdom in Early Modern Europe* (Cambridge, Mass.: Harvard University Press, 1999), p. 136.

37. Cummings, *The Literary Culture of the Reformation*, comments on the use of the Psalms by Henrician courtiers thus: "The Psalms become a covert means of expressing the laments of these latter days" (p. 224).

38. Matthew Parker, *The Whole Psalter translated into English Metre* (London, 1567), RSTC, 2729, image 10.

39. Roger Ascham, *The Schoolmaster*, in *Roger Ascham, English Works*, ed. William Aldis Wright (Cambridge: Cambridge University Press, 1904), p. 247. Further references to this text will be made in the body of the text by page number.

40. Respectively, *Psalmorum omnium: iuxta Hebraicam veritatem paraphrastica interpretatio authore Ioanne Campensi . . .* (London, 1534), RSTC, 2354; and *A paraphrasis vpon all the Psalmes of Dauid, made by Ioannes Campensis . . .* (London, 1539), RSTC, 2372.6.

41. *The First Tome or Volume of the Paraphrase of Erasmus upon the New Testament*, trans. Nicholas Udall (London, 1548), RSTC, 2854. Reference to this text will be made in the body of the text by image number.

42. For example, *The Arundel Harrington Manuscript*, ed. Hughey, 2:106.

43. Compare, for example, Surrey, Psalm 54: "Myne old fere [compan-

ion] and dear friend, my guide that trapped me; / Where I was wont to fetch the cure of all my care, / And in his bosom hide my secret zeal to God" (Psalm 54; 54.23–25), with Campensis (1534 edition), paraphrase of Psalm 54.12:

> Non enim ex professo inimicus probro affecit me; tolerabile esset illud; neque palam hostis erexit sese adversum me, cuius vitare potuissem consortium. Sed tu homo quem prefeci rebus meis, qui veluti dux fuisti mihi, et arctissima familiaritate coniunctus. Mutuo enim et suaviter secreta nostra communicavimus, et in domo dei versati sumus concorditer.

44. The significant exception to the case I make here for Surrey's closeness to Campensis is the translation of Psalm 54, where lines 32–48 find almost no echo in either Campensis or the Vulgate.
45. *SR*, 34 Henry 8, 3: 894.
46. Ibid., 896.
47. Christopher St. German, *An Answer to a Letter* (London, 1535), RSTC, 21558.5. For discussion of this text in its context, see John Guy, "Scripture as Authority: Problems of Interpretation in the 1530s," in Alistair Fox and John Guy, *Reassessing the Henrician Era: Humanism, Politics and Reform 1500–1550* (Oxford: Blackwell, 1986), pp. 199–220.
48. St. German, *An Answer to a Letter*, Chapter 7.
49. Ibid.
50. Thomas Becon, *David's Harp*, in Becon, *The Early Works*, ed. John Ayre (Cambridge: Cambridge University Press, 1843), pp. 264–303.
51. Ibid., p. 288.
52. *Tudor Royal Proclamations*, ed. P. L. Hughes and J. F. Larkin, 3 vols., Vol. 1: *The Early Tudors (1485–1553)* (New Haven: Yale University Press, 1964), 1: 373–376.
53. William Tyndale, "A Prologue Showing the Use of Scripture," in *Tyndale's Old Testament*, ed. David Daniell (New Haven: Yale University Press, 1992), p. 8. Further references to this Prologue in this chapter will be made by page number in the body of the text.
54. See Chapter 4 and, especially, Chapter 6 in this volume.
55. For Tyndale's literalist hermeneutics, see Chapter 4 in this volume. For the absolutism of the *Obedience of a Christian Man*, see Duerden, "Justice and Justification."

56. Becon, *David's Harp*, ed. Ayre, p. 288.
57. "The death of his saints is precious in the sight of the Lord."
58. 2 Corinthians 12:10; Philippians 1:1–29.
59. Becon, *David's Harp*, ed. Ayre, p. 275.
60. Ibid., p. 290.
61. Ibid., p. 274.
62. John Foxe, *Acts and Monuments* [. . .] (1563 edition), [online]. (hriOnline, Sheffield). Available from *http://www.hrionline.ac.uk/johnfoxe, Acts and Monuments*, 3: 524–525.
63. Discussed in Greenblatt, "The Word of God in an Age of Mechanical Reproduction," p. 97. The source is John Foxe, *Acts and Monuments*, 8: 1151.
64. See Brian Cummings, "Iconoclasm and Bibliophobia in the English Reformations, 1521–1558," in *Images, Idolatry and Iconoclasm in Late Medieval England*, ed. Jeremy Dimmick, James Simpson, and Nicolette Zeeman (Oxford: Oxford University Press, 2002), pp. 185–206 (at p. 203).
65. See further Chapters 6 and 7 in this volume.
66. For the history of the relation between Scripture and the Church, see George H. Tavard, *Holy Writ or Holy Church?* (London: Burns and Oates, 1959). See further Chapters 6 and 7 in this volume.
67. See further Chapter 7 in this volume.
68. William Tyndale, *An Answere unto Sir Thomas Mores Dialogue*, ed. Anne M. O'Donnell and Jared Wicks (Washington: Catholic University of America Press, 2000), p. 49.
69. Ibid., p. 49.
70. Ibid.
71. For the quarrel between Tyndale and Joye, see Charles C. Butterworth and Allan G. Chester, *George Joye, ?1495–1553: A Chapter in the History of the English Bible and the English Reformation* (Philadelphia: University of Pennsylvania Press, 1962), chap. 9.
72. William Tyndale, *Tyndale's New Testament*, ed. David Daniell (New Haven: Yale University Press, 1989), p. 16. Further references in this chapter to Tyndale's Prologue concerning Joye will be made by page number in the body of the text.
73. William Tyndale, *The Parable of the Wicked Mammon*, in *Doctrinal Trea-*

tises and Introductions to Different Portions of the Holy Scriptures, ed. Henry Walter (Cambridge: Cambridge University Press, 1848), pp. 37–126 (at p. 39).

74. Thus David Daniell, *The Bible in English: Its History and Influence* (New Haven: Yale University Press, 2003), pp. 168–169.

75. William Tyndale, *The Pathway into the Holy Scripture,* in Tyndale, *Doctrinal Treatises,* ed. Walter, pp. 7–28 (at p. 7).

76. Tyndale, *The Parable of the Wicked Mammon,* ed. Walter, p. 44.

77. Tyndale, *Tyndale's New Testament,* ed. Daniell, p. 3.

78. See Cummings, *The Literary Culture of the Reformation,* p. 200, for this point.

79. Tyndale, *Tyndale's Old Testament,* ed. Daniell, p. 3.

80. Tyndale, *An Answere unto Sir Thomas Mores Dialogue,* ed. O'Donnell and Wicks, pp. 13–23.

81. George Joye, *An apologye made by George Ioye* (London, 1535), RSTC, 14820. All further references to this text in this chapter will be cited by image number in the body of the text.

82. One might note that Joye changes the Latin Vulgate reading "dux" (leader) here to "fellow."

83. Stephen Gardiner, *A declaration of such true articles as George Ioye hath gone about to confute as false* (London, 1546), RSTC, 11588. All further references to this text in this chapter will be cited by image number in the body of the text.

84. See further Chapter 7 in this volume.

6. History as Error

1. Cited from John Leland and John Bale, *The Laboryouse journey and serche of Johan Leylande for Englandes antiquitees* (London, 1549; reprinted in facsimile, Amsterdam, 1975), RSTC, 15445, f. D7v.

2. Cited from "A Fruitful Exhortation to the Reading and Knowledge of Holy Scripture," in *"Certain Sermons or Homilies" (1547) and "A Homily against Disobedience and Wilful Rebellion" (1570),* ed. Ronald B. Bond (Toronto: University of Toronto Press, 1987), pp. 61–67 (at p. 60).

3. For historiographical cultures that are especially subject to the "virus" of the past (that is, revolutionary cultures that repudiate the past as

error), see the excellent study by Anthony Kemp, *The Estrangement of the Past: A Study in the Origins of Modern Historical Consciousness* (New York and Oxford: Oxford University Press, 1991).

4. Alexander Alesius, *Of the auctorite of the word of god agaynst the bisshop of London* (Strassburg, 1544), RSTC, 292, image 5. All further references to this text in this chapter will be cited by image number in the body of the text.

5. For the history of the relation between Scripture and the Church, see George H. Tavard, *Holy Writ or Holy Church?* (London: Burns and Oates, 1959). See further Chapter 7 in the present volume. For the specific issue of unwritten verities in England, see Thomas Betteridge, *Tudor Histories of the English Reformations, 1530–1583* (Aldershot, Hants.: Ashgate, 1999), pp. 92–95. See also Thomas Cranmer, *The Confutation of Unwritten Verities* (1556), in Cranmer, *Miscellaneous Writings and Letters of Thomas Cranmer*, ed. John E. Cox (Cambridge: Cambridge University Press, 1846), pp. 272–274.

6. For evangelical hostility to councils, see Chapter 4 in this volume.

7. He also cites Revelation 22:18–19, promising plagues on anyone who adds to the "prophecy of this book" (image 20).

8. See Chapter 4 in this volume. When Max Weber discusses the "rationalization" of Protestant society, he designates the application of single protocols to previously heterogeneous groups; he does not mean to suggest a more "rational" system. See Max Weber, *The Protestant Work Ethic and the Spirit of Capitalism*, trans. Talcott Parsons (New York: Scribner's Sons, 1958; first published in German, 1904), p. 25.

9. Martin Luther, *On the Bondage of the Will*, in *Luther and Erasmus: Free Will and Salvation*, trans. E. Gordon Rupp, A. N. Marlow, Philip S. Watson, Paul Althaus, and B. Drewery (Philadelphia: Westminster Press, 1969), p. 127.

10. Ibid., p. 129.

11. Ibid., p. 131.

12. William Tyndale, *The Obedience of a Christian Man*, ed. David Daniell (London: Penguin, 2000), p. 179. For an even more virulent account of the plagues that will befall any of the "marked men" who add anything to or subtract anything from Scripture, see John Champneys, *The harvest is at hand, wherin the tares shall be bound, and cast into the fyre and brent* (London, 1548), RSTC, 4956, image 14.

13. See also William Tyndale, *Tyndale's Old Testament*, ed. David Daniell (New Haven: Yale University Press, 1992), p. 85.

14. See Henri de Lubac, *Exégèse médiévale: les quatres sens de l'Écriture*, vols. 41, 42, and 59 of *Théologie*, 2 vols. in 4 (Paris: Aubier, 1959–1964); Beryl Smalley, *The Study of the Bible in the Middle Ages* (Notre Dame, Ind.: University of Notre Dame Press, 1964); and Gilbert Dahan, *L'Exégèse Chrétienne de la Bible en Occident Médiéval XII–XIV siècle* (Paris: Cerf, 1999).

15. Galatians 4:22–26; 1 Corinthians 10:11 (though the force of the historical idea is lost in the frequent translation of *figura*, the Vulgate reading, in this passage as "example"; thus Tyndale, *Tyndale's New Testament*, ed. Daniell, p. 252).

16. Tyndale, *The Obedience of a Christian Man*, ed. Daniell, p. 156.

17. Dahan, *L'Exégèse Chrétienne*, p. 436.

18. Erich Auerbach's essay remains the most perceptive: "Figura," in *Scenes from the Drama of European Literature* (Minneapolis: University of Minnesota Press, 1984; first published 1959), pp. 11–26.

19. See Chapter 4 in this volume.

20. Augustine of Hippo, *Sancti Aurelii Augustini de doctrina christiana, libri IV,* Corpus Christianorum Series Latina 32 (Turnholt: Brepols, 1962), 3.15.23, p. 91. The translation is mine.

21. The General Prologue to the Wycliffite Bible translates the passage just cited from the *De doctrina Christiana* promoting charitable readings. See *The Holy Bible . . . made from the latin Vulgate by John Wycliffe and his Followers*, 4 vols., ed. Josiah Forshall and Frederic Madden (Oxford: Oxford University Press, 1850), Prologue, 1: 44–45. The same Prologue reaffirms the four-fold method, laying emphasis on the literal as the basis of the other three mystical senses (1: 37–53). Wyclif's own ultra-realist hermeneutics, by contrast, claimed that, from God's perspective, the whole of Scripture is literal, to which the properly disposed reader has access. For Wyclif, that is, Scripture is not its material instantiations, but an idea in the mind of God, accessible only to certain readers. See *De veritate sacrae scripturae* (1377–1378) for these positions. Daniell inaccurately describes Wyclif's defense of scriptural inerrancy as "orthodox" (David Daniell, *The Bible in English: Its History and Influence* [New Haven: Yale University Press, 2003], p. 71). For the extremity of Wyclif's unusual position, see James Simpson, "Desire and the Scriptural Text: Will as Reader in *Piers Plowman*," in *Criticism*

and Dissent in the Middle Ages, ed. Rita Copeland (Cambridge: Cambridge University Press, 1996), pp. 215–243, and Kantik Ghosh, *The Wycliffite Heresy: Authority and the Interpretation of Texts* (Cambridge: Cambridge University Press, 2002), pp. 22–66, and further references.

22. Desiderius Erasmus, *Enchiridion Militis Christiani, An English Version*, ed. Anne M. O'Donnell, EETS, 282 (Oxford: Oxford University Press, 1981), p. 45.

23. Ibid., p. 49.

24. John Fisher, *Sermon Made Agayn the Perncyous Doctryn of Martin Luther*, in *The English Works of John Fisher*, ed. John E. B. Major, Early English Text Society, extra series 27 (London: Trübner, 1876), pp. 311–348 (at p. 315).

25. William Tyndale, *The Pathway into the Holy Scripture*, in Tyndale, *Doctrinal Treatises and Introductions to Different Portions of the Holy Scriptures*, ed. Henry Walter (Cambridge: Cambridge University Press, 1848), p. 28.

26. *The First Tome or Volume of the Paraphrase of Erasmus upon the New Testament*, trans. Nicholas Udall (London, 1548), RSTC, 2854, image 10. See further Chapter 4 in the present volume.

27. All the citations in this paragraph are from Tyndale, *Tyndale's Old Testament*, ed. Daniell, p. 4.

28. Ibid., p. 8.

29. The tension between the past as wholly relevant and as wholly foreign is embedded within philological humanism from its fifteenth-century beginnings; as Anthony Grafton says, some humanists wished to "make the ancient world live again, assuming its undimmed relevance and unproblematic accessibility," while others sought to "put the ancient texts back into their own time, admitting . . . that success may reveal the irrelevance of ancient experience and precept to modern problems." See his *Defenders of the Text: The Traditions of Scholarship in an Age of Science, 1450–1800* (Cambridge, Mass.: Harvard University Press, 1991), pp. 26–27; see also pp. 42–43. See also Debora Shuger, *The Renaissance Bible: Scholarship, Sacrifice and Subjectivity* (Berkeley: University of California Press, 1994), pp. 22–23 and 48–53.

30. See also Elizabeth Eisenstein, *The Printing Press as an Agent of Change*, 2 vols. in 1 (Cambridge: Cambridge University Press, 1979), p. 367: "Vernacular Bible translation took advantage of humanist scholarship

only in order to undermine it by fostering patriotic and populist tendencies."

31. Tyndale, *The Pathway into the Holy Scripture*, ed. Walter, p. 8.
32. For which see Heinrich Bornkamm, *Luther and the Old Testament*, trans. Eric W. Gritsch and Ruth C. Gritsch (Philadelphia: Fortress Press, 1969), pp. 81–87, and Althaus, *Die Theologie Martin Luthers*, pp. 83–86.
33. Tyndale, *Tyndale's Old Testament*, ed. Daniell, p. 88.
34. For the evangelical preference for explicit statement over narrative, see Chapter 4 in this volume.
35. Tyndale, *Tyndale's Old Testament*, ed. Daniell, p. 84.
36. For Cranach's close relations with Luther, see Joseph Leo Koerner, *The Reformation of the Image* (Chicago: University of Chicago Press, 2004), pp. 76–78.
37. For Luther's admiration for these images, see ibid., pp. 246–247.
38. Thomas More, *A Dialogue Concerning Heresies*, ed. T. M. C. Lawler, Germain Marc'hadour, and Richard Marius, 2 Parts, in *The Complete Works of St. Thomas More*, 6 (New Haven: Yale University Press, 1981), 1: 118.
39. Ibid., 1: 196/23–24.
40. Ibid., 1: 196/25–26.
41. The historical durability of the Church was not, as it was for More, an important argument for the other Catholic controversialists in the early stages of the anti-Lutheran campaign. See David V. N. Bagchi, *Luther's Earliest Opponents: Catholic Controversialists, 1518–1525* (Minneapolis: Fortress Press, 1989), and his summary article, "Luther's Catholic Opponents," in *The Reformation World*, ed. Andrew Pettegree (London: Routledge, 2000), pp. 97–108.
42. Antwerp, 1541. RSTC, 4070.5; the second edition, from which these citations are drawn, was published in London in 1547 (RSTC, 4071). All further references to this text in this chapter will be made by image number in the body of the text.
43. Luther also held that the evangelical Church was the true, old Church; see Althaus, *Die Theologie Martin Luthers*, pp. 287–290.
44. See further Mary Jane Barnett, "From the Allegorical to the Literal (and Back Again): Tyndale and the Allure of Allegory," in *Word, Church and State: Tyndale Quincentenary Essays*, ed. John T. Day, Eric Lund, and Anne M. O'Donnell (Washington: Catholic University

Press of America, 1998), pp. 63–73. For later Protestant reabsorption of allegory, see Barbara Kiefer Lewalski, *Protestant Poetics and the Seventeenth-Century Religious Lyric* (Princeton: Princeton University Press, 1979), pp. 111–144.

45. Luther also frequently made the identification of Jewish and Catholic practice. See Bornkamm, *Luther and the Old Testament:* "The godless arrogance of the Jews was nothing but the haughtiness of the Roman Church of [Luther's] day" (p. 19). For a routine example of the alignment of Jewish idolatry with Catholic idolatry, see Martin Luther, "Preface to the Prophets," in *Luther's Works*, 35, *Word and Sacrament*, 1, ed. E. Theodore Bachmann (Philadelphia: Muhlenberg Press, 1960), pp. 268–273. For a full range of Jewish hermeneutic practices and religious observances being lined up with Catholic practices, see also Tyndale, "Prologue to the Prophet Jonah," in Tyndale, *Tyndale's Old Testament*, ed. Daniell, pp. 636–637.

46. Tyndale, *Tyndale's Old Testament*, ed. Daniell, p. 148. All further references to Tyndale's Old Testament in this chapter will, unless otherwise specified, be made by page number in the body of the text.

47. For this feature of the English cultural revolution of the 1530s to 1550s, see James Simpson, *Reform and Cultural Revolution* (Oxford: Oxford University Press, 2002), chap. 1.

48. Tyndale, *The Obedience of a Christian Man*, ed. Daniell, p. 160. All further references to the *Obedience* in this chapter will be made by page number in the body of the text.

49. For other examples of tropological readings in Tyndale, see Tyndale, *Tyndale's Old Testament*, ed. Daniell, pp. 8 and 85.

50. Tyndale, *The Obedience of a Christian Man*, ed. Daniell, pp. 164–165.

51. Tyndale, *Tyndale's Old Testament*, ed. Daniell, p. 11.

52. Ibid., p. 191.

53. Bornkamm, *Luther and the Old Testament:* "Luther detested the Jews and loved the Old Testament" (p. 1). By Bornkamm's uneasy account, although "kindly hearted" Luther (p. 21) had a "passionate stand" on the question of Judaism, this "did not obscure his approach to the Old Testament" (p. 7). On pp. 144–146, we read about the necessity to stone Moses the lawgiver to death, discussing this passage from Luther's "Table Talk," no. 1371: "Tentati soln Mosen todt schlagen. Wenn einer in tentatione ist oder apud tentatos, so schlag er nur

Mosen todt und werff alle stein auf in. Wenn er aber wider gesundt wirt, so soll man im legem predigen, quia afflicto non est addenda afflictio." (Those in temptation should strike Moses dead. When a man is in temptation or among those in temptation, let him strike Moses dead and throw stones upon him. When he is recovered, so a man should preach the Law, for the afflicted should not be subject to affliction.) My translation. Cited from *Luther's Werke* (http:// luther.chadwyck.com), *Tischreden*, 2, no. 1371. Bornkamm's book was written before the Second World War, but had to wait until 1948 for publication (Bornkamm, *Luther and the Old Testament*, p. ix).

54. William Tyndale, *A briefe declaration of the sacraments expressing the fyrst oryginall how they came vp* (London, ?1548), RSTC, 24445, image 10. Further references to this text in this chapter will be made by image number in the body of the text.

55. For a brilliant analysis of the same strategy at work in the drama of John Bale, see David Scott Kastan, "'Holy Wurdes' and 'Slipper Wit': John Bale's *King Johan* and the Poetics of Propaganda," in *Rethinking the Henrician Era: Essays on Early Tudor Texts and Contexts*, ed. Peter C. Herman (Urbana and Chicago: University of Illinois Press, 1994), pp. 267–282.

7. Thomas More and Textual Trust

1. For some recent classics of pragmatism, see Richard Rorty, *Contingency, Irony, Solidarity* (Cambridge: Cambridge University Press, 1989), and Stanley Fish, *Is There a Text in This Class? The Authority of Interpretive Communities* (Cambridge, Mass.: Harvard University Press, 1980). For a critique of both Rorty's and Fish's impoverished, faithless understanding of all reading "communities" (religious or otherwise), see James Simpson, "Faith and Hermeneutics: Pragmatism versus Pragmatism," *Journal of Medieval and Early Modern Studies*, 33 (2003): 215–239.

2. William Roper, *The Life of Sir Thomas More*, in *Two Early Tudor Lives*, ed. Richard S. Sylvester and Davis P. Harding (New Haven: Yale University Press, 1962).

3. Ibid., p. 208. All further references to this edition in this chapter will be cited by page number in the body of the text.

4. E. J. Devereux, "Elizabeth Barton and Tudor Censorship," *Bulletin of the John Rylands Library*, 49 (1966): 91–106 (at p. 100).

5. *The Life and Letters of Sir Thomas Wyatt*, ed. Kenneth Muir (Liverpool: University of Liverpool Press, 1963), p. 196.

6. Ibid., p. 197.

7. Ibid., p. 210.

8. See Chapter 5 in this volume.

9. Thomas Wyatt, *Penitential Psalms*, in *Sir Thomas Wyatt, The Complete Poems*, ed. R. A. Rebholz (London: Penguin, 1978), lines 364–374, p. 205.

10. *SR*, 26 Henry VIII, c. 13, 3:508; see further John Bellamy, *The Tudor Law of Treason: An Introduction* (London: Routledge and Kegan Paul, 1979), pp. 31–34.

11. See G. R. Elton, *Policy and the Police: The Enforcement of the Reformation in the Age of Thomas Cromwell* (Cambridge: Cambridge University Press, 1972), p. 231. Further references to this work in this chapter will, unless otherwise specified, be made by page number in the body of the text.

12. For Elton's admiration for Cromwell—suffering under so many bureaucratic burdens, yet so efficient—see, for example, ibid., pp. 164–170, and p. 423, where we read how "it was something of a blessing" that England had such a "cool and discriminating chief of police" in a "sad time of violence and revolution."

13. For Elton's determination to see Cromwell as the architect of a limited monarchy, see Rosemary O'Day, *The Debate on the English Reformation* (London: Methuen, 1986), pp. 119–124.

14. For a more complex account of the discursive environment, see Ethan H. Shagan, *Popular Politics and the English Reformation* (Cambridge: Cambridge University Press, 2003), p. 221.

15. Cited in Elton, *Policy and the Police*, p. 231.

16. For the imposition of legal practice and the use of English in Wales in a statute of 1536, see *SR*, 27 Henry VIII, c. 26, 3:536–569; for the "rationalization" of English liturgy, see *The booke of the common praier and administracion of the Sacramentes and other rites and ceremonies of the Churche* (London, 1549), image 3: "Where heretofore, there hath been great diversity in saying and singing in churches within this realm: some following Salisbury use, some Hereford use, some the use of Bangor, some of York, and some of Lincoln: Now from henceforth, all

the whole realm shall have but one use." For discussion, see Ramie Targoff, *Common Prayer: The Language of Devotion in Early Modern England* (Chicago: University of Chicago Press, 2001), p. 17. One might also mention the imposition of the mandatory use of the *Book of Homilies* in 1547, designed to standardize evangelical preaching in every parish church: "All parsons, vicars, and curates shall read in their churches every Sunday one of the homilies, which are and shall be set forth for the same purpose by the king's authority." Royal Injunctions of 1547, number 32, cited in *"Certain Sermons or Homilies" (1547) and "A Homily against Disobedience and Wilful Rebellion" (1570)*, ed. Ronald B. Bond (Toronto: University of Toronto Press, 1987), p. 4.

17. For the novelty of adverbs in Henrician treason legislation, see Bellamy, *The Tudor Law of Treason*, pp. 33–34.

18. *Sir Thomas Wyatt, The Complete Poems*, ed. Rebholz, lines 359–361, p. 205.

19. For which see the penetrating essay of Erich Auerbach, "The Arrest of Peter Volvomeres," in his *Mimesis: The Representation of Reality in Western Literature*, trans. Willard R. Trask (Princeton: Princeton University Press, 1968; first published in German in 1946), pp. 50–76.

20. Linguistic pragmatism, though of course not called thus until the twentieth century, is a perennial feature of hermeneutic thought. See, for example, Cicero's brilliant defense of a pragmatic reading of wills, in his *De inventione:* "All cases are not covered by exceptions expressed in writing, but some that are self-evident are covered by exceptions understood but not expressed. Then it may be urged that nothing at all could be done either with laws or with any instrument in writing, or even about our every day conversation and the orders issued in our own homes, if everyone wished to consider only the literal meaning of the words and not to follow the intentions of the speaker." *De inventione*, ed. H. M. Hubbell (Cambridge, Mass.: Harvard University Press, 1949), 2.47.140, p. 309. More makes the same point in the *Confutation;* see Thomas More, *The Confutation of Tyndale's Answer*, ed. Louis A. Schuster, Richard Marius, James P. Lusardi, and Richard J. Schoeck, in *The Complete Works of St. Thomas More*, 8, 3 Parts (New Haven: Yale University Press, 1973), 1:264/7–17. For the pragmatic tradition in the classical and early Christian period, see Kathy Eden, *Hermeneutics and the Rhetorical Tradition: Chapters in the Ancient Legacy and Its Humanist Reception* (New Haven: Yale University Press, 1997).

21. For the mode of debate that More was engaged in, see further Chapter 8 in the present volume, and John M. Headley, "Form and Style in the *Responsio,*" in Thomas More, *Responsio ad Lutherum,* ed. John M. Headley, in *The Complete Works of St. Thomas More,* 5, 2 Parts (New Haven: Yale University Press, 1969), 2:804–823 (at pp. 804–810).

22. See Chapter 8 in this volume.

23. Thomas More, *The Confutation of Tyndale's Answer,* ed. Schuster et al., 2:658/10–15. For the likely Erasmus source, see Desiderius Erasmus, *De Libero Arbitrio (On the Freedom of the Will)* in *Luther and Erasmus: Free Will and Salvation,* trans. E. Gordon Rupp, A. N. Marlow, Philip S. Watson, and B. Drewery (Philadelphia: Westminster Press, 1969), p. 43.

24. Cited from David V. N. Bagchi, *Luther's Earliest Opponents: Catholic Controversialists, 1518–1525* (Minneapolis: Fortress Press, 1989), p. 90.

25. For the text of *Exsurge Domine,* see *Enchiridion Symbolorum, Definitionum et Declarationum de Rebus Fidei et Morum,* ed. Henricus Denzinger and Adolfus Schönmetzer (Barcelona: Herder, 1967), pp. 357–362.

26. Bagchi, *Luther's Earliest Opponents,* p. 247.

27. Ibid.; for the official Church's unwillingness to support opponents of Luther, see especially p. 266.

28. Council of Trent, Session 4, 8 April 1546, in *Enchiridion Symbolorum,* ed. Denzinger and Schönmetzer, p. 364.

29. Ibid., p. 365.

30. For the controversialists' defense of the divine right of the Pope, see Bagchi, *Luther's Earliest Opponents,* pp. 53–65.

31. For More's defense of translation of the Scriptures into English, see Chapter 2 in the present volume. For John Fisher's approval of vernacular scriptures, see Richard Rex, *The Theology of John Fisher* (Cambridge: Cambridge University Press, 1991), p. 149.

32. For the two versions of the *Responsio,* see More, *Responsio ad Lutherum,* ed. Headley, 2:732–774.

33. Henry VIII, *Assertio septem sacramentorum aduersus Martin Lutherum* (London, 1522), RSTC, 13079.

34. For arguments about the authorship of the *Assertio,* see John M. Headley, "The Controversy," in More, *Responsio ad Lutherum,* ed. Headley, pp. 715–731 (at p. 720–721).

35. Henry VIII, *Assertio,* images 67–69.

36. Luther's response can be found in *Contra Henricum Regem Angliae,* in *Luther's Werke (http://luther.chadwyck.com),* 10.2:180–222.

37. For the circumstances of the *Responsio*'s composition, see John M. Headley, "Background and Circumstances of Composition," in More, *Responsio ad Lutherum*, ed. Headley, 2:775–803 (at p. 791 for the likelihood of More's being commissioned).
38. Ibid., 2:775–803.
39. Ibid., 2:797. It should be mentioned that More stood in an established English tradition of defending unwritten verities (developed in response to Lollardy, from the late fourteenth century), although he nowhere refers to prior English theorists. See James Simpson, *Reform and Cultural Revolution, 1350–1547* (Oxford: Oxford University Press, 2002), chap. 9, and Kantik Ghosh, *The Wycliffite Heresy: Authority and the Interpretation of Texts* (Cambridge: Cambridge University Press, 2002). For the Reformation debate in England, see Peter Marshall, "The Debate over 'Unwritten Verities' in Early Reformation England," in *Protestant History and Identity in Sixteenth-Century Europe*, ed. Bruce Gordon, 2 vols. (Aldershot, Hants.: St. Andrews Studies in Reformation History, 1996), 1: 60–77.
40. More, *Responsio ad Lutherum*, ed. Headley, 1:51.
41. Ibid., 1:93.
42. Ibid., 2:882, and further references.
43. For the history of the relation between Scripture and the Church, see George H. Tavard, *Holy Writ or Holy Church?* (London: Burns and Oates, 1959). Tavard makes the important point that the doctrine of unwritten verities is a late medieval development; see ibid., chap. 3.
44. More, *Responsio ad Lutherum*, ed. Headley, 1:101/5–6. Translation by Scholastica Mandeville.
45. Ibid., 1:101/12–13. Translation by Scholastica Mandeville.
46. Ibid., 1:100/1. For an alternative defense of unwritten verities from a practical and pastoral perspective, see Richard Smith, *A brief treatyse settynge forth diuers truthes necessary both to be beleued of Chrysten people, & kepte also, whiche are not expressed in the Scripture* (London, 1547), RSTC, 22818. Smith retracted the treatise, pretty obviously under duress, in his *A godly and faythfull retractation* (London, 1547), RSTC, 22822.
47. More, *Responsio ad Lutherum*, ed. Headley, 1:101/3–4.
48. See Tavard, *Holy Writ or Holy Church?*, pp. 120 and 134–135.
49. More, *Responsio ad Lutherum*, ed. Headley, 1:101/19–27. For the metaphor of Scripture being written on the heart elsewhere in More, see Thomas More, *A Dialogue Concerning Heresies*, ed. T. M. C. Lawler,

Germain Marc'hadour, and Richard Marius, 2 Parts, in *The Complete Works of St. Thomas More*, 6 (New Haven: Yale University Press, 1981), 1: 142–144. For its use by other Catholic controversialists, see Tavard, *Holy Writ or Holy Church?*, p. 120. See also the penetrating essay by Jamey Hecht, "Limitations of Textuality in Thomas More's *Confutation of Tyndale's Answer*," *Sixteenth-Century Journal*, 26 (1995): 823–828.

50. More, *Responsio ad Lutherum*, ed. Headley, 1:100/22.

51. Published as *A dyaloge of syr Thomas More knyghte* . . ., RSTC, 18084 and 10885. For a survey of More's views in the *Dialogue*, and of his objections to the Tyndale Bible more broadly, see Heinz Holeczek, *Humanistische Bibelphilologie als Reformproblem bei Erasmus von Rotterdam, Thomas More und William Tyndale* (Leiden: Brill, 1975), pp. 279–358.

52. *Concilia*, ed. Wilkins, 3:711–712.

53. John Fisher, *A sermon had at Paulis by the commandment of the most reuerend father in god my lorde legate, and sayd by Iohan the bysshop of Rochester* (London, 1526), RSTC, 10892, image 4. Thomas M. C. Lawler makes the contrast between Fisher's and More's approach: see his "A General View of the Dialogue: An Anatomy of Heresy," in More, *A Dialogue Concerning Heresies*, ed. T. M. C. Lawler et al., 2: 440. All further references to the *Dialogue Concerning Heresies* in this chapter will be cited, unless otherwise specified, by volume, page, and line number in the body of the text.

54. For the household setting, see Germain Marc'hadour, "In His Own House," in More, *A Dialogue Concerning Heresies*, ed. T. M. C. Lawler et al., 2: 487–494, although Marc'hadour makes no mention of the improvised prison in More's garden. For discussion of the interrogation and imprisonment on More's own property, see Stephen Greenblatt, "The Word of God in an Age of Mechanical Reproduction," in *Renaissance Self-Fashioning, from More to Shakespeare* (Chicago: University of Chicago Press, 1980), pp. 74–114 (at pp. 74–75, and notes). See also Richard Marius, *Thomas More: A Biography* (New York: Knopf, 1984), p. 404.

55. More, *A Dialogue Concerning Heresies*, ed. T. M. C. Lawler et al., Book 1, chaps. 12–19.

56. Ibid., Book 1, chaps. 20–31.

57. For the Lesbian rule, see Eden, *Hermeneutics and the Rhetorical Tradition*, p. 13.

58. For More's use of sources in the *Dialogue,* see Germain Marc'hadour and Thomas M. C. Lawler, "Scripture in the *Dialogue,*" in More, *A Dialogue Concerning Heresies,* ed. T. M. C. Lawler et al., 2:494–534 (at p. 495 for 400 or so scriptural references; at pp. 526–530 for his secondary use of the fathers of the Church; and pp. 532–535 for his extremely limited if admiring use of Aquinas).

59. It is significant that when More comes to defend the allegorical sense of Scripture in the *Confutation,* he almost entirely restricts himself to passages that were allegorized by New Testament writers themselves, thus simultaneously not giving his opponents any ground and depriving them of ground. It is also significant that this defense should be so brief. See More, *Confutation of Tyndale's Answer,* ed. Schuster et al., 2:634–637. For a more forthright defense of figural allegory made in 1521, see, for example, John Fisher, *Sermon Made Agayn the Perncyous Doctryn of Martin Luther,* in *The English Works of John Fisher,* ed. John E. B. Major, Early English Text Society, extra series 27 (London: Trübner, 1876), pp. 311–348 (at pp. 315–316), though Fisher also takes care to justify figural allegory via St. Paul's own statements.

60. For More's understanding of the viciousness of the evangelical God, see also his story of the illiterate merchant's wife in the *Confutation.* He imagines the woman asking Robert Barnes about how to perceive the tokens of salvation derived from Scripture when she cannot read. More imagines Barnes's response thus: "All those that are elect of God shall be secretly moved and taught inwardly, and shall by the instinct of the spirit of God . . . perceive the true word of God upon the hearing and shall understand it as Tyndale sayth that the eagle perceived her prey. And the tother sort whom God hath not chosen, though they hear it shall not understand it . . . but be deceived by the false and not perceive the true for anything that they can do" (p. 897). More then imagines the woman's response: she simply cannot accept that God would leave her in "darkness and ignorance" for no other reason than "he list to choose [another] and to leave me unchosen" (2:898).

61. More, *Confutation of Tyndale's Answer,* ed. Schuster et al., 2:901/6–17.

62. Ibid., 1:388/17–18.

63. Headley points out that More "never lost the opportunity to recognize the book [the *Assertio*], together with its understanding of the papacy, as having been written by the king" (More, *Responsio ad Lutherum,*

ed. Headley, 2:721). William Roper reports that More had tried to persuade Henry VIII to treat papal supremacy in the *Assertio* "more slenderly" (see Roper, *The Life of Sir Thomas More*, ed. Sylvester and Harding, p. 235).

64. More, *Confutation of Tyndale's Answer*, ed. Schuster et al., 1:342/12. See also Chapter 4 in the present volume.

65. Ibid., 2:921.

66. Ibid., 2:924–27.

67. Ibid., 2:938/16–23. More's failure to promote papal supremacy stands out in stark contrast to most other controversialists; see Bagchi, *Luther's Earliest Opponents*, pp. 63–65.

68. Luther, *On the Bondage of the Will*, in *Luther and Erasmus*, trans. Rupp et al., p. 132.

69. For later medieval theory on the existence and function of different rhetorical modes in Scripture, see A. J. Minnis, *Medieval Theory of Authorship: Scholastic Literary Attitudes in the Later Middle Ages* (London: Scolar Press, 1984), pp. 118–159.

70. Compare More's defense of a rhetorical culture in Book 1 of *Utopia* (1516); see *The Utopia of Sir Thomas More*, ed. Edward Surtz and J. H. Hexter, in *The Complete Works of St. Thomas More*, 4 (New Haven: Yale University Press, 1965), p. 99.

71. See also More, *Confutation of Tyndale's Answer*, ed. Schuster et al., 1:248.

72. Ibid., 1:248/8–25. John Fisher makes the same point, but uses a musical analogy to make it: with regard to Scripture and its interpreters, he says that there is "no discord, no repugnancy, no contradiction of one part of it with another. It is like . . . of a songe where be many singers that diversely descant upon the plain song: but for as much as they all agree without any erring, without any mistuning, they make all but one song and one harmony." See John Fisher, *A sermon had at Paulis by the co[m]mandment of the most reuerend father in god my lorde legate, and sayd by Ioh[a]n the bysshop of Rochester* (London, 1526), RSTC, 10892, image 17.

8. The Tragic Scene of Early Modern Reading

1. See Chapter 1 in this volume.

2. Two notable dates in that history are as follows: 1483, the Spanish In-

quisition established, 1542, the Roman Inquisition established. For a survey see F. H. Reusch, *Der Index der verbotenen Bücher: Ein Beitrag zur Kirchen- und Literatur-geschichte,* 2 vols. (Aalen: Scientia, 1967; first published 1883–1885). In England, Arundel's Constitutions of 1409 signal a remarkably aggressive campaign of censorship, directed against vernacular scripture among other targets. For a survey of censorship legislation in England between 1350 and 1550, see James Simpson, *Reform and Cultural Revolution, 1350–1547* (Oxford: Oxford University Press, 2002), pp. 333–343.

3. Thomas More, *A Dialogue Concerning Heresies,* ed. T. M. C. Lawler, Germain Marc'hadour, and Richard Marius, 2 Parts, in *The Complete Works of St. Thomas More,* 6 (New Haven: Yale University Press, 1981), 1:31/8–12. Further references to the *Dialogue* in this chapter will, unless otherwise specified, be made by volume, page and, where appropriate, line number in the body of the text.

4. For the historical accuracy of this statement, see R. I. Moore, *The Formation of a Persecuting Society* (Oxford: Blackwell, 1987), p. 5, for the proposition (defended throughout the rest of this remarkable book) that around 1100 "socially sanctioned violence began to be directed, *through established governmental, judicial and social institutions,* against groups of people defined by general characteristics such as race, religion or way of life" (author's emphasis). The examples of each group that he chooses are Jews, heretics, and lepers. For Augustine of Hippo's theology of persecution, which stopped short of inflicting death on heretics, see Alexandra Walsham, *Charitable Hatred: Tolerance and Intolerance in England, 1500–1700* (Manchester: Manchester University Press, 2006), pp. 40–41.

5. Thomas More, *Utopia,* ed. Edward Surtz and J. H. Hexter, in *The Complete Works of St. Thomas More,* 4 (New Haven: Yale University Press, 1965), p. 271. Further references to this edition in this chapter will be made by page number in the body of the text. For an argument that the humanist vision of *Utopia* is in fact designed in the interests of a punishing and extremely centralized power, see Simpson, *Reform and Cultural Revolution,* pp. 229–238.

6. See More, *A Dialogue Concerning Heresies,* ed. Lawler et al., 2:719, for More's inaccuracy.

7. Burning of heretics was very rare up to the fourth century, and be-

tween 383 and 1022 there are no recorded cases. See Moore, *The For-mation of a Persecuting Society,* p. 13 and passim.

8. The punishment of burning for heresy in England was first instituted in 1401, with the statute *De heretico comburendo* (*SR*, 2 Henry IV, c. 15, 2: 125–8).

9. See More, *A Dialogue Concerning Heresies,* ed. Lawler et al., 2:724. The canon law reference can be found in *Corpus Iuris Canonici,* 2nd ed., ed. A. Friedberg, 2 vols. (Leipzig: Bernard Tauchnitz, 1879–1881), Cause 23, Questions 5 and 6, 1: 928–50.

10. The linking of heresy with sedition was a tactic used in the persecu-tion of Lollardy. See M. E. Aston, "Lollardy and Sedition, 1381–1431," *Past and Present,* 17 (1960): 1–44.

11. Thomas More, *In Defense of Humanism: Letter to Martin Dorp, Letter to the University of Oxford, Letter to Edward Lee, Letter to a Monk,* ed. Daniel Kinney, in *The Complete Works of St. Thomas More,* 15 (New Haven: Yale University Press, 1986), p. 71.

12. Thomas More, *Responsio ad Lutherum,* ed. John M. Headley, in *The Com-plete Works of St. Thomas More,* 5, 2 Parts (New Haven: Yale University Press, 1969), 1:85. Further references to this text will, unless other-wise specified, be made by volume, page, and line number in the body of the text.

13. Thomas More, *The Confutation of Tyndale's Answer,* ed. Louis A. Schuster, Richard Marius, James P. Lusardi, and Richard J. Schoeck, in *The Com-plete Works of St. Thomas More,* 8, 3 Parts (New Haven: Yale University Press, 1973), 1:13. Further references to this text will, unless other-wise specified, be made by volume, page, and line number in the body of the text.

14. For an explicitly opposed narrative of Bilney's martyrdom, see John Foxe, *Acts and Monuments* [. . .] (1570 edition), [online]. (hriOnline, Sheffield). Available from *http://www.hrionline.ac.uk/johnfoxe, Acts and Monuments,* 8:1150–1152.

15. See Alistair Fox, *Thomas More: History and Providence* (Oxford: Blackwell, 1982), pp. 119–120, for more examples.

16. Stephen Greenblatt, "The Word of God in an Age of Mechanical Re-production," in *Renaissance Self-Fashioning, from More to Shakespeare* (Chi-cago: University of Chicago Press, 1980), pp. 74–114 (at pp. 74–75). In his *Apology* More denies whipping anyone but two people in his

garden, the son of a servant spreading heretical views within More's own household and a man of heretical persuasion who had become mentally ill. See Thomas More, *The Apology*, ed. J. B. Trapp, in *The Complete Works of St. Thomas More*, 9 (New Haven: Yale University Press, 1979), pp. 117–118. All further citations from this work in this chapter will be cited by page and line number in the body of the text.

17. David Daniell, *The Bible in English: Its History and Influence* (New Haven: Yale University Press, 2003), p. 243.

18. Ibid., p. 243.

19. The key dates for heresy legislation in England are given in *An Answere Unto Sir Thomas More's Dialoge*, ed. Anne M. O'Donnell and Jared Wicks (Washington: Catholic University of America, 2000), pp. 419–420. I cite from p. 420: "1677, 29 Charles II, Ch. 9 abrogated the writ *De heretico comburendo* and substituted ecclesiastical penalties such as excommunication for the death penalty in punishing heresy (*Statutes* 5:850)."

20. For the Henrician blurring of heresy and treason, see Simpson, *Reform and Cultural Revolution*, pp. 336–337. For some examples and the theory, see Walsham, *Charitable Hatred*, pp. 52–53. See also Ethan H. Shagan, *Popular Politics and the English Reformation* (Cambridge: Cambridge University Press, 2003), p. 51 and passim.

21. Cited from Diarmaid MacCulloch, *Reformation: Europe's House Divided* (London: Allen Lane, 2003), p. 392.

22. John A. F. Thomson, *The Later Lollards, 1414–1520* (Oxford: Oxford University Press, 1965), pp. 237–238. I thank Professor Anne Hudson for help on this matter.

23. Hard statistics for More's persecution are difficult to find. My source for the actual figure of 6 derives from John Guy, *Thomas More* (London: Arnold, 2000), p. 112. The names derive from Richard Marius, *Thomas More: A Biography* (New York: Knopf, 1984), pp. 386–406.

24. These figures derive from G. R. Elton, *Policy and the Police: The Enforcement of the Reformation in the Age of Thomas Cromwell* (Cambridge: Cambridge University Press, 1972), pp. 387–398. Elton wants to refute the belief that the figures reveal Cromwell's tenure as especially savage. He has recourse to the fact that these people were, after all, acting against the law (laws that Cromwell had framed): the regular religious, for example, "had in fact become guilty in law" (p. 399).

25. Alec Ryrie, *The Gospel and Henry VIII: Evangelicals in the Early English Reformation* (Cambridge: Cambridge University Press, 2003), pp. 23–24 and Appendix 1.

26. For which see Anthony Fletcher and Diarmaid MacCulloch, *Tudor Rebellions*, 5th ed. (Harlow, Essex: Longman, 2004), pp. 57–58.

27. Figures and comment cited from MacCulloch, *Reformation*, p. 392. For a somber narrative of sixteenth- and seventeenth-century confessional persecutions in England, see Walsham, *Charitable Hatred*, pp. 106–159.

28. See Chapter 1 in this volume.

29. More, *In Defense of Humanism*, ed. Kinney, p. 71.

30. More, *The Confutation of Tyndale's Answer*, ed. Schuster et al., p. 3/5–6.

31. Ibid., pp. 11/36–12/2.

32. Thomas More, *The Answer to a Poisoned Book*, ed. Stephen Merriam Foley and Clarence H. Miller, in *The Complete Works of St. Thomas More*, 11 (New Haven: Yale University Press, 1985), p. 3/16–23. Further references to this text will be made by volume, page, and line number in the body of the text.

33. I am guided by the succinct formulation of Stephen Greenblatt: More's work, he says, "longs to disappear, to cede place to multiple voices, to tradition and ultimately to the institution as the living expression of the Christian consensus. More's commitment to the disappearance of the text paradoxically commits him to an endless text." Cited from Greenblatt, "The Word of God in an Age of Mechanical Reproduction," p. 104.

34. Thomas Becon, *News out of Heaven*, in *The Early Works*, ed. John Ayre (Cambridge: Cambridge University Press, 1843), pp. 37–58 (at p. 51).

35. C. Augustin, "Hyperaspistes I: La doctrine d'Érasme et de Luther sur la *claritas scripturae*," in *Colloquiua Erasmiana Turonensia*, 2 vols. (Paris: Vrin, 1972), 2:737–748 (at p. 739).

36. William Tyndale, *Tyndale's Old Testament*, ed. David Daniell (New Haven: Yale University Press, 1992), p. 4.

37. For the textual understanding of sixteenth-century philology, see especially Anthony Grafton, *Defenders of the Text: The Traditions of Scholarship in an Age of Science, 1450–1800* (Cambridge, Mass.: Harvard University Press, 1991), chap. 1, especially pp. 42–43. See also Seth Lerer, *Error and the Academic Self: The Scholarly Imagination, Medieval to Modern* (New York: Columbia University Press, 2002), Introduction and

chapter 1, and further references. For distinctions between different kinds of humanism that extend beyond the narrow, fifteenth-century version, see James Simpson, "Humanism," in *Dictionary of the Middle Ages*, Supplement 1, William Chester Jordan, Editor in Chief (New York: Charles Scribner's Sons, 2004), pp. 279–282.

38. For More's verbatim citation, see John M. Headley, "Form and Style in the *Responsio*," in More, *Responsio ad Lutherum*, ed. Headley, 2:804–823 (at pp. 804–810). For use of the same laborious and ineffective method by other Catholic controversialists, see David V. N. Bagchi, *Luther's Earliest Opponents: Catholic Controversialists, 1518–1525* (Minneapolis: Fortress Press, 1989), p. 81.

39. More, *In Defense of Humanism: Letter to Martin Dorp*, ed. Kinney, p. 69.

40. *The Life and Letters of Sir Thomas Wyatt*, ed. Kenneth Muir (Liverpool: University of Liverpool Press, 1963), p. 197.

41. More, *A Dialogue Concerning Heresies*, ed. Lawler et al., 1:23.

42. More, *Responsio ad Lutherum*, ed. Headley, 1:21/1–2. I have altered the translation of *virtutes* in this passage from "virtues" to "strengths."

43. More, *The Confutation of Tyndale's Answer*, ed. Schuster et al., 1:419/26–28).

44. For the text of the *Treatise Concerning the Division between the Spirituality and the Temporality*, see More, *The Apology*, ed. Trapp, Appendix A.

45. For More's analysis and repudiation of the tactic of airing contentious issues in the voice of others, by introducing them with "some say," see *The Apology*, ed. Trapp, pp. 86–88, 94, 104.

46. Tyndale, *Tyndale's Old Testament*, ed. Daniell, p. 3.

47. See Chapter 2 in this volume.

48. More, *Confutation of Tyndale's Answer*, ed. Schuster et al., 1:139/16–21.

49. William Tyndale, *An exposycyon vpon the v.vi.vii. chapters of Mathewe* (Antwerp, 1533), RSTC, 24440. I cite by image number from the 1536 edition (London, 1536), RSTC, 24441.3.

50. For the hidden though profound identities between More and Tyndale, see Greenblatt, "The Word of God in an Age of Mechanical Reproduction," pp. 109–114.

51. For evangelical opposition to imagination, see James Simpson, "The Rule of Medieval Imagination," in *Images, Idolatry and Iconoclasm in Late Medieval England*, ed. Jeremy Dimmick, James Simpson, and Nicolette Zeeman (Oxford: Oxford University Press, 2002), pp. 4–24.

52. Thomas Elyot, *Pasquil the playne* (London, 1533), RSTC, 7672. Further references to the *Dialogue* in this chapter will be made by image number in the body of the text.

53. William Tyndale, *The Obedience of a Christian Man*, ed. David Daniell (London: Penguin, 2000), p. 24.

54. Cited in Elton, *Policy and the Police*, p. 196.

55. "A Fruitful Exhortation to the Reading and Knowledge of Holy Scripture," in *"Certain Sermons or Homilies" (1547) and "A Homily against Disobedience and Wilful Rebellion" (1570)*, ed. Ronald B. Bond (Toronto: University of Toronto Press, 1987), pp. 61–67 (at p. 64).

56. Tyndale, *The Obedience of a Christian Man*, ed. Daniell, p. 145. For Tyndale's hostility to the realm of the imaginative, see also Greenblatt, "The Word of God in an Age of Mechanical Reproduction," pp. 112–114.

57. For the preference for explicit discourse, see Chapter 4 in this volume. For Luther's dismissal of "poetae," see Bagchi, *Luther's Earliest Opponents*, p. 78. For Luther's dismissal of skepticism in favor of assertion as a mode of writing, see Martin Luther, *On the Bondage of the Will*, in *Luther and Erasmus: Free Will and Salvation*, trans. E. Gordon Rupp, A. N. Marlow, Philip S. Watson, and B. Drewery (Philadelphia: Westminster Press, 1969), pp. 105–109.

58. More, *A Dialogue Concerning Heresies*, ed. Lawler et al., 1:132/11–16.

59. For a broader account of the closing down of fiction in the 1530s and 1540s, see Alistair Fox, *Politics and Literature in the Reigns of Henry VII and Henry VIII* (Oxford: Blackwell, 1989).

60. More, *In Defense of Humanism*, ed. Kinney, p. 107.

61. More, *The Confutation of Tyndale's Answer*, ed. Schuster et al., 1:178/17–21.

62. William Barlow, *A dyaloge describing the originall grou[n]d of these Lutheran faccyons* (London, 1531), RSTC, 1461, images 2–3.

Index